I0569454

JOURNEY THROUGH TIME

JOURNEY THROUGH TIME

THE CATHOLIC CHURCH AND CHRISTIAN INITIATION

Kravitz & Sons
INNOVATORS IN PUBLISHING, MARKETING AND ADVERTISING

Kravitz and Sons LLC
1301 Farmville Blvd, Suite 104
Greenville, NC 27834

© 2025 Laurence F. Aucella. All rights reserved.

No part of this book may be reproduced, stored in a retrieval system, or transmitted by any means without the written permission of the author.

Published by Kravitz and Sons LLC.

ISBN: (sc) 979-8-89639-212-5
ISBN: (e)   979-8-89639-213-2

Library of Congress Control Number: 2025904383

Because of the dynamic nature of the Internet, any web addresses or links contained in this book may have changed since publication and may no longer be valid. The views expressed in this work are solely those of the author and do not necessarily reflect the views of the publisher, and the publisher hereby disclaims any responsibility for them.

Abstract

The purpose of this study was to explore variables both demographic and motivational in the examination of how these factors influence and may predict success in the completion of the RCIA process. The researcher utilized a reliable and valid (coefficient alpha = 0.984) survey in a double-blind study of completers of RCIA in different counties of the state of Connecticut. A total of twenty participants completed surveys printed in English or Spanish (n=20). A Pearson Chi Square Test indicated (x^2 (7) = 42.8, p< .01) statistical significance at the alpha level of .01. Moreover, a Phi coefficient 0 of 0.52 demonstrated a relatively medium-to-large effect. Thus, the RCIA processes are working very well in these urban settings in Connecticut. However, further research is required with a large sample size in the replication of this study. Furthermore, a causal comparative study germane to half year and full year catechumenates is warranted. Finally, a noted weakness remains evident in church record keeping and tracking of neophytes.

Chapter I
Introduction

It is important to know the demographic and motivational factors which may influence individuals to enter the Rite of Christian Initiation of Adults (RCIA). More specifically, what makes a person want to convert to Catholicism. Essentially, a person may be searching for meaning in one's life or seeking a personal relationship with the Lord Jesus Christ. Historically, converts have made enormous contributions to the Roman Catholic Church in the United States as well as to the betterment of American society as a whole. It is interesting to note that most catechumens in the first three centuries of the early Christian Church, came from the poorer classes; however, the church drew from a cross section and was able to socially bring them together in a cohesive and genuine community[1, 2]

Certainly, the development of the Roman Catholic Church in the American territory had early roots in the discovery of Puerto Rico by Cristoforo Colombo under the auspices of the Catholic Monarchs of Spain in 1493.[3] In fact, it was not until June 29, 1908, that the Holy See no longer regarded the United States as missionary territory. Essentially, the signing of the Sapienti Consilio by Pope Pius X moved away the jurisdiction from the Congregation of the Propagation of the Faith at the

Vatican since this office basically provides oversight for churches still in development in foreign lands.[4]

The Roman Catholic Church in America grew after the American Revolution, primarily because of European Catholic immigrants. In a sense, the first Catholic celebration of independence in the United States took place on Sunday July 4, 1779, in Philadelphia at St. Mary's Chapel according to the "Pennsylvania Packet" dated July 10, 1779: "On Sunday, last (being the anniversary of the independence of America), his Excellency the president, and the honorable the members of Congress, attended divine worship in the forenoon in Christian Church... At the noon, the president and Chief Magistrates of this state, and a number of gentlemen and their ladies, went, by invitation from the honorable the Minister of France, to the Catholic chapel, where this great event was celebrated by a well-adapted discourse, pronounced by the Minister's chaplain, and a Te Deum, solemnly sung by several good voices, accompanied by the organ, and other kinds of music."[5]

However, it was the major influx of immigrants who impacted the growth of the Roman Catholic Church in the latter part of the 19th century and well into the 20th century in the United States. In respect to the positive nature and influence of converts to Catholicism, it was the quality of contribution to their respective communities which stood out and became their trademark.[6]

Certainly one of the prime examples was Elizabeth Ann Bayley Seton (1774 -1821), a widower who joined St. Peter's in New York City.[7] Essentially, she converted from the Episcopal Church since she believed that the Roman Catholic Church is the "right faith". The founder of the Sisters of Charity which was the first community for religious women in the United States, Saint Elizabeth Ann Seton is the pioneer of American Catholic schools.[8] In September of 1808, Elizabeth founded a school for girls on Paca Street adjacent to St. Mary's College and Seminary in Baltimore. The following year, she moved her school to Emmitsburg, Maryland which officially opened on Februaty22, 1810 and was called St. Joseph's Academy and Free school. The enrollment reached sixty students by 1817.[9]

It is important to point out that Elizabeth with her daughter Kate had professed solemn and private vows before Bishop John Carroll on March 25, 1809. Moreover, in January of 1812, Archbishop John Carroll approved the Daughters of Charity for Elizabeth's Emmitsburg-based Sisters of Charity, making the title of "Mother" for Elizabeth, who was selected the superior.[10] Finally, Elizabeth and eighteen women had taken vows as a group as Sisters of Charity.

Although Mother Elizabeth Ann Seton died in 1821 just eight years later, the sisters' community had approximately sixty sisters by the time of her death. When Elizabeth had initially decided to convert to Roman Catholicism, she stated, "I will go peaceably and firmly to the Catholic Church, for its faith if so important to our salvation, I will seek it, where true faith began, seek it among those who received it from God Himself."[11] Furthermore, "The first end [of the congregation] I propose in our daily work is to do the will of God; secondly, to do it in the manner He wills; and thirdly, to do it because It is His will."[12] Mother Elizabeth became the first canonized saint born in the United States in 1975 via Pope Paul VI.[13]

Other examples of converts who have made significant contributions in various ways include the entire Barber Family of Claremont, New Hampshire, who converted to Catholicism in 1816. Mrs. Barber and her daughters all became nuns while her only son became a Jesuit. Moreover, the Jesuit initiated the first Catholic parish in Claremont.[14] The significance of Catholic converts must not be understated. In fact, during the next few decades, converts included six future bishops including Archbishops James Roosevelt Bayley of Baltimore and James Wood of Philadelphia. Moreover, there were priests such as Thomas S. Preston, long to be a conservative force in New York Catholic affairs, and Isaac Hecken with his friends who in 1858 founded the Paulist Fathers.[15] Cornelia Peacock Connolly and her husband Pierce, an Episcopalian clergyman, became a Roman Catholic priest in 1835. Pierce eventually became a Roman Catholic priest in 1844 after signing a paper indicating a formal act of separation from his wife who became a nun. She resettled in England and started the sisters of the Holy Child Jesus in 1846.[16]

Orestes A. Brownson, the editor of the Boston Quarterly Review from 1838 to 1842, had converted to Catholicism in 1844. Moreover, he had edited the Brownson's Quarterly Review from 1844 to 1864 and 1873 to 1875. Some people have regarded this period of time as an American "Oxford Movement".[17] Levi Silliman Ives, an Episcopal Bishop of North Carolina, became a convert in 1852 and perform various social welfare work in the New York milieu.[18]

John R.G. Hassard and Joseph Ripley Chandler, a well-known journalist, converted to Catholicism. Interestingly enough, Mr. Chandler was once a Grand Master Mason in President Buchanan's administration.[19] Even in the scientific realm, astronomer William H. Anderson and physicians William Edmonds Horner (1839) and Moses L. Linton (1844) became converts. Dr. Linton founded the first American medical monthly, the St. Louis Medical and Surgical Journal, as well was the president (1845) of the first American conference of the St. Vincent de Paul Society.[20]

Finally, David Goldstein, a convert and founder of the Catholic Truth Guild with Martha Moore Avery in 1917, defended the Roman Catholic Church against attack. The Catholic Truth Guild was commonly referred to as The Campaigners for Christ and both Goldstein and Avery went on a lecture tour throughout the United States. After Avery's death in 1929, Goldstein continued a nationwide lecture tour until 1941. Moreover, Goldstein was a prolific writer, his works include *Autobiography of a Campaigner for Christ* (1936), *Letters, Hebrew-Catholic, to Mr. Isaacs* (1943), and suicide bent: *Sangerizing Mankind* (1945) as well as numerous newspaper articles.[21]

It is, then, well worth examining demographic and motivational factors involved in the conversion process. Since the RCIA is the established mechanism which the Roman Catholic Church has developed, it is imperative to explore variables which not only leads to conversion but may predict success in completion of RCIA.

STATEMENT OF THE PROBLEM

Essentially, the Rite of Christian Initiation of Adults (RCIA) is a restoration of the early Christian practices via the second Vatican Council (SC, nos.64-66).[22] It is read as follows:

"64. The catechumenate for adults, comprising several distinct steps, is to be restored and brought into use at the discretion of the local ordinary. By this means the time of the catechumenate, which is intended as a period of suitable instruction, may be sanctified by sacred rites to be celebrated at successive intervals of time.

"66. Both rites for the baptism of adults are to be revised, not only the simpler rite but also, taking into consideration the restored catechumenate, the more solemn rite. A special Mass 'For the Conferring of Baptism' is to be inserted into the Roman Missal.[23]"

It is important to note that RCIA is a sacramental process which is a reflection of the conversion experience.[24] In essence, the RCIA is one rite which is composed of various periods and steps, which includes the following:

(1) Period of Evangelization and the Pre-catechumenate
(2) Rite of acceptance into the Order of Catechumenate
(3) Period of the Catechumenate
(4) Rite of Election on Enrollment of Names
(5) Period of Purification and Enlightenment
(6) Celebration of the Sacrament of Initiation
(7) Period of Mystagogy or Post-Baptismal catechesis.[25]

This is recognition that typical conversion to Christ is a gradual process. In reality, the RCIA facilitates this process. In a sense, it is a process of surrendering to God; it is a dying to oneself so that a new life can emerge.[26]

This is analogous to the steps germane to the death and dying literature. The end point is the acceptance of death. Therefore, it is seeing things as they are and actually embracing it. Conversion may be defined as a punctuated change of turning to a more authentic embrace via understanding, discernment, and acceptance.[27]

Therefore, the focus of the present study was to consider selected demographic variables and motivational factors germane to those who enter the Rite of Christian Initiation of Adult process in order to predict success in completing RCIA and remaining a practicing Roman Catholic. In an attempt to better understand this population and the variables which influence their decision to participate in RCIA, the researcher considered the following questions:

1. What differences exist across the various ethnic groups represented in this study with respect to those participants who have completed RCIA?

2. What differences exist across the socio-economic status of participants represented in this study with respect to those individuals who have completed RCIA?

3. What differences exist across the participant's level of formal education in this study with respect to those individuals who have completed RCIA?

4. What differences exist across the age group of participants represented in this study with respect to those individuals who have completed RCIA?

5. What difference exists across those participants who felt fulfilled spiritually as a result of experiencing RCIA with respect to those individuals who have completed RCIA?

6. What differences exist across those participants who had a person in one's life who influenced one to enter RCIA and those who did not have such a person with respect to diose individuals who have completed RCIA?

7. What differences exist across those participants who had a person in one's life that helped one remain and complete RCIA and those who did not have such a person?

SIGNIFICANCE OF THE STUDY

Certainly, the importance of this study is multifaceted. A definitive weakness of the RCIA in the Northeast of the United States of America is that there is a little or no tracking of those who completed the RCIA. Informal inquiries with pastors, priests, and RCIA coordinators have concurred with this notion.

Essentially, only the number of individuals who have completed the RCIA are reported to their respective diocese. The researcher of this study spent much time conducting field work with an RCIA group for a four-year period. This includes attending the weekly group meeting, a weekend retreat with the RCIA group, and the Easter Vigil Mass each year during this time span.

Therefore, the researcher of this study is seeking to explore both demographic and motivational variables germane to follow up of these completers of the RCIA in a selected urban area of Connecticut. This is the initial empirical study of RCIA utilizing inferential statistical methods to examine data.

DEFINITION OF TERMS

ACTS OF THE APOSTLES – The fifth book of the New Testament. Traditionally accepted as the work of Saint Luke. Acts is a continuation of the narrative of Luke's gospel, presenting a history of the Church from the ascension of Christ and the descent of the Holy Spirit to the period when Saint Paul preached in Rome. It mentions the acts of Peter, Paul, and James, although only Paul's acts are given fully and connectedly, the establishment and expansion of the Church from Jerusalem to the ends of the earth, and from a Jewish beginning to a Gentile expansion. It is believed that acts were most likely written approximately A.D. 63 which is when the narrative breaks off after Paul had been under house arrested in Rome for two years (Acts 28:30).[28,29,30]

ALPHA AND OMEGA. The first and last letters of the Greek alphabet (A, W). The expression is a divine tide in the book of Revelation where it means that everything in creation begins and ends with God, who is

Lord of all (Rev. 22:13). Alpha and Omega are the words spoken by Jesus of himself (Rev. 1:8).[31,32]

ANTIOCH. One of the most prominent cities in the Roman Empire and capital city of Syria. It was first built in 300 B.C. by Seleucus I Nicator on the Orontes River in Syria and named after his father Antiochus. Antioch was situated in a fertile region which had provided grain, olives, grapes, and fish, as well as being well-positioned for trade routes. Antioch was the third largest city of the Roman Empire, a center of Greek culture.

Essentially, the church at Antioch was the first to reach out to the Gentiles in a systematic fashion. Basically, it was at Antioch that the followers of Christ were first called Christians. It is important to note that it was in Antioch where Saint Peter and Saint Paul disagreed about the issue of circumcision of new Gentile converts (Gal 2:11-14).[33,34]

ANTIOCH OF PISIDIA. Pisidian Antioch was founded by the Seleucids in the early third century B.C. The city was a prominent in the Roman colony in the Roman province of Galatia when Saint Paul and Barabbas met with resistance among the Jews. In fact, they were forced to leave the city by officials under the influence of local Jewish leaders. Paul and Barabbas were welcome by the Gentiles. They did return to Antioch of Pisidia.[35]

APOSTLES. It is the title used in the New Testament to denote the twelve closest disciples of Jesus, the Christ. The word "apostle" is used eighty times in the New Testament. Essentially, it implies that the apostle is sent in the service of Jesus Christ. However, the strict definition in Acts 1:21-22 indicates that an apostle is "one of the men who have accompanied us during all the time that the Lord Jesus went in and out among us, beginning from the baptism of John until the day when he was taken up from us."[36]

APOSTOLIC FATHER. Consisted of mostly bishops who had succeeded the apostles such as Saint Clement of Rome (Pope Clement I), Papias, Hermas, Saint Polycarp of Smyrna, and Saint Ignatius of Antioch. For some time, their writings were held in quasi-canonical esteem?[37, 38]

APOSTOLICAM ACTUORITATEM. The Decree on the Apostolate of Lay People was issued on November 18, 1965, by the second Vatican Council. The Latin title translated to English is apostolic activity. It stresses that the laity are made sharers in the priestly, prophetic, and kingly office of Christ. One of its important provisions is the recognition that, while preserving the necessary link with ecclesiastical authority, the laity has the right to establish and direct associations as well as to join existing ones.

The decree allots for three types of corporate lay apostolates: (1) those which "owe their origin to the free choice of the laity and are run at their own discretion", but always having the approval of legitimate ecclesiastical authority", (2) those specially chosen by the bishops and "without depriving the laity of their rightful freedom" never the less have received a "mandate" from the hierarchy, and (3) those so closely associated with the hierarchy that they are "hilly subject to the superior ecclesiastical control in regard to the exercise of these charges".[39, 40]

AUTHORITY. In theocratic societies, such as the Catholic Church, God founded a particular society by supernatural revelation. Since God himself founded the Catholic Church, He structured it Himself, and passed on the authority to its leaders, The Sacred Liturgy depends totally on the authority of the Church, in this case, the Apostolic see (title of the bishopric of Rome). It applied to the pope and the persons and offices directly under his authority. [41, 42]

BAPTISM. (Greek, "immersion" or "dipping") The rite of cleansing with water. First practiced by John the Baptist and then by the apostles. Basically, John's baptism established by Jesus, the Christ. Essentially, repentance and baptism are the initial step of the Christian life (cf. Acts 2:37-38) and essential to Christian mission (Matt 28:19). Moreover, adult baptism is just one small part of the total initiation rites found in the Rite of Christian Institution.[43, 44]

CATACOMBS. Subterranean galleries used as burial grounds by the Christians of the first centuries. According to Roman law, they were immune from disturbance. Thus, Christians were safe here during persecutions and they celebrated the Eucharist on top of the tombs of martyrs. Basically, the Catacombs' existence was well known to the imperial authorities. Catacombs were regarded as sacrosanct by the Romans. In reality, the greatest development of the Catacombs actually was secured during the fourth century, a time of peace between the Church and the Roman Empire.[45,46,47]

CATECHUMENATE. In the early church, the period of preparation for baptism culminating in the scrutinizes or prayers of healing on the third, fourth, and fifth Sundays of Lent and the actual reception of baptism during the Easter Vigil. From St. Cyril of Jerusalem (ca. 315-86) there exists a series of homilies used for initiating catechumens and preached in the Church of the Holy Sepulchre.

In this day and age, usually accommodated to the liturgical year and enhanced by scriptural celebrations, certainly brings these adults to an understanding of the beliefs and obligations which they will accept. The faithful, primarily via sponsors, give good example and support in teaching them how to live the Christian way of life. Essentially, it is via fitting liturgical rites, the Church cleanses the catechumens a little at a time and strengthens them.[48,49]

CATHOLIC. The word "Catholic" in its original meaning is general or universal from the Greek words Katholikos, It was first used by Saint Ignatius of Antioch (A.D. 3 5-107) in his letter to the Smyraeans which states the following: "Where so ever the Bishop shall appear, there let the people be, even as where Jesus is there is the Catholic Church" (Smyr. 8:20). In this day and age, it applies to the church membership, the creeds, churches, institutions, clergy, and hierarchy who follow the same teachings of Christ as given to the Apostles. [50,51,52]

CHRISTIAN. A follower of Christ. The term "Christian" was initially used by followers of Christ at Antioch approximately A.D. 40-44, according to Acts 11:26. It is also used in only two other places in the New Testament, Acts 26:28, it is used by King Herod Agrippa when speaking to Saint Paul. Moreover, in I Peter 4:15-16, "But let none of you suffer as a Christian, let him not be ashamed, but under the name let him glorify God." A Catholic Christian further accepts the teachings of the Roman Catholic Church, participates in the Eucharistic liturgy and sacraments. [53,54]

CONFESSION. In Catholic theology, confession refers to the act of admitting personal sin toa qualified priest in order to receive sacramental pardon or absolution (sacrament of Penance). Essentially, per church law (Fourth Lateran Council, 1215), Catholics are required to go to confession annually in order to fulfill their Easter duty. Moreover, the Council of Trent decreed that Catholics must confess their mortal sins according to kind and number. According to Pope St. Pius X (1903 - 14), the young children may be admitted to the sacrament once they reach the age of reason about the age of seven. Although, penitents have committed only venial sin, they should seek confession as a means of obtaining God's merciful forgiveness and to benefit spiritually (Reconciliation et Poenitentia, 1984).[55,56]

CONFIRMATION. One of the Sacraments of Christian Initiation; those baptized receive this Sacrament ordinarily from a bishop, by the laying on of hands and anointing with chrism and prayer... be sealed with the Gift of the Holy spirit. Distinct ritually from Baptism, Confirmation is the complement to Baptism which not only perfects it but also orientates the confirmed person toward the Eucharist.

Essentially, baptized person after confirmation may complete their initiation via participation in the Eucharist. The proper Mass allows appropriate texts from the Lectionary during the Liturgy of the Word. After the Gospel the candidates are presented to the bishop, who then renders a homily on the readings. The Baptismal promises are renewed, and the imposition of hands by the bishop. Finally, each candidate is anointed with chrism during the recitation of the formula, and the sign of peace is allotted to each person. [57, 58]

CONSECRATION. The words of institution of the Eucharist, Jesus words of institution which is repeated by the priests as the culminating moment of the Mass during which the substance of the bread and wine is changed into the Body of Christ, the Transubstantiation, which connects the same sacrifice Christ instituted at the Last supper. Essentially, the formula of consecration is uniform for all the approved canons of the

Mass which reads as follows: "Take this, all of you, and eat it: this is my body which will be given up for you ... Take this, all of you, and drink it: this is the cup of my blood, the blood of the new and everlasting covenant. It will be shed for you and for all so that sins may be forgiven, do this in memory of me". According to Saint Ambrose, it is Christ Himself who consecrates in the priest. In fact, the Eucharistic Prayer is the heart of the Mass and the Consecration is the heart of the Eucharistic prayer.[59,60]

CONSTITUTION ON THE SACRED LITURGY. (Sacrosanctum Concilium) It was the first document issued by the Second Vatican Council on December 4,1963. Pope Paul VI (Giovanni Battista Montini) stated that "the first subject to be examined and also the first, in a certain sense, because of its intrinsic value in the life of the Church." Essentially, the Constitution presents broad and various principles to govern the adaptation of the Liturgy. Four main points were stressed: (1) the pastoral character of Liturgy, (2) the Liturgy's importance for the missions, (3) the need to incorporate the vernacular into Liturgy, and (4) a push to revisit concelebration. The first chapter is germane to the nature of the liturgy and its importance in the life of the Church. It is thought that the most significance change that resulted from the Second Vatican Council was the promotion of the faithful's participation in Church fife. This document emphasizes the faithful's participation in the liturgy with the resultant liturgical significance of the parish and the diocese. Moreover, pastoral life in liturgical action is promoted.

Basically, the second chapter pertains to the place of the Holy Eucharist in Liturgy, stressing the importance of the community of believers not to be mere silent spectators but rather fully collaborate with the priest during the Mass. Chapter three indicates the purpose of the sacraments, stressing that they are signs that instruct us, their relationship to the sacramentals, and how the sacraments and sacramental are revised and allow the vernacular in their celebration. Chapter four is germane to the Divine Office as the liturgical prayer of the Church and inviting the faithful to celebrate the Hours as well. The key terms utilized include the Mystery of Christ and the Paschal Mystery, the fulfillment of God's plan for reconciliation of mankind. This Christ centered approach to the liturgical year is the theme of the fifth chapter.

In essence, the liturgical year unfolds the whole Mystery of Christ from incarnation to ascension which includes the hope of the Second Coming. The sixth chapter has to do with the strong musical tradition of the church. It addressed the teaching and practice of music in seminaries. The final chapter is germane to sacred arts and furnishings.

The Church has made good use of the various works of artists as long as they are in full accordance with the Faith and piety. Saint John Paul Il's apostolic letter dated December 4, 1988, was in celebration of the twenty-fifth anniversary of the Constitution. He wrote that it "was undertaken in accordance with the conciliar principals of fidelity to tradition and openness to legitimate development, and so it is possible to say that the reform of the liturgy is strictly traditional..." (n,4). Furthermore, "it is a matter of the organic growth of a tree becoming ever stronger the deeper it sinks its root into the soil of tradition" (n.23)[61, 62, 63]

CONSUBSTANTIAL. According to the Council of Nicaea in A.D. 325, the Three Persons of the Blessed Trinity are of one and the same substance although distinct and separate.[64]

CONTRITION. It is the virtue of sorrow for one's sins. According to the Council of Trent, "sorrow of heart and detestation for sin committed with the resolution not to sin again" (D. S. 1676,1705). Essentially, contrition is the initial step of the four parts of the Sacrament of Penance and is followed by confession, an act of penance and absolution. However, it is only an act of contribution which is necessary for remission of sin. In essence, supernatural contrition is regarded as 'perfect" if in fact the reason of sorrow is for the true love of God. Basically, imperfect contrition is less complete although still of faith but not truly for the love of God, lamenting evil for a secondary reason such as fear of the wrath of God. Imperfect contrition is also commonly referred to as attrition.

The act of contrition is a prayer and a formula which not only expresses sincere sorrow for sin but also a firm resolution to sin no more. The traditional prayer is as follows; O my God, I am heartily sorry for having offended you and I detest all my sins because of Your just punishments, but most of all because they offend You, my God, who are all good and deserving of all my love. I firmly resolve, with the help of your grace, to no sin no more." Certainly, those who cite this prayer can gain a partial indulgence. [65, 66, 67]

CONTUMACY. In Canon Law, contempt of court is Germane to a party to an ecclesiastical case or controversy via the respondent who willfully refuses to appear before an ecclesiastical court. Essentially, the general law of the Church demands that the order to appear be repeated three times before proceedings declaratory of contumacy take place. Therefore, one forfeits all or some of his rights before the tribunal (Canons 1592-1595). Moreover, the use of contumacy happens in die matter of ecclesiastical penalties.

In essence, one who refuses to desist from edictal behavior is regarded as state contumacious and thus renders oneself liable to censure (Canon 1347). A prolonged of contumacy may result in the increase of the penalty (Canons 1326, 1364). The main penalties are as follows: "(1) The trial proceeds in the absence of the contumacious person, and presumably to his detriment; (2) presumption of guilt, but not sufficient for conviction; (3) a pecuniary fine at the discretion of the judge; (4) suspension; (5) excommunication may be inflicted, and if the contumacious party be not absolved within one year he may be proceeded against as suspected of heresy (Council of Trent, Sess. XXV, Ch. iii de Ref); (6) loss of the right of appeal from a definitive sentence, in all cases of true contumacy. Presumptive contumacy does not carry this penalty." According to Canon 1358, it is upon withdrawal from contumacy that one has a canonical right to remission of a censure. [68, 69]

CONVENTUAL MASS. Missa Conventualis, it is part of the office that, in essence, Mass is to be celebrated daily in those communities. Basically, it completes, with the canonical Hours, the official public service of God in such a place. It is commonly referred to as a "chapter' Mass (missa Capituli) since it is said or sung in all Cathedrals or/and collegiate churches. It is most fitting that conventual Masses are sung with the full participation of all members of the community. The term "conventual" refers to all aspect of the monastic or religious life.[70,71, and 72,]

CONVERSION. Conversion is a change of heart; it is a "turning to God" or a "returning to Him". Essentially, conversion means turning from the ways of sin and towards the ways and life of the Lord Jesus Christ. In the New Testament, Jesus preaches conversion as a preparation for the coming of the Kingdom. Certainly, the call to conversion and true repentance is a central theme of the New Testament.

According to the Catechism of the Catholic Church "Jesus calls to conversion. This call is an essential part of the proclamation of the kingdom: 'The time is fulfilled, and the Kingdom of God is at hand; repent, and believe in the gospel' In the Church's preaching this call is addressed first to those who do not yet know Christ and his Gospel. Also, Baptism is the principal place for the first and fundamental conversion. It is by faith in the gospel and by Baptism that one renounces evil and gams of new life. Conversion is brought about as a result of hearing the word of God; however, Christian conversion has both an interior and exterior component which originates in the mind and heart. A change of mind, metanoia in Greek is the New Testament reference for repentance. According to Saint Thomas Aquinas, conversion consists in preparation, merit and glory, and that there are special graces correlative to each. According to Saint Ambrose, "there are water and tears: the water of Baptism and the Tears of repentance".[73,74,75, 76.]

CONVERT. A person who turns away from a life of sin to a life of moral goodness. The rite of Christian initiation of adults is the mechanism in the Roman Catholic Church which facilitates the conversion experience. Thus, the catechumenate process is assisting a potential convert to awaken to the stirrings of God to a renewed life, a transformative one which affects every dimension of the convert's life. In a denominational sense, it refers to a person who accepts a new religious affiliation.[77, 78]

CORNELIUS. A Roman centurion in charge of the Italian cohort at Caesarea, and the first Gentile to convert to Christianity (Acts 10:1-11: 18; cf. 15:6 – 11). Essentially, Cornelius was a God-fearing man who was strongly attracted to the Jewish teaching of monotheism. Therefore,

Cornelius who received a heavenly vision sent his men to find Peter in Joppa, approximately thirty-six miles south of south of Caesarea. Peter, who received a vision as well had responded to the request of Cornelius. When Peter arrived to the house of Cornelius, Peter instructed him in the Gospel, and the Holy Spirit came upon Cornelius and his household and they received the gift of tongues. Peter had commanded them to be baptized in the name of the Lord. [79, 80, 81]

CREATION. It is God's free activity by which He brings all things into existence. Essentially, God creates out of nothing (ex nihilo) since He starts with no pre-existing matter, and He parts with nothing of His own being.

Only God himself is sheer existence. Basically, God creates out of nothing by the power of His Words. Moreover, His creation proceeds according to an orderly plan and has a definite purpose. All that God creates is good. [82, 83, 84.]

DEAD SEA SCROLLS. Manuscripts and fragments of manuscripts written mostly in Hebrew and Aramaic found between 1947 and 1956 in the cave's northwest of the Dead Sea, in the vicinity of Khirbet Qumran. It is believed that these works are thought to be the remains of an extensive library of a community of Essenes residing in this area from C.125 B.C. to about A.D. 66-70. It seems likely that these manuscripts were kept in caves in order to preserve them and keep them from harm, particularly during the Jewish rebellion against the Roman Empire. The manuscripts were enclosed in jars, and they were mostly written in Hebrew; one-fifth was in Aramaic, and a few were in Greek.[85, 86, 87]

DIDACHE. (Gr. "teaching"). A work from around the end of the first century, (A.D. 60-90) by an unknown author of western Syria or eastern Asia Minor. It is an early Christian manual on morals and Church practice, known by the first word of its Greek title:" The teaching (Didache) of the twelve Apostles". Essentially, the Didache is divided into three parts: (1) the two Ways, the Way of life, and the Way of Death; (2) a liturgical manual treating of baptism, fasting, confession, and Holy Communion; (3) a treatise germane to ministry. There are sixteen chapters in total. The Last chapter contains a prophecy of the approaching end of the World and refers to the Antichrist. By and large, it depicts the life of the early Christian community such as baptism by immersion, station fasts on Wednesday and Friday, recitation of the Lord's Prayer three times daily and confession of sins. [88, 89, 90]

DIPTYCHS. Two-leveled folders of wood or metal hinged in the center on which were written the names of the living and the dead. Essentially, departed Christians including catechumens who were to be remembered in the Canon of the Mass. Certainly, among the dead, the Saint had a privileged place. Thus, originally, "canonization meant to be named in the "Canon of the Mass." [91,92]

PAPAL PRIMARY. It is the authority if the Bishop of Rome as pastor of the universal Church, inherited from Peter who was promised the primacy when Jesus states that Peter was to be the "rock" on which Jesus would build His Church (Matt 16:18 cf. John 1:42). Moreover, Jesus gave the keys of the Kingdom to Peter which means it is the start of an office to be filled by successors. Jesus told Peter to "feed my lambs, feed my sheep" (John 21: 15-17). It was at the First Vatican Council that further definition described that the success of Peter in the primacy are the Bishops of Rome. Thus, this doctrine affirms that the Bishop of Rome at any time is in reality the holder of the primacy. Moreover, it does not simply rest on the fact that Peter worked and died as Bishop of Rome but rather on a positive ordinance of Jesus, the Christ who revealed this and notwithstanding the second Vatican council s mention of collegiality; the basic elements of the primacy have not been modified. [106, 107]

PAROUSIA. It is a Greek term for arrival or presence; it denotes a person's presence as distinct from his absence (I Cor. 16:17; 2 Cor. 10:10; Phi 2; 12). Essentially, it refers to the Second Coming of Christ in all His glory to judge the living and the dead. According to Acts 1:11, "This Jesus, who was taken up from you into heaven, will come in the same way as you saw him *go* into heaven, will come in the same way as you saw him go into heaven". Moreover, "For as often as you eat this bread and drink the cup, you proclaim the death of the Lord until he comes" (I Cor. 11:26). "Then they will see the Son of Man coming in the clouds with great power and glory* (Mark 13:26). At this point in time, the world will be transformed by fire into a new heaven and a new earth (2 Pet. 3:12-13). [108,109]

RITE OF CHRISTIAN INITIATION OF ADULTS. *(RCIA)* It is the process by which adult converts are received into full communion of the Roman Catholic Church via the three sacraments of initiation: Baptism, Confirmation, and the Holy Eucharist. It takes place in various stages which begins at an Inquiry phase or pre-Catechumenate.

Essentially, a person learns of the Church and indicates an interest in becoming a Christian Catholic. The Catechumenate phase incorporates a process of spiritual formation as one's faith grows while receiving religious instruction. The day of election marks the completion of this stage. This election phase means that the candidate is fit for the sacraments. The first Sunday of Lent is a starting point and the rite includes scrutinies, presentations, and anointing.

Finally, the last initiation phase takes place at the Easter Vigil when catechumens are baptized, confirmed, and receive their First Holy Communion. However, the follow-up period during the Easter season is called mystagogia which is a vital time for further spiritual growth and reflection. Moreover, the Christian neophytes become part of the Christian Community of believers and continually grow in faith. Thus, mystagogia is a post baptismal experience marked by a new experience of the sacraments and the Christian community by which they continue to grow into a deeper personal relationship with Jesus. [108, 109]

SUCCESS. Completion of the Rite of Christian Initiation of Adults process via receiving the sacraments of initiation. However, the fullest meaning of success is continual growth in a personal relationship with our Lord Jesus, The Christ and acceptance of His most perfect Holy Will. Mystagogia is in a sense the beginning of this new journey. [110]

TRINITY. God the Father, Jesus the Son, and the Holy Spirit comprise the blessed Trinity. Three divine persons are of one divine nature and the same substance (although distinct and separate). (Refer to Consubstantial)

DELIMINATIONS AND LIMITATIONS OF THE STUDY

This study is limited to the Rite of Christian Initiation of adult groups in urban settings in Connecticut. This study is further limited by the research design, methodology, instruments, and statistical analyses which will be utilized at the $P<.05$ alpha level.

ORGANIZATION OF THE STUDY

This study is organized into five chapters. Chapter one includes an introduction, statements of the problem, significance of the study, definition of terms, delimitations and limitations; Chapter two presents a review of the literature related to the study. Chapter three describes research design and procedures. Chapter four contains a statistical analysis of the data and a review of the research findings. Chapter five includes a summary, conclusion, and recommendations.

CHAPTER II
REVIEW OF RELATED LITERATURE

The review of literature related to this study includes three sections. The first section addresses a historical, biblical, and theological overview of early Christianity. The quintessence of the early church approach to its mission as it understands and accepts mission was a process guided by the Holy Spirit. Essentially, the church comes to fruition only when it dawns on the disciples that in reality, they comprise the beginning of a church separate from Judaism.

In a sense, mission is the "mother of the church". Although, Pentecost is typically thought of as the birthday of the church, rather, it is logical to infer that the church evolved as the disciples came to the realization that they are called to spread the good news of the resurrection of Jesus, the Christ to the very ends of the Earth. Therefore, Saint Paul believed that the mission is not completed until "the full number of the Gentiles enter in" (Rom: 1 1:25). [111]The invitation is for all peoples, Jews and Gentiles.

The second section is germane to the history, development, and organization of Catholicism in the United States of America. Certainly, the impact of immigration on the increased growth of the Roman

Catholic Church in America as well as the quintessential role of converts to Catholicism was vitally important to the mission of Catholicism in the United States. In fact, Winthrop Hudson had indicated that "the most spectacular development in American religious life in the latter half of the nineteenth century was the growth of the Roman Catholic Church."[112]

The third section addresses the role of the second Vatican council in the reinstatement of the catechumenate and order of Christian Initiation of adults. The Evangelii Nuntiandi (on evangelization in the Modem World), Pope Paul Vi's apostolic exhortation promoted the renewal of catechesis as a work of evangelization in terms of the mission of the church. Although the Rite of Christian Initiation of adults (RCIA) has its roots in the early Church, its promulgation in 1972 via Pope Paul VI began a significant change in modern times germane to conversion to the Catholic Christian Community in a sacramental process.[113]

HISTORICAL, BIBLICAL, AND THEOLOGICAL OVERVIEW OF EARLY CHRISTIANITY

During the first three centuries of Christianity in Rome, most Christians were of lower status in society, but there were exceptions. Moreover, this seems to correlate with references in the gospels that Jesus spent the majority of his time with the poor and needy.[114] Essentially, the early Christians had a keen sense of the conflicting beliefs and goals between the Church and the empire. [115] Tertullian of Carthage, a lawyer who was an early Church Father, states that the blood of the martyrs was a seed which produced Christians. [116, 117]

A biblical reference to martyrdom (I Corinthians 13:1-3) suggests that the apostle Paul actually equates being a martyr as a gift of the Holy Spirit.[118] It is important to note that conflicts arose when Christians were not welcome in synagogues since they were considered false Jews. Therefore, Christians sought to gather in private homes on Sundays for the "Breaking of the Bread."[119] At first, the early Christians did not necessarily believe that they had founded a distinctive new religion, but rather they were Jews who firmly believed that the Messiah had come.[120] It was in Antioch that the followers of Jesus were first referred to as "Christians".[121] The apostle Paul typically would first visit the synagogue in order to preach the good news that Jesus rose from the dead. In other words, Jesus is the Messiah; He is the Christ.[122]

Since most converts were either Jews or God-fearers (Gentiles), the conversion experience with the God-fearers or Gentiles actually beginning with Cornelius, a Roman Centurion; the need for a formal introduction and instruction of Christianity became necessary. Therefore, the birth of the Catechumenate emanated from this notion.[123] Basically, there were two essential parts which comprised the Christian service, 'the service of the Word" and the "service of the table". In the beginning of the Mass, scriptures were read with an interpretation in order to instruct the catechumens who were dismissed prior to the service of the table, namely Holy Communion.[124]

According to the book of Acts, mostly everyone was baptized immediately upon conversion. However, as the church grew and became increasingly Gentile, the development of the catechumenate emerged as the Salient feature of a process of a defined preparation for Baptism of new converts. By and large, the catechumenate was composed of instruction on Christian doctrine including the meaning of the creed or baptismal formulary. This process would last about three years by the third century.

Catechumens would typically fast on Friday and Saturday prior to their baptism early Easter Sunday morning. The catechumens were separated by gender and went into the water completely naked and were provided with white robes upon leaving the water. These neophytes were anointed and then marched in procession to meet the rest of the congregation and received Holy Communion. The neophytes drank water as a sign that they were cleansed inside and outside.

Moreover, they were provided with both milk and honey. This served as a sign of entering the Promised Land. Neophytes were baptized in the name of the Father, Son, and Holy Spirit while kneeling in the water and having water poured over their heads three times. This is germane to adult baptism with no solid evidence of the baptism of infants in early Church history.[125] However, it was the public conversion of Cornelius and his household which marked a punctuated change in that Christianity is not restricted to the Jews. The apostle Peter needed to expound on this point to followers in Jerusalem.[126]

Essentially, Cornelius receives a vision to send for Peter at Joppa. He sent two servants and a devout soldier in order to retrieve Peter. During this time, Peter while in prayer slips into trance and recurring vision, Cornelius' men arrive at this time when Peter is pondering the meaning of his vision. At the direction of the Holy Spirit, Peter meets them and travels to Caesarea to see Cornelius. After Cornelius welcomes him into a crowded house filled with Cornelius' relatives and some close friends, Peter verbalizes the "good news of peace proclaimed through Jesus Christ who is Lord of all."[127] Moreover, Peter baptizes them in the name of the Lord Jesus Christ and remains with them a few days. Then Peter returned to Jerusalem to inform the community of this situation.[128]

According to Peter, the Holy Spirit came upon these Gentiles, "just as it had upon us at the beginning." The Jerusalem community understood, and their response was "if this be so, then God has granted life-giving repentance even to the Gentiles."[129] The Cornelius public experience differed from that of the conversion of the Ethiopian eunuch which was a "private and isolated event". Certainly, the conversion of Cornelius and his entire household redefined in the minds of the Jerusalem community, the notion of blessing of the messianic age by which Jews and Gentiles share in the resurrection and life of Christ.[130']

It is important to note that most of these beginning gentile converts who were referred to as "God-fearers" were familiar with Judaism and Jewish customs.[131] In the strictest sense, Paul did not believe that he was preaching and teaching about a novel religion, but rather via the resurrection of Jesus, the Christ, it is the fulfillment of a promise made to the people of Israel.[132] Paul's methodology was first to go to the synagogue and contact the Jewish community. In feet, in Antioch of Pisidia, Paul and Barnabas were well received by its Jewish populace until the invitation to the Gentiles or God-fearers was made. Essentially, the trend was that Paul's message was typically rejected by the Jewish people and accepted by the Gentiles.[133] Antioch of Syria was a pluralistic society where the followers of Jesus were first called 'Christians".

Basically, Jewish and Gentile converts coexisted there. Another important variable in this equation of converts to Christianity is the migration of Jewish Christians of Hellenistic tendencies from Jerusalem.[134] There were two major cities called Antioch, one of which was first constructed in 300 B.C. by Seleucus I Nicator on the Orontes River in Syria. It was located about seventeen miles from the sea in a fertile religion along a trade route from the east and west. In Antioch of Syria, Paul and Peter had discussed the issue of circumcision of new Gentile converts.[135] Antioch of Pisidia was where Paul and Barnabas made their first missionary journey and subsequently returned although they were ejected from the city by officials who were influenced by Jewish leaders.[136]

Barnabas and Paul indicated that, "it was necessary that the word of God be spoken to you first, but since you reject it and condemn yourselves as unworthy of eternal life, we now turn to the Gentiles." (Acts 13:46).[137] The gentiles reacted in a positive manner and praised the Lord. Barnabas and Paul did not halt preaching to the Jews; however, the pattern is clear. Paul had concluded that Israel will be converted only after the "full number of Gentiles enter in" (Romans 1 1:25).[138] Paul was well-traveled. He brought the gospel message to the island of Cyprus and the various cities of Asia Minor. He went to Greece as well as Rome and perhaps Spain.[139]

The fact that his Epistles became part of Christian sacred scripture indicates a decisive and continuing impact on the Church.[140] Although Paul, Barnabas, John, Mark, and the other apostles taught, preached, and healed in the known world, there were many others who went from place to place with them. These various nameless Christians were likely merchants, slaves, and other occupations that brought their faith and witness to those they had encountered. Unequivocally, this contributed to the spread of Christianity.[141] It is believed that both Peter and Paul suffered martyrdom in Rome during Nero's persecution.

Tradition indicates that Peter was crucified upside-down at his request. Paul was very likely beheaded, which was befitting for a Roman citizen.[142] It is thought that Peter and Paul's deaths were circa A.D. 67. Some believed that Peter may have died just three months after Nero's great fire in A.D. 64. While Peter had experienced, "Quo Vadis?" ("Where are you going?"). Thus, Peter turned around and accepted his martyrdom. According to the apostle John (John 21:18), Peter's death was foretold by Jesus.[143, 144]

In First Clement, both Peter and Paul are mentioned. Essentially, First Clement serves as an important document which indicated the martyrdoms of Peter and Paul in Rome. Moreover, First Clement referenced only two apostles by name, Peter and Paul. In fact, it is the primary source for the belief that Paul reached Spain. It is important to point out that Paul's death may have served as a precursor for the turmoil in Corinth. Therefore, the very purpose of Clement's letter (First Clement) is due to the after effect of Paul's death on the Corinthian community.[145]

Clement is referenced in Paul's letter to the Philippians (4:3). The dating of First Clement is debatable. Eusebius, the father of Church history (Circa 263 - 340), places the episcopacy of Clement of Rome with the reign of Domitian (AD 81- 96). Thus, First Clement was thought to be dated in Circa A.D. 95. However, it is hypothesized that an earlier date is highly likely such as A.D. 70 or 80.[146, 147] First Clement 1:1 state, "Owing to sudden and repeated misfortunes and Calamities which have be fallen us..." This has typically referred to as the persecution of the church by Domitian; however, the eruption of Mount Vesuvius outside Naples in A.D. 79 may serve as an alternate hypothesis.[148]

Moreover, the names of the legates, Claudius Ephebus and Valerius Vito, who were the couriers of the letter to Corinth were freed slaves of the household of the Emperor Claudius (+A.D. 54) and his wife Valeria Messalina (+A.D. 48). According to Roman law, a slave could not be freed prior to age thirty years.[150] Thus, the messenger would likely be too old to deliver Clement's letter as late a date of A.D. 95.

It is reasonable to believe that there exists plausible evidence to support an earlier date. It was not uncommon to find undated letters at this time since none of the several letters of the New Testament are explicitly dated.[151] Another caveat is Germane to First Clement's reference to the Jerusalem Temple in the present tense. It is unequivocal that the Jerusalem temple was destroyed in A.D. 70 under Vespasian by his son Titus.[152] Basically, Clement refers to sacrifices being offered which points toward early in A.D. 70 since the temple was brought down in July of that year.[153] First Clement's reference to the repeated crises may possibly be during the "year of four emperors" in A.D. 69.[154] It is unclear that Clement was writing as a pope. Essentially, the evidence weighs in the direction that First Clement is not a monepiscopal or papal letter. Although First Clement is an intervention of Clement of the Roman Church in the internal affairs of the church at Corinth, he was not perse acting in a papal role.

Perhaps, this intervention is rather a phase of the process of developing papacy. Basically, primacy is the notion that the Roman Church utilized a certain oversight over the other churches while papacy indicated that the bishop of Rome is the person whose authority is in force.[155] Although First Clement did not assert authority, however two apostles, Peter and Paul, both exercised their authority and were martyred in Rome.[156] By and large, Peter and Paul were the apostles who mainly promoted the mission to the Gentiles.

Moreover, First Clement served as a continuation of communication and intervention started by Paul, notwithstanding, the harsh climate of the Roman authorities, "of the continuous and unexpected evils".[157] Certainly, First Clement reveals insight into the presbyterial form of church government. Essentially, First Clement posits that the presbyterate actually comes from the apostles. It is clearly of apostolic origin.[158] Thus, first clement regarded the presbyterate to be normative in nature. One may conclude that First Clement was most likely written Circa A.D. 70 and Clement was a presbyter at that time and later was elected bishop in apostolic succession which originated with Peter.[159]

The very doctrine of apostolic succession has its place within First Clement. There is evidence that First Clement was read in the Sunday assemblies at Corinth as early as the second century.[160] Another early Christian document which is anonymous and originally did not have a title is referred to as the Didache or the "Teaching of the Twelve Apostles." Essentially, the Didache is very different than First Clement. Another title for the Didache is "Training of the Lord through the Twelve Apostles to the Gentiles." The framers of the Didache were not the twelve apostles nor even the founders of the Didache. It is a product of various years of oral tradition.[162] It is the unfolding of a comprehensive an organized process of formation for use of gentile converts.

The Didache is composed of five topical parts which include the following: (1) "Training program in the way of Life' (44% of the total document) Did. 1:1- 6:2, (2) "Regulations for Eating, Baptizing, Fasting, Praying (22% of the total document) Did. 6:3 -11:2, (3) "Regulations for Hospitality/Testing various classes of visitors "(15% of the total document) Did. 11:3 - 13:2, (4) "Regulations for First fruits and for offering a pure sacrifice (10% of the total document) Did. 13:3 — 15:4, and finally (5) "Closing apocalyptic Forewarnings and hope (9% of the total document) Did. 16:1-8 .[163]

It is important to note that 'the Way" is correlated with the Lord Jesus' ministry on Earth. There exists a certain form of unity and natural progression within the Didache. Essentially, the Didache is composed of 2190 words of which 504 are New Testament words, 497 are classical, and 479 are contained in the Septuagint.[164] Evidence suggests that the Didache was developed without the framers relying on the gospels.[165] In fact, the Didache does not resemble First Clement nor the epistles of Ignatius.[166] While the Didache utilizes certain terms such as "teachers," "apostles," and "prophets," First Clement does not exactly use this verbiage. In fact, the Didache emphasizes the danger of a false apostle or prophet.

Essentially, the utilization of the term apostle varies between the Didache, First Clement, and the synoptics.[167] Basically, this term became an honor or title which was claimed by individuals after, the time of the original Apostles; thus, it became important to discern between a true one or a false one.168 According to First Clement, it is the presbyters who replace the Apostles. Thus, apostolic succession of bishops via the continuous series of presbyterial appointments was the rule. However, bishops appointed presbyters not bishops.[169]

It is important to note that First Clement does not demonstrate monepiscopoi First Clement is not a monepiscopal letter; rather, it seems to be an intervention of the Roman Church into the life of the Corinthian church or community.[170] Both Peter and Paul were in authority and died at Rome. First Clement is a key witness to the martyrdom of Peter and Paul. Moreover, it is the source leading to the belief that Paul had traveled to Spain. Unequivocally, First Clement knew only two apostles, namely Peter and Paul.[171] In regard to Paul, it can be hypothesized that his death had a very different effect on the Church of Rome as opposed to the Corinthian community. Certainly, the church at Corinth accepted and obeyed Paul and his death had an adverse effect. While Paul was a stabilizing influence in the Corinthian community during his life, it seems that Paul was more revered in Rome after his death.[172] The fact that First Clement is addressed to a Pauline Church at Corinth and has a corrective approach just as Paul's letters to this community, lends support to a continuation of the Pauline trajectory. Moreover, the confluence of the Petrine and Pauline trajectories, the effects of the combined influence of Peter and Paul impacted the notion of Roman primacy and papacy.[173]

Essentially, First Clement is evidence of an initial part of the process toward Roman primacy and papacy which supports the hypothesis of an early Circa AD. 70 dating of this letter.[174] It is apparent that First Clement was cognizant of the various pluralistic approaches germane to Church order. However, he regarded the presbyterate as normative.[175] Of course, First Clement is not sacred scripture, but it does provide insight into the makings of the early Church order. At the very least, First Clement is in direct line with Paul's interventions as well as promoting the presbyterial structure.[176] He believed that that the presbyterate came from the Apostle. Thus, First Clement stressed that the presbyterial way actually ensures and preserves the integrity of the community's faith. [177] Moreover, it is not per se opposed to charisms, nor is it in conflict with eschatological belief. [178]

It is important to note that First Clement's intervention was successful. Although Eusebius, Christian historian, dated First Clement Circa A.D. 96, it is thought an earlier date Circa A.D. is more likely.[179] Basically, First Clement does not really demonstrate monepiscopacy and since the date of the destruction of the Temple is certain; thus, First Clement referenced the Jerusalem Temple in his argument, reinforces the hypothesis of an earlier date. First Clement used the present tense germane to the Jerusalem temple and described the four different types of Jewish sacrifices being offered in the Jerusalem temple. Moreover, Christian converts from Judaism were free to practice the temple worship, which included sacrifice.[180]

The epistles of Ignatius were composed in AD. 107- 110 when Ignatius, the third bishop of Antioch, was condemned to death via the imperial authorities.[181] It was on Ignatius' way to martyrdom that he wrote seven letters, his sole extant authentic writings.[182] Ignatius was brought to

Rome under heavy guard as he was sentenced to die in the arena to wild beasts. The letters were addressed to various Christian communities at Ephesus, Magnesia, Tralles, Rome, Philadelphia, and Smyrna. His letters resulted from visitors he had received during his journey.[183] Essentially, Ignatius' first stop was the city of

Smyrna which is where Polycarp, a disciple of Saint John, was bishop.[184] Ignatius had written four of his letters to respectively the Churches of Ephesus, Magnesia, Tralli, and Rome. Moreover, he wrote two letters to the Churches of Philadelphia and Smyrna and one to Bishop Polycarp.[185]

Ignatius referred to himself as "the bearer of God" in his letters.[186] Basically, Ignatius was the second bishop after the apostles of one of the most ancient churches. Since a number of Christians from Asia Minor came to visit him, thus Ignatius held conversations with them. Moreover, he had a Christian amanuensis with him who had actually written the letters dictated by Ignatius. It is known that Ignatius had seen a bishop, two elders, and a deacon from the church in Magnesia including Bishop Polybius of Tralles and Bishop Onesimus of Ephesus. It is believed that Onesimus is one and the same person mentioned in Saint Paul's letter to Philemon. By and large, most scholars concur that Ignatius' letter to the Church of Rome is the most significant letter in terms of comprehending Christian persecution and martyrdom during the second century.[187]

Essentially, Ignatius described the Church of Rome as the "Church beloved and enlightened... which has the presidency in the country of the Romans, worthy of God, worthy in its holiness, and pre-eminent in love." It is important to note that Ignatius utilized the term "bishop" in his letter which may connote a monepiscopacy in Rome. Basically, Ignatius described a tripartite hierarchy composed of three orders that is namely, bishop, presbyters, and deacons.[188] Ignatius indicated that his goal is to become an imitator of the passion of Jesus. Although Christians in Rome had contemplate freeing Ignatius, he very strongly discouraged them. In reality, Ignatius only wanted their prayers. Bishop Polycarp of Smyrna inquired about Ignatius from Christians in Philippi although there is no evidence from the Christian Philippians of a response to the letter. In fact, Ignatius had died soon after his arrival in Rome.[189]

In the year A.D. 155, Bishop Polycarp was sought and arrested. The proconsul urged Polycarp to worship the emperor and "to revile Christ".[190] Polycarp's response is clear; "eighty-six years I have served Him and He has never done me wrong. How, then, should I be able to blaspheme my King who has saved me?"[191] The proconsul had ordered "out with the atheists" and Polycarp indicated, "Yes, out with the atheists" while pointing to his accusers'. Authorities of Rome considered Christians to be atheists since they worshipped an invisible God or rather had no visible gods.[192]

Marcus Aurelius, the Roman emperor from the year A.D. 161 to 180, was relatively more refined than other emperors of Rome in this era. Moreover, he wrote a number of "Meditations", which were meant to be private. Although he was a forward thinker, he regarded Christians to be stubborn.[193] Since there were a number of natural disasters, epidemics, and misfortunes, Christians had absorbed the blame. Although it is not known whether or not Marcus Aurelius actually believed that the Christians were responsible for these occurrences or phenomena of nature, nevertheless he whole heartedly supported the persecution of Christians.[194,195]

Justin of Neapolis, the premier Christian scholar of his time, founded a school in Rome and taught "the true philosophy" which is Christianity. According to Justin, he discovered and defined "the missing piece of Socrates' puzzle, namely the good news of Jesus, the Christ."[196] Basically, Justin died as a martyr. He was beheaded in Rome. Essentially, Justin wore the pallium which signified him as a philosopher, but he was truly a Christian apologist as well.[197]

Certainly, his two apologies as well as the dialogue with the Hebrews, Tryphon is his only known works. Justin martyr's writings provide insight into the organization of the Christian communities and worship He described Jesus as the fulfillment, "the logos, the eternal word, eternal reason, and creative reason."[198] Justin and many Christians were martyred during the reign of the enlightened Emperor Marcus Aurelius who wore the pallium.[199,200] A letter that the churches of Lylon and Vienne in Gaul sent to Christians in Phrygia and Asia Minor indicated that persecution was unexpected, "like a bolt of lightning". Moreover, the letter states that the place, where many Christians were held, were filled to the point that some Christians actually died of suffocation.[201]

By and large, the entire second century and most of the third century, persecution of Christians took place. However, it depended on certain factors. [202] Although it was illegal to be a Christian, the Roman authorities as a rule would not systematically seek Christians. It was mostly situational based upon an accusation. Certainly, it was important for Christians to have neighbors of good will.[203]

Since Justin was addressed by his rival Crescentius this brought attention to him. Other scenarios include the forming of a mob in Lyons and Viene which was the catalyst for Christian persecution.[204] It was not only the case of the worst emperors since persecution of Christians were at times heightened with better emperors. There were misconceptions about Christians which added to the confusion and chaos.[205]

It was difficult for the more cultured pagans to accept that those of a poorer class knew truth which was unknown to the upper class. They believed that Christians were barbarians. Moreover, the Christian religion came from the Jews who were regarded as a primitive people whose best teachers never reached the status of Greek philosophers.[206] Therefore, Christian apologists had a daunting task. Justin was the most famous of the early apologists; however, "the Letter to Diognetus" is the earliest known apology of an unknown author or possibly a man named Quadratus.[207] It has been aptly depicted as "the pearl of early Christian apologetics". Perhaps the letter written to a Greco-Roman pagan may be regarded as a treatise.[208] Certainly, it was the work of an enlightened Christian with classical academic training utilizing Addisonian type sentences to make a specific point. It is thought that Diognetus may have been one of Marcus Aurelius' tutors.[209] Interestingly, enough knowledge of the text came about by accidental discovery in Constantinople in 1436 by an Italian scholar, Thomas of Arezzo, in a fish shop underneath wrapping paper. This letter was provided to a German scholar, namely Johannes Reuchlin, and it found a place in the University Library of Strasbourg. Moreover, there were at least five copies made which accounts to its modern-day survival, since the library was destroyed during the Franco-Prussian War on August 24, 1870.[210] It is important to note that our knowledge base of early Christian apology typically involved a few textual witnesses.[211]

Furthermore, apologetics in the ancient Christians church were the result of martyrdoms as well as via reasoning though the spoken and written word.[212] The author of the letter to Diognetus stressed that reason alone is insufficient; rather, God provides the ability to hear the truth.[213]

Essentially, the Greeks and Romans were polytheistic. Thus, attacking Greco-Roman paganism is indicative of the formulary of the second-century Christian church for defending the faith in a pluralistic culture.[214] The author formed his argument by clearly stating that the gods and goddesses are merely a product of human invention or imagination.[215] Defining the idolatry and then indicating that Christians are not subject to this bondage completes his case. In fact, the author depicted this idolatry as "the locus of demonic activity".

Thus, the act of worshipping the Greek and Roman gods is actually, "fellowship with demons".[216] Finally, conversion to Christianity means that one realizes that the gods are a "grand illusion" and most importantly, freedom from the demonic powers and activity.[217] In essence, Christians believed that any deviation from sole worship of Jesus Christ is to deny Him. Christians tended to avoid civil ceremonies since it involved sacrifices and vows to the pagan gods. Similarly, Christians would not become soldiers for the same reasons as well as pacifist convictions. Moreover, many Christians abstained from the study of classical literature in which the pagan gods prevailed. The main question was the teachings of Socrates, Plato, Aristotle, and the stoics. While some Christians opposed this association, such as Tertullian, other Christians such as Justin sought the correlation between Christianity and classical wisdom.[218] Basically, Justin focused on the notion of Logos which is a Greek word meaning both "word" and "reason". Justin felt that in a sense that Socrates, Plato, and others "were Christians" since their wisdom in reality came from Jesus, the Christ. The distribution is that the ancient philosophers had a partial knowledge of Logos while those who know the incarnation know Him more "fully". Therefore, Justin's contribution was to pave the way for a Christian philosophy via a connection to classical wisdom regardless of pagan elements.[219]

However, it was Tertullian who began the usage of theology in the Latin language. The exact dates of his birth and death are unknown but Tertullian at Carthage toward the end of the second century had received an education in rhetoric, philosophy, history, and law.[220] Essentially, his most well-known work, *Apologeticus,* addresses the unjust treatment of the authorities toward the Christian church.[221] Altogether, thirty-one of his works survived where he finds fault in the presuppositions and practices of the pagan religion. Moreover, Tertullian dismissed the notions of Socrates, Plato, and Aristotle. His famous phrase, what does Athens have to do with Jerusalem? What does the academy have to do with the Church?"[222, 223] His mindset was strict due to the threats of the various heresies which emerged during this era.

Perhaps, the greatest threat to Christianity was Gnosticism. Some Jews embraced Gnostic beliefs as a result of the fall of Jerusalem and the destruction of the Temple in A.D. 70. However, it was the infiltration of Gnostocism into Judeo-Christian Tradition which made it a growing threat.[224] The adoption of the name of Christ in Gnosticism greatly distorted Jesus' role and even disputed His birth. Ducetism, a Greek word meaning "to seem" described these beliefs such as that the body of Jesus seemed to be fully human but not in reality. Essentially, the Gnostics believed that there is secret knowledge that Christ, a heavenly messenger, came to earth in a spiritual matter unlike human. Thus, people must learn the secret knowledge known to the Gnostic teachers. Basically, Gnosticism denied important and essential Christian doctrines including creation, incarnation, and the crucifixion and resurrection of Jesus. Therefore, Gnosticism posed a serious threat to Christianity during the entire second century.[225]

The formation of the sacred scripture was a process. However, the Gospel, the book of Acts, and the Pauline Corpus were firmly recognized by the early Christian Church by the conclusion of the second century. Moreover, the book of Revelation was clearly accepted as scripture in the third century. As a result of the conversation of Constantine, questions arose for those in leadership within the Roman Empire.

Essentially, they felt that the words were too harsh. Certainly, by the end of the fourth century, the books of the New Testament were unequivocally established.[226] During the first four or five centuries, there were many Gospels and various writings germane to the acts of Mary and the apostles. However, they were never considered to become part of the canon.

Essentially, the non-canonical Gospels of the second century were Gnostic while the writings in the third century were composed of Pious stories about Jesus.[227] Moreover, there existed various creedal formulas which were highly similar with some variation based upon the church in a particular city. Basically, a "daughter" church adopted the creedal formulary which it had acquired from the "mother" church with small changes.

The creeds were the Church's response to tire heresies. Actually, the Apostle's Creed was developed in Rome in the year circa A.D. 150. Thus, the ancient form of the Apostle Creed is referred to as "R" by scholars. It was called "the symbol of the faith" by the Christians community at that time. It was the method of discerning between a true believer from a heretic?[228] Essentially, the churches in North Africa and Gaul utilized various forms of R while the churches in Syria, Egypt, and Asia Minor used their own version. Basically, the Apostle's Creed has a simple tripartite scheme, developed around the Father, Son, and Holy Spirit. According to Rufinus (ca. 345- 410), the twelve apostles collectively composed it by each contributing a phrase.[229] However, he simply recounted a legend with no basis in reality.[230] The early creed was likely constructed to combat the heresy of Marcion and the Gnostics. The most extensive part of the early creed is germane to the Son of God, Jesus the Christ.

Since the Christology of Marcion and the Gnostics radically deviated from the early Christian Church, it was vitally important to affirm that Jesus was born, crucified, died, and rose again. Moreover, Jesus, the Christ will come again to Judge which is a concept that Marcion rejected. In fact, Marcion and the Gnostics did not even accept the fact of the birth of Jesus. Thus, it was paramount to point out that Jesus is the Son of God who is the Creator of all things and rules over this world and over all reality. In order to specifically date a historical fact, the creed mentions Pontius Pilate.[231] However, the authority of the church and unity became issues. The early church was made of various assemblies centered around their bishops. Basically, the bishop represented the unity of the church membership with each other and the Lord Jesus Christ.[232] Furthermore, there was a fraternity of bishops who gathered together to affirm a uniform faith to counter the heresies. The bishop was the head of the local Eucharistic assembly who exerted a control of membership which is referred to as "the power of the keys". This episcopal practice of "the power of the keys" was a consensus of church members.[233]

Hegesippus, a Jewish Christian, discovered widespread uniformity in the local churches contrary to the inconsistencies and contradictions of the Gnostics. Moreover, he found that the local bishops lead by word and example due to their communion with Jesus Christ. Certainly, over time the early Church became known in a recognizably identical form rich in its tradition.[234]

Aside from Tertullian, another Christian of influence from Africa, namely Cyprian, viewed the church as a corporate body established and rooted in Christ. Moreover, he purported that the Church does not exist without the office of the bishop. In fact, he consulted his own clergy and congregation on the issue of absolution germane to those Christians who fell into heresy. Once he had apologized for ordaining a sub-deacon and a lector without seeking consent from his clergy.[235]

Evidence exists in the Didascalia (Syriac) indicating the rights and jurisdiction of the episcopal office. It is known that the church of Rome in the year 251 was composed of a bishop, sixty-four presbyters, seven deacons, seven subdeacons, forty-two acolytes, fifty-two exorcists, readers, and doorkeepers as well as about 1,500 widows and needy people.[236] Basically, the bishop was responsible for everyone and the poor, especially the widows and orphans was a particular responsibility of the bishop. Moreover, bishops with their clergy often met on /Mondays with Christians who had disputes within the assembly. The emphasis was to have a resolution prior to the gathering of the Eucharist by next Sunday.[237]

It was during the persecution of Decius (250) that certain Christians in Africa composed of priests and bishops had offered sacrifice to pagan gods in order to avoid torture of death. According to Cyprian, the episcopacy as a whole maintained faith fullness although certain bishops faltered. By coming together in councils, bishops expressed their fidelity to Christ, the one true faith.[238] Essentially, the early church used the term catholic meaning universal. However, Catholic referred to "according to the whole" as well. This reference to catholic distinguished the early church from the various heretical sects. Thus, the Catholic church was the Church "according to the whole" meaning all of the apostles and evangelists. Moreover, it was only the church called catholic which contained the whole apostolic witness.[239] The bishops of Asia Minor met ingroups during the second century in order to combat the Montanists. / More specifically, in the year 268, Eastern church bishops met at Antioch to defend the faith against Paul of Samosata as well as in the year 314 as a more collected group of western and African bishops to thwart the Donatists.[240'] The Arian heresy, the date of Easter, and other matters were discussed at Nicea in 325. Since religious agreement became a priority under Constantine, he convoked these councils. However, it took some time for the Council of Nicea to have widespread acceptance.[241] These were certain assumptions Germane to councils over time besides from the fact of the guidance and presence of the Holy Spirit. In essence, conciliar meetings had authority as mediators of the faith, expectations of a positive reception to their decrees, and their own perception of being bound to the Holy Scriptures.[242] It is important to note that the acceptance of council teaching in the early Church was a complex process involving a twofold test. This meant that there was a consensus of the entire Church as well as correlates to the scriptures and tradition.[243] Basically, ecumenical conciliar decision by which the Collectivity of Bishops were to impact the faith and make a significant difference such as requiring new creedal formulations.

The recognization of the Roman patriarch was made official in 325 at Nicea and in the East, Rome was regarded as one of the five great patriarchates. Moreover, African churches realized that local and regional decisions could be appealed and ratified in Rome. It was Damasus, the Roman Bishop, who clarified that Peter is the foundation of his office. In fact, Pope Damasus' successor, Siricius, indicated in a letter to Bishop Himerius of Terragona in 385 that "Peter fives on each pope".[245]

Certainly, various theological controversies existed within Christianity. Initially, there was an issue germane to the relationship between Jewish and Gentile converts. The Gnostic threat to the early

Church was real and significant. Bishop Cyprian of Carthage dealt with the argument over restoration of the lapsed.[246]

It was during the persecutions of Decius and Valerian that Cyprian had to flee in order to continue the pastor his flock although from a distance. Cyprian was martyred in 258. By calling for a synod of bishops, Cyprian took a leadership role in this issue of lapsed Christians (lapsi). Novatian was temporary in charge of the Church of Rome, as a result of the death of Fabian. Cornelius was made pope when it was deemed safe to hold the election. Essentially, Novatian was not in favor of readmitting the elapse back into the fold while Cornelius who became Bishop of Rome made a path for the lapsi to return after a public penance.[247]Basically, it was the degree of the offense or apostasy such as sacrificati or offered sacrifice, thurificati or offered incense, and libellatici or received certificates; which determined the length and extent of public penance.[248]'

As a result of the election of Pope Cornelius in 250, Novatian became a rival Bishop of Rome in a sense although martyred in the persecution of Valarian (257-258).[249] Without doubt, the martyr was the ideal of unqualified witness of Christ to the world. However, the most common form of witness particularly of the second and third centuries were those of ordinary Christians in a casual informal way. The Christian faith spread mostly via existing relationships such as family, acquaintances, business associates, and the Jewish Diaspora/Gentile God-fearer connections. Christianity moved thru person-to-person influence.[250]

Continuing on this point, the household very often included slaves, freed persons, various hired workers, tenants, and partners in trade or craft. Thus, Christianity was an urban movement for the most part, growing very rapidly in the Greco-Roman cities of Asia Minor.[251] One must not underestimate the value of the conduct of ordinary Christians in spreading the good news of Christ. This pre-Constantinian era church required this concerted effort of ordinary Christians particularly that of women. Christians absolutely prohibited abortion and more women than men tended to convert, especially a good number of high-status women.[252]

Essentially, Christians subculture women had a higher or better status in a sense than women overall in the Greco-Roman environment.

Thus, it is logical that this is reflected in the Christian condemnation of infanticide (mostly female infanticide) and abortion. Moreover, Christian women married at an older age and chose their husband in comparison to pagan women. Basically, Christians took care of widows instead of encouraging them to remarry. The good news of Christ extended to gender, class, culture, and race. Since women were in the majority within the Christian community, they most likely married non-Christian men. According to Tentallian, wives were a positive influence in the conversions of their husbands.[253]

Thus, Christian women had a shared role in hosting Christian gatherings. Without doubt, Christian women spread the good news of Christ to where they typically gathered: the laundry, the marketplace, and in the care for the poor. [254] Due to insufficient evidence, it is unclear of the role of women in official ministry in the second century. However, any official role was not present by the conclusion of the third century.[255] It is noteworthy to mention that the Didascalia Apostolorum points to the role of deaconesses as mainly caring for sick women as well as helping at baptisms for women. Finally, the significant role of women in spreading the Christian faith during the post-apostolic age in light of a subordinate status of women and cultural norms is remarkable.[256]

A well-known martyrdom in 203 a year after the edict of Septimius Severus was issued, was that of Perpetua and Felicitas.

In essence, there were five catechumens who were martyred. Basically, Perpetua and her companions were arrested. The others were the slaves of Felicitas and Revocatus and the other men named, Saturninus and Secundulus. Perpetua's father attempted to convince her to save herself by renouncing the Christian faith. Moreover, Felicitas was pregnant and wanted her life spared for the time being only to deliver her child. This prayer of Felicitas came to fruition since she gave birth in her eighth month to a girl who was adopted by another Christian woman.

Both Perpetua and Felicitas were martyred together in the arena, being attacked by a crazed cow. The two bleeding women stood together in the middle of the arena and with the kiss of peace said their goodbyes to each other prior to death by sword. As to the three men, they were martyred in the arena with Saturninus and Revocatus who died first and bravely as well as Secundulus who the beasts did not initially attack. Secundulus indicated that a leopard would kill him which became a self-fulfilling prophecy.[257]

The formalization of the catechumenate was present which was a highly significant ecclesial development for the future of the church. The writings of Hippolytus and Tertullian contain reference made to the catechumenate. The rapid growth of Christian faith in the Roman Empire was significant. In fact, approximately ten percent of the fifty million people of the Roman Empire is estimated to have been Christian. However, the Christian faith in urban areas grew relatively quicker than the rural population.[258] Perhaps, it was the open social networks and practical paths in an urban situation which was conducive to this phenomena. Similarly, there existed a Christian community in Edessa which was a city situated between two ancient trade routes as well as the capital of Oshroene which served as a buffer of the warring empires of Rome and Persia.[259]

Interestingly enough, the earliest documented record in history of a public church building was located in Edessa during the reign of Abgar VIII towards the end of the second century. Barbaisan of Edessa had written of the importance of unity of Christ.[260] Basically, Christians of Oshroene had a relationship with Christians of the West and of the East.

Since Oshroene became a Roman colony in 214, it was politically under the Roman Emp.re. However, it had closer religious and cultural ties to Persia. Moreover, there was a Christian community in Arbela, the capital of the Adibene Kingdom in the empire of Persia. Tatian the Assyrian, theologian and former pupil of Justin Martyr, brought the Syriac gospels to Asia.

Essentially, he chronologically arranged the gospels into a history. It is known that the Peshitta, a Syriac version of the Old Testament existed in the church of Asia by the conclusion of the second century.[261] Tatian was a radical ascetic which means that perhaps ascetic monasticism had its roots in Syria rather than in Egypt. An important difference existed between ascetics of Egypt who retreated and resided in caves and ascetics of Syria who were mainly wandering missionaries. There is evidence that there were various Christian communities all across the Persian Empire as far as what we referred to as northern Afghanistan.[262]

A migration pattern commencing in 226, was that the eastern church moved its organizational center to the Persian capital of Selencia-Ctesiphon as well as its theological center to the city of Nisibis. This phenomenon was the result of the Sassanid dynasty of Persia subplanted the Parthian Kings of Persia for approximately a four-hundred-year span. An important caveat is that the language remained Syriac.[263]

Evidence suggests that it was Christian merchants who first brought the faith to the kingdom of Armenia, northwest of Edessa. Basically, Gregory the Illuminator, influenced by the church of Cappadocia, baptized Tiridates I the king of Armenia. Thus, in approximately 301, Armenia became the first nation to become officially Christian.[264] By this time, the Christian faith existed in India since the Apostle Thomas and the teacher Pantaenus were likely in India. It is known that there was considerable travel, trade, and emigration between India and the Roman Empire around this time. In fact, it is thought that Thomas made his way in both Northwest and Southwest India.[265]

By and large, the Christian faith had spread across the continent of the East as much as the West into Europe. There was a type of pulling effect on these buffer kingdoms between Rome and Persia. Basically, Parthian rulers did not bring nor fostered a unified cultural and religious way of life. Analogously to the Pax Romana environment of the West, the room for growth of Christianity in Asia filled this vacuum of the Parthian dynasty.[266]

Constantine's edit of toleration provided freedom and respectability for fourth century Christians in the West. The year 313 for the church in the Roman Empire was similar in a sense to the year 226 for Syrian Christianity[267] However, the difference is that Constantine, who believed that the Christian God was very powerful, would support him as long as he was good to the Christians Although Constantine did not have a full comprehension of Christianity, he was sincere in his effort to serve the cause of Christians.[268]

Moreover, the Pax Romana provided relative peace, calm, and stability as well as a superb network of roads for Christians to travel. Essentially, Greek was a language for communication and business trade.[269] Certainly, the conversion of Constantine effected theological debate. Constantine promoted church unity since he felt that the Church would keep the empire together. Thus, he utilized his authority to foster theological agreement upon Christians. Other views which threatened Christianity were defended. Prior to this influence of Constantine, issues in the church took longer to resolve often via long debate. In fact, Constantine intervened in the Arian situation.

Basically, the roots of the Arian controversy preceded Constantine.[270] His mission for reforming the Roman Empire was contingent on the Christian Church of being one mind. Thus, synods and councils were necessary for the local Christian Church to transition from its existence as an illegal and secretive entity to a larger and accepted one. Basically, Christians in the post apostolic age formed a local Church and various representatives were known from certain places such as the church of God in Corinth, Smyrna, or Roma.

Church unity was evident at the level of Eucharistic celebrations within the congregation. However, issues with the wider Christian Community in terms of the date of Easter penitential discipline and battling heresies required synods.[271] Conversely, heresies such as the Arian one could no longer be contained locally due to the newfound freedom after the year 313. Thus, the problem of Arius, a priest from Alexandria not only affected the various churches of Asia Minor but in addition, the churches of the west. Moreover, Pelagianism started in Rome but extended to the churches of Africa and Jerusalem.[272] Essentially, Bishop Alexander of Alexandria took issue with Arius who was a popular presbyter.

The Arian motto was that "there was when he was not." Thus, Arius claimed that the word (Logos) was not coeternal with the Father. Moreover, Anus indicated that the word or Logos was not God rather the first creature.[273] However, Bishop Alexander countered with the fact that the Word was divine and thus it could not possibly been created. In essence, he maintained that the word was co-eternal. Bishop Alexander was supported in his argument by a deacon named Athanasius. Basically, Alexander in his role as bishop publically condemned the teachings of

Arius. This disagreement was a dividing point which threatened the church. Constantine had dispatched Bishop Hosius of Cordoba, his advisor in Church matters, to settle this dispute.[274] Since Bishop Hosius was unsuccessful in resolving this issue Constantine called a council of Bishops from all over the Roman Empire.'

This council of Nicea became known as the First Ecumenical Council which took place in 325 drew approximately three hundred bishops from the Greek-speaking East as well as the West.[275] Ironically, bishops who were imprisoned, tortured, or exiled not long ago were invited to attend the council with expenses paid by Constantine. According to Eusebius of Caesarea who was physically present indicated that there were Syrians, Cilicians, Phoenicians, Arabs, Persians, and Scythians in attendance. Moreover, representatives from Pontus, Galatia, Pamphylia, Cappadona, Asia, Phrygia, Thrace, Macedonia, Achaia, Epirus, and Spain made it to the council.[276] Essentially, the agenda included approving standard procedures for allowing the lapsi to return, the election and ordination of presbyters and bishops, and developing the order of precedence of the episcopal seas. Last but not least, the bishops needed to discuss and rule on the controversy of Arius.[277] Since Arius did not hold a seat in the council, this task fell upon Eusebius of Nicomedia.

Essentially, Bishop Alexander of Alexandria along with his deacon Athanasius opposed the teachings of Arius. Basically, Constantine, who called for the council, remained neutral, not really taking an official position.[278] Although Arius and Athanasius were not bishops, they openly debated with each other. There exits no writing record of this debate. In reality, Eusebius of Caesaran promoted the notion of writing a theological statement to be signed by all in agreement. This was no easy task since there was not only Greek and Latin spoken but various secondary languages.[279] Moreover, most of the Latin-speaking bishops of the West regarded Arianism as an issue among Eastern followers of Origen. They simply felt that Tertullian's theological position of "three personas and one substance" sufficed.[280]

At first, the belief was to find common ground. However, this was not to be. The majority of bishops soundly renounced Eusebius of Nicomedia who had stanchly promoted Arius' teachings. This led to the creation of a creed which would express the true faith of the

Church. Essentially, Eusebius of Caesarea recommended the creed of his own church while Constantine indicated that "homoousios" ("consubstantialem" in Latin) be included in the wording of this creed. It was likely that Hosius of Cordoba suggested this to him. In actuality, the main thrust of this theological document was based on the creed of Caesarea with additional verbiage which strongly rejected Arianism. This formulary with some adjustment became the basis for the Nicene Creed, which remains the most universally accepted Christian creed.[281]

On June 19, A.D. 325, Hosius of Cordoba was the very first signature while Arius, Theomas, and Secundus absolutely refused to sign the theological document or creed. As a result, they were excommunicated. This action likely prompted Eusebius of Nicomedia to agree to the creed, although very reluctantly.[282,283]

By and large, The First Ecumenical or Council of Nicea did not avert the controversy of Arianism mostly due to Eusebius of Nicomedia repeated efforts to undermine the creed. In fact, he sought the favor of Constantine who permitted Eusebius of Nicomedia to be reinstated in Nicomedia which was Constantine's summer residence. Moreover, Constantine was persuaded to even restore Arius from exile to communion with the church. [284,285] The bishop of Constantinople was confronted with the difficult decision of whether or not to comply to Constantine's order. However, Arius suddenly died in 336 after leaving the imperial palace due to a medical issue.[286]

One of the signers of the Nicene Creed in 325 was John the Persian "of the churches of the whole of Persia and in the great India".[287] By and large, Synods via the Persian Church in the years 410 and 424, confirmed and secured the Council of Nicea. Moreover, it decreed that the organization of this East Syrian Christian Church would be in the Persian capital of Seleucia-Ctesiphon by placing their bishop there. Essentially, the catholicos of all the churches in Persia was under their bishop who was equal to the other patriarchs including the bishops of Rome, Alexandria, and Constantinople.[288] Regardless of this transition of the Syrian period to the Persian period, the language of the church was still Syriac.

It is known that Constantine had dispatched a letter addressed to the Shah of Shahs in Persia in the hope of protecting Christians in that region. However, there is no indication that the letter was ever read by the Shah of Shahs. In Persia, the state religion of Zoroastrianism strictly opposed the Christian faith not only was a double tax made against Christians, their churches in the fourth century. Basically, an addict of toleration was established for the Christians in Persia in 409. However, the persecution of Christians was renewed in 420.[289] Thus, East Syrian Christians were in the minority, Christians tended to migrate near certain trade routes into northeastern Persia and eventually across central Asia. In the mid-fourth century Thomas of Cana, a Persian Christian merchant thought to be of Armenian descent, with approximately four hundred Christians, found their way to Cranganore where a Christian community had existed.290

One may hypothesize that these Christian communities were composed of Persians who were forced to flee the fierce persecutions in Persia. Cosmas, the Indian Navigator, discovered a Persian Christian community on the Island now known as Sri Lanka.[291] In fact, this Persian Christian Church had a Bishop appointed from Persia around the southwestern part, Malabar. Essentially, this Persian Christian community had a component of Jewish culture and faith embedded within the group.[292] Basically, an indication that Christianity spread beyond Persia to India, was evidence of the caste system a commixture of Christian faith and Indian culture. These Christians communities still utilized Syriac in their liturgies, and they used rice cakes and palm vine for the Eucharist.[293']

The death of Alexander, Bishop of Alexandria in 328, just three years after the Council of Nicea, left a void which was filled by Deacon Athanasius. Eusebius of Nicomedia influenced Constantine to exile Athanasius as well as other Nicene Christians. In fact, it was Eusebius of Nicomedia who had baptized Constantine on his death bed. Basically, Constantine's sons succeeded him. Constantine H, Constants, and Constantins U gained authority over different regions of the Rome Empire. Constantine II controlled Gauls Great Britain, Spain, and Morocco while Constantins ruled the East and Constants seized mostly Italy and North Africa. Essentially, this initially favored the

Nicene group with the eldest son of Constantine restoring Athanasius and others from exile to good standing.[294] However, Constantins was influenced by the Arians, and he was able to remove Athanasius again. Basically, Constantins was required to find a more moderate middle ground due to circumstances. As a result of Constantine's death, many of his relatives were killed with the exception of his three sons who rose to power. It is believed that Constantins was behind the killing of his relatives. Julian was a first cousin to the three sons who shared the power of being emperors. In fact, Julian who became known as the apostate and his half-brother Gallus survived the family massacre. Julian was simply a six-year-old boy at the time and Gallus was very ill which was likely the reason for their lives being spared.

Essentially, Julian and Gallus were not regarded as a threat. They were baptized and became readers of the church.[295] Actually, Constantins provided the title of Caesar to Gallus in the year 351 which placed various power and territories under his control. Over time, Constantins mistrusted him and had Gallus beheaded.[296] However, Julian was immersed into philosophical studies at Athens and adopted the pagan religion of classical Greece. Constantius offered the tide of Caesar to Julian who became a superb administrator and very capable general.[297]

However, Constantius pitted himself against Julian after preparation to attack Persia. The army of soldiers became rebellious and joined Julian making him Augustus, the supreme ruler. When Constantius troops fought against the Julian regime, Constantius was Killed in the year 361 and Julian became the undisputed sole emperor.[298] By and large, Julian had strongly rejected the Christian faith. Although he did not directly persecute Christians, he had barred them from teaching classical literature and tended to ridicule them.[299] Julian's literary work, "Against the Galileans," contradicted the teachings of Jesus. It was not until Bishop Cyril of Alexandria about eighty years later that written Christians response was made.[300] Moreover, Julian chose to have the Temple in Jerusalem to be rebuilt in defiance of the Christian faith. Julian was killed in a military campaign against the Persians by being struck by an enemy spear.[301]

In retrospect, it was the wish of Bishop Alexander of Alexandria that his deacon Athanasius be his successor as bishop. Although Athanasius sought the peace and solitude of the desert, he would accept the role of bishop reluctantly several weeks after Alexander's death.[302] Athanasius' fundamental stance was that if Jesus was not God, then He would not be able to redeem mankind. Thus, the Logos did not simply "enter into" a human according to Arius. Although Athanasius was exonerated from false allegations which were made to the Synod of lyre, he was unable to gain access to the emperor in Constantinople. This was mainly due to the nefarious behavior of Eusebius of Nicomedia who exerted influence in blocking Athanasius' efforts. However, Athanasius jumped onto a horse while the Emperor Constantine was riding somewhere, holding the horse's bridle. This did not resolve Athanasius' situation. It was not until Athanasius gained support from Julius, bishop of Rome when presenting the Nicene argument personally to him. As a result, the Roman clergy joined Athanasius and the Nicene cause?[304] When Constantius acquired compete control in the year 353, he forced bishops to accept heresy of Arianism. When the emperor deployed troops to Alexandria, Athanasius was ordered to leave. However, Athanesius utilized an old imperial order in his possession to avert this threat.

Basically, Athanasius after a series of situations including an incident when celebrating communion in a local church, was able to retreat to the monks in the desert. It was the monks who provided protection by moving him place to place.[305] Shortly thereafter, a council at Sirmium had firmly rejected the tenets of the Nicene cause which was a low point for the Church. Thus, this council became known as the "Blasphemy of Sirvaium".[306]

In summary, Julians reign was supplanted by Jovian who favored Athanasius who returned from exile for the final time. He went to Alexandria and then to Antioch. However, Jovian had a short-lived tenure as emperor and died a few months later. Thus, Jovian was succeeded by Valens, another pro-Arian. However, there was no further conflict for Athanasius. He was allowed to remain in Alexandria until his death in the year 373.

The Second Eumenical Council in Constantinople in 381 strongly confirmed the doctrine of the council of Nicea.[307] There existed this dichotomy between Antioch and Alexandria in terms of representing Christologies. While in Antioch the focus was more on both the human and divine natures of Jesus, the thinking in Alexandria was that a total union of human and divine existed. However, the divine had absorbed the human.[308]

It was Apollinarius, bishop of Laodicea (Asia Minor) who followed the ways of Athanasius. However, he was condemned by Pope Damasus.[309] Athanasius posited that Jesus is the Savior of mankind. He reasoned that a new creation was necessary in terms of radical reformation and restoration. As a result of sin, humanity became corrupt. Moreover, the work of salvation is not less than that of the work of creation. Thus, our re-creator cannot be less than our Creator. Athanasius had realized that some believed that Jesus, the Son was of the same substance as God, the Father could be misconstrued to mean that there is simply no distinction between the two. Thus, some would not concur with "of the same substances (homosusius); however, it was more palpable to state, "of a similar substance (homoiousios).[310]

In the year 362, a synod took place to discuss this matter. Basically, Athanasius found it acceptable to refer to the Father, Son, and Holy Spirit as of one substance" and that one may posit that "of three substances was also allowable. His main concern was that "of three substances" should not be mistaken for three gods and "of one substance" should not be misconstrued as not recognizing the three. More specifically, one must comprehend the distinction among the three.[311] Essentially, it was Basil, the bishop of Caesarea, a true advocate for the Nicene cause, who not only combated die pro-Arians but also strong reaffirmed the Trinitarian doctrine via various theological treaties. Basil had died a few months prior to die council of Constantinople in 381 where the Nicene doctrine would be strongly confirmed, die fruition of Athanasius and Basil's efforts.[312]

Basil of Caesarea and his brother Gregory of Nyssa were known as the Cappadocian Fathers. Moreover, Gregory of Nazianzus was one of the "Great Cappadocian Fathers who produced hymns in the Greek-speaking church.[313] It was during the year 380 when the Emperor Theodosius entered Constantinople that Gregory, "The Theologian", was made the bishop of Constantinople. The Second Ecumenical Council in 381 of which Gregory presided over was disputed and Nectarius, the evil governor of Constantinople was elected the new bishop.[314,315]

Gregory, a humble and sensitive person, indicated that "We have divided Christ, we who so loved God and Christ."[316] Moreover, Gregory's farewell address included, "my children, I beg you, jealously guard the deposit [of faith] that has been entrusted to you, remember my suffering."[317]

However, in the end, the Council of Constantinople reaffirmed the Nicene Doctrine germane to the divinity of Jesus the Son as well as the doctrine of the Trinity. Basically, the clarification of "ousia" (essence) and "hypostasis" (substance) of which the Cappadocian Fathers determined as the translation of the Latin word, "persona" was discussed during the Council. Thus, the agreed upon formulary indicated one essence (ousia) in three person or hypostases.[318] It is noteworthy to mention Macrina, the sister of Basil and Gregory of Nyssa, who was arranged to marry a young relative which was the norm at that time. When the young man had died suddenly, Macrina vowed herself to celibacy. Essentially, Macrina lived a life of contemplation and played an important role in Basil's spiritual development.[319] However, it was the death of his brother Naucratius who had died suddenly which affected Basil. Naucratius was humble of heart and had rejected worldly pomp which Basil embraced. Thus, Basil became humble and radically changed his ways. Macrina supplied moral support and spiritual direction to Basil. Basically, Macrina, her mother and other spiritual women retreated to Annesi to live the monastic life. Thus, Basil was turned onto the monastic way and became the great teacher of monasticism in the Greek-speaking church.

In a sense, Macrina could be regarded as the founder of Greek monasticism.[320] Due to Basil's efforts, this spread of monasticism in Egypt into Palestine and die Sinai Peninsula was attempted to be integrated into the life of the local church. Basil became known as the father of Eastern Orthodox monasticism. In essence, the Byzantine monasticism maintained its movement although not an institution. Moreover, it had kept the union of asceticism and mysticism in correlation of the primitive church. Byzantine monasticism really did not develop the strong missionary character of western or East Syrian traditions but highly significant.[321]

Lastly, Gregory of Nyssa was Basil's younger brother who had a good education and sought solitude. He married a young woman and after some years she died and Gregory joined the monastic way of life. It was via Basil's influence that Gregory became the bishop of Nyssa, a small territory. Gregory was a staunch proponent of the Nicene cause and was a member of the council of Constantinople in 381.[322] Previously, he went into hiding to avoid the pro-Arians. Ultimately, Theodosius, the Emperor, made Gregory an advisor in matters germane to theology. Thus, this required Gregory to travel, and he went as far as Arabia and Mesopotamia. However, he preferred a simple life of contemplation. Basically, Gregory went back to the monastic life and no information is available of his death.[323]

Another important figure in the fourth century was Ambrose, bishop of Milan. Auxentius, a bishop of Milan who died in 373, was appointed by an Arian emperor. Ambrose who was governor of Milan unexpectedly became the next bishop. Initially, he attended the election as a role of trouble shooter. However, in doing, so he became elected as bishop. Being only a catechumen at the time, Ambrose went through the process in record time only eight days during which he was baptized and covered certain ministerial orders.[324]

Ambrose's brother Uranius Satyrus, governor of another province, came to his aid. Also, their sister Marcellina was a Christian living a semi-monastic life in Rome. However, it was his tutor in theology, Simplicianus, who taught him the rudiments of Christian doctrine. Essentially, Ambrose became a considerable theologian and wrote a treatise, "Duties of the Clergy". This work addressed the formation of the clergy and has been referred in the developing of a good understanding of Christian ministry for church leaders for many years.[325]

Ambrose had endured many difficulties during his bishopric. He had received numerous refugees in Milan as a result of the Goths Mao raided nearby areas. In fact, Ambrose had golden vessels and ornaments of the church melted in order to meet the ransom demands of the Goths who had taken prisoners. Moreover, Ambrose interceded to save a child whose half-brother Gratian was killed when ruling the western part of the empire, Maximus, the new ruler, wanted this child's (Valentianian II) territories. Ambrose was able to avert an invasion by Maximus and kept peace. However, Valentinian's mother Justina who requested Ambrose help actually went against Ambrose at a later time. Years later, Justina tried to get rid of Ambrose ironically via Maximus, but Theodosius intervened successfully against Maximus. Somehow Valentinian was killed in the process, and Theodusius would emerge as the one and only ruler of the empire?[326] It was Theodosius who would allow for the council of Constantinople to take place in 381. Certainly, Theodosius was a strong advocate for the Nicene doctrine. Although Ambrose would need to stand up against Theodosius at times over injustices, in the end they were friends. When the Nicene Christian rulers Theodosius was nearing death, he requested Ambrose at his side on his death bed?[327]

The Germanic queen of the Marcomanni Fritigil, who heard of Ambrose had wanted a document about the Christian faith written by him. Ambrose had complied with her wish. However, Ambrose died on April 4, 397, Easter Sunday, before Fritigil reached Milan to meet and thank him?[328]

Ambrose's sister Marcellina and a woman named Paula with her daughter Julia Eustochium would have a profound influence upon Jerome, a contemporary of the fourth century, Jerome was ordained a presbyter in Antioch and was at Constantinople during the Council.

Essentially Jerome, who studied and enjoyed classical literature, experienced a conversion to a deeper Christian life. He had lived a very worldly life and turned away from it and sought the monastic way of living. However, Jerome studied Hebrew since the Old Testament must be divine. This knowledge would serve him well when Bishop Damasus would make Jerome his personal secretary.[329] Jerome's task was very comprehensive which was to translate the Hebrew Old Testament and Greek New Testament into Latin. The work became known as the versio vulgate or Vulgate later in the Middle Ages. Initially, Jerome translated the Gospels which were completed prior to Damasus' death in 384.[330] Due to rumors of a sexual nature with Paula, a wealthy widow who financed his work, Jerome was required to exit from Rome. Siricius, the bishop who replaced Damasus, was against Jerome who stated that he was leaving "from Babylon to Jerusalem" when Jerome was deported from Rome.[331]

Basically, Jerome was not tactful nor cared what others thought of him Paula and her daughter left Rome taking a different route to

Jerusalem. Jerome and Paula would later found two monastic places in Bethlehem one for men with Jerome's supervision and one for women under Paula's tutelage.[332] In 384, Jerome influenced Paula's eldest daughter Blesilla to live a celibate life, prayer, fasting and study of the scripture. Moreover, Blesilla learned Hebrew but died four months later in November 384. Jerome wrote to Paula indicating that Blesilla is with Mary and the saints?[333]

However, Augustine was in Rome during this time not yet a Christian but a Manichaean. His mother, Monnica, had visions of Augustin being a Christian.[334] Certainly, Rome was a historic city but Roman emperors at this time tended to be northward to cities such as Trier and Milan due to proximity to the routes from Rome to the Balkans. However, Rome was the residence of two thousand senators although they also had estates in various provinces. In fact, Augustine taught in the house of his Manichaean friend by which Augustine would become known to potential pupils.[335]

Essentially, Augustine was initially a student of rhetoric. He was born in 354 at Tagaste in North Africa. It was due to a man named Romanianus that he was able to go to Carthage in order to study. There Augustine found a concubine that had a son from her named Adeodatus.[336]

Manichaeism was founded by Mani who was born in Persia circa 215. His doctrine borrowed parts of Zoroastrianism, Buddhism, Gnosticism, and Christianity.[337] Basically, Manichaeism recognized along series of prophets including Mani himself. Manichaeism spread throughout the Mediterranean basin by the fourth century. He believed in two principles, light and darkness. In essence, Mani posited that the human condition is a commixture of light which is spiritual and darkness which is matter. He believed that salvation was the separation of these two elements. Thus, the mingling of the two result is evil. Thus, procreation must not happen.[338] In 275, Mani was skinned alive per order of the Persian emperor?[339] Nine years prior to Augustine's conversion to the Christian faith, he was a Manichae?[340] However, it was Simplicianus who had previously tutored Ambrose during his catechumenate who too influenced Augustine.

Basically, Simplicianus brought the philosophy of Neoplatonism to Augustine as a means to an end which would hopefully be Christianity. Essentially, it was via Neoplatonism that Augustine was to realize God and soul in an incorporeal fashion.[341] At first, Augustine was more interested in listening to Ambrose's sermons in terms of rhetoric and articulation. It was not the content of Ambrose's sermon but how he had delivered it. When Ambrose had provided interpretations of scripture passages which was obscure to Augustine, thus then the meanings became palable to Augustine.[342] Although Augustine had decided to become Christian, he had experienced an internal struggle. Moreover, it was the conversion of a famous philosopher, namely Marius Victorinus, who translated the writing of the Neoplatonist to Latin which profoundly affected Augustine?[343]

Damasus was the Bishop of Rome when Augustine had arrived in the city. There existed a division among Christians due to the Arians. In the years 383 to 384, Rome was experiencing a serious food shortage. The etiology of this situation was likely a succession of poor harvests. Thus, not only did food shortages result, but inflation of the cost of various staple foods as well. Certainly, this shortage forced the poor to do without or they would rather fall into personal debt in order to survive?[344] Essentially, Damasus who lead the Christian community for approximately twenty years, often visited popular burial sites of Rome's Christian martyrs, and made known their presence.

In fact, Damasus had a new church for Laurentius of Rome (Saint Laurence d.258) positioned around the campus Martius across the rival racing-factions where situated their stables near the "Greens". Out of all the Christian martyrs, it was Laurentius who was the most dedicated to the poor and needy.[345,346]

Actually, Damasus was actively involved in excavations to rediscover the remains of the martyrs. An inscription in the cemetery near Via Salaria is read (as translated into English), "the tomb was hidden under the hill's furthest mound, stated as this, Damasus reveals, because he preserves the bodies of the pious."[347]

It is important to note that Damaus had written and promoted the significance of virginal life. Moreover, Damasus fostered a rule that his senior clergymen must maintain their celibacy. He had opposition from a certain Helvetius, a former Christian ascetic. who denied the virginity of the Blessed Mother Mary. Also noteworthy, Jerome had not only wrote letters to Paula's daughter, but to men as well in support of celibacy.[348]

Later in life, Augustine would write as well for men to be celibate.[349] Meanwhile, Augustine was formally converted to the Christian faith when he and his son Adeodatus was baptized by Ambrose at Easter in 387?[350] Thus, Augustine had left his teaching position and his concubine of many years. With his mother Monnica and his son Adeodatus, Augustine decided to return to Tagaste. However, at the seaport of Ostia in Rome, Monnica took ill and died.[351,352] Thus, Augustine, Adeodatus, and some friends stayed in Rome for several months. Augustine would later write in his writings, "Confessions", "glad to weep before you [God] about her and for her, about myself and for myself. Now I let flow the tears which I had held back so that they ran as freely as they wished. My heart rested upon them, and it reclined upon them because it was your ears that were there, not those of some human critic"?[353]

It is important to reflect upon Augustine's personal experience as a catechumen. Essentially, Augustine as well as his son, Adeudatus, Alypius and others had their names accepted and took part in the preparation class. Initially, they were called competentesor seekers who participated in a certain routine of mainly solid instruction and strict discipline?[354] The process of his catechumenate entailed attending class twice a day for thirty days in Lent. Basically, during the week at the third and ninth hour of each day Augustine had participated in services of worship and heard Ambrose's homilies.

Both Augustine and Alypius had already adhered to a vow of celibacy. The process involved a strict diet and abstinence of worldly pleasures. In fact, the bodies of the Candidates were checked for "signs of demons"[355] Augustine and the other candidates were required the books of the Old Testament including Ecclesiasticus, Proverbs, and Wisdom.

Certainly, Ambrose's sermons contained various people of the Old Testament and provided a moral to the story. Moreover, Ambrose covered New Testament incidences such as the Samaritan woman of the well and the Lord Jesus raising Lazarus from the dead?[356] On April 18, 387, Palm

Sunday, Ambrose revealed the words of the creed and expounded on each creedal statement in detail. The candidates were to learn it and commit the creed to memory. There existed a particular power of secrecy about the creed as part of a Christian initiation?[357] Ambrose parsed out the creed into three groups of four, thus twelve parts in all, analogously "like the twelve apostles. During Holy Week, Ambrose increased his preaching daily and covered the creation would one day write and teach from this sermon of creation as well as expound on it. On Holy Thursday, Ambrose focused on penance and forgiveness with the entire congregation. Early Easter Sunday, the Catechumeans were brought together for baptismal rite of immersion. The candidates were completely dressed in white clothing and approached Ambrose as he cited die Ephphatha, rite of opening, as he touched their ears and nose, according to the Gospel of Mark's account of Jesus using this word in the healing of a deaf man (Mark 7: 32-35)[358]

Being anointed by both a priest and a Deacon, the candidates entered the baptistery facing west, renouncing Satan, and looked east into the rising sun, turning to Christ. The Candidates took off their clothes, men and women in different areas of the Church. Women were brought to the smaller baptistery by the Old Basilica. Augustine and the other me cathechumeans or candidates were likely in the octagonal baptistery in the New Basilica which was sixty feet wide with pillars and mosaics with a particular pattern of a black and white floor.[359] Ambrose would also strip himself of clothes with the men and anoint them with oil. Thus, the candidates would submerge their heads into the water three times, one for each person in the Blessed Trinity. When they had left the water, Ambrose anointed them again on their heads.[360] Ambrose had washed the feet of each candidate not only in reference to the Lord Jesus washing the feet of the Apostles, but also Ambrose was washing out "the venom of the serpent". Thus, washing the candidates' individual sins as well as original sin. Basically, Ambrose's prayer included filling the candidates with the Holy Spirit, "with inner light".[361] After being sealed and washed, they processed to the New Church dressed in white as they sang Psalm 23. The congregation sang as the candidates turned converts and entered the church as they prepare to receive the Eucharist, Holy Communion. During every day of Easter week, concluding the Saturday after Easter, Ambrose brought the new converts together and provided additional instruction and reflection, expounding on the deeper meanings of the sacraments and the Lord's Prayer.[362]

After the death of Monnica, Augustine returned to Tagaste and sold most of his property. Augustive and Adeodatus went to Cassiciacum with some close friends. Adeodatus died in 390 at the age of age of seventeen?[363] Augustine was focused on prayer, study, and writing at Cassiciacum. In 391, he went to a village called Hippo to meet a friend Bishop Valerius would recruit Augustine as a co-bishop in Hippo, around four years later?[364]

Basically, there was a rule in place which did not allow for two bishops for a single church. Essentially, Valerius wrote to Aurelius, bishop of Carthage, requesting permission due to his old age and illness to have Augustine share responsibility in the bishopric. Valerius received a positive response via letter from Aurelius. Bishop Megalius of Calama, while visiting the church in Hippo with other bishops, reinforced the bishopric on Augustine.[365]

It was in the summer of 396, less than a year later, that Augustine began writing the confessions that he was now serving as co-bishop in Hippo. The bishops had maintained that there were precedents not only in Africa but "across the sea" as well.[366] At that time, Megalius in charge of the diocese of Numidia was the senior bishop, in other words, he served as bishop the longest. Essentially, Megalius was not pleased with appointing Augustine according to his letter to Valerius, which fell into the hands of the Donatists around four years later.[367]

The Donatists emerged early in the fourth Century when Caecilian, a new bishop of Carthage, was named in 311. Since his appointments was considered invalid and Caecilian was unwilling to face his accusers, a group of bishops, he was replaced by Majorinus. Caecilian was popular in Cathage and Rome had remained in communion with him. Essentially, Donatus succeeded Majorinus as bishop and a schism had formed in North Africa. Thus, two 'churches' existed in North Africa with the Donatists opposing the Christian Catholic Church.[368] A significant number of Donatists were in Hippo at the time Augustine's bishopric.

Basically, Augustine's view was that the church was composed of a mixture of various people with varying levels of commitment and participation in the sacraments. Moreover, Augustine pointed out that it is, in reality Christ, who baptizes via the clergy. Thus, the body of Christ encompasses those who receive the sacraments from Jesus the Christ regardless of the degree of holiness of the clergy.[369] According to Augustine, "there is no other Catholic Church than that which according to the promise is spread abroad throughout the whole world.[370] Acts of violence conducted by the Donatists lead to the calling of a conference consisting of equal number of 284 on each side in June of 411. In essence, the Donatists became known as heretics and determined illegal. Augustine took a harsh stance utilizing reason and argument towards the Donatists.

Over time, many of the Donatists returned to the Catholic Church in Hippo and other villages and cities as well.[371] Augustine had attended the council at Carthage on August 28,397 as bishop of Hippo. It is believed that Valerius died prior to the council. Essentially, Augustine's wirings against the Donatists were approximately between the years 400 to 412.[372] In the year 410, Rome fell to the barbarians since civil wars had weakened Rome's strength and frontier systems.

Essentially, core provinces in the west went one by one. It was a long process, and the Roman Empire was still more powerful than any other single force.[373] Augustine's major work, *City of God* was his response to the fall of the earthly city.

The first chapter of the *City of God* begins as follows: "For this earthly city belong the enemies against whom I have to defend the city of God. Many of them, indeed, being reclaimed from their ungodly error, have become sufficiently creditable citizens of this city; but many are so inflamed with hatred against it, and are so ungrateful to its redeemer for His Signal benefits, as to forget that they would now be unable to utter a single word to its prejudice, had they not founding its sacred places, as they fled from the enemy's steel that life in which they now boast themselves. Are not those very Romans, who were spared by the barbarians though their respects for Christ, become enemies to the name of Christ? The reliquaries of the martyrs and the churches of the apostles bear witness to this; for in the sack of the city they were open sanctuary for all who fled to them, whether Christian or Pagan....And they ought to attribute it to the spirit of these Christian times, that, contrary to the custom of war, these blood-thirsty barbarians spared them, and spared them for Christ's sake, whether this mercy was actually shown in promiscuous places, or in those places specially dedicated to Christ's name, and of which the very largest were selected as sanctuaries, that full scope might thus be given to the expansive compassion which desired that a large multitude might find shelter there."[374]

Augustine s baptizer Ambrose died on Easter Saturday 397. Due to recent discoveries, some of Augustine's long-lost sermons were published in 1994 by Francois Dolbeau. Basically, Augustine's homilies for the five-month period following Ambrose's death was germane to health. However, he likely began with those six homilies about the days of creation during Easter Week. Augustine initially gives thanks to the Lord for his congregation's love and thanksgiving. He followed with expounding on Psalm 60:11 in the Latin text.[375]

Essentially Francois Dolbean discovered the long lost sermons in the Mainzs Cathedral library of which thirteen correlated with titles in a group of thirty sermons that Benedictine Scholar Donatien De Bruyne founding 1931 in Possidius (Augustine's associate) collection in the library at Hippo. Moreover, Benedictine Cyrille Lambotin 1935 indicated that this collection of Sermons happened between Ascension Day in May, 397 and the council of Carthage on August, 397.[376]

Augustine was mostly preaching in Carthage and other local areas during this time. Although none of these sermons have a year date, Lambot was able to date them. Moreover, Dolbean is fairly accurate based upon available data. Interestingly, the sermons coincidences with the "confessions" which was likely completed by this time might serve as supporting evidence of the hypothesis of Lambot's determination of the dates.

Thus, Augustine was preaching and teaching on the word confession in terms of "confession of sins" as well as "confession (testifying) in praise of God".[377] Possidius described Augustine on his death bed in Hippo "and, lying in his bed, he had the pages, in fours, placed against the wall, and in the days of his weakness, he would gaze at them and read, and he would weep copiously and continuously."[378] Augustine died at the age of seventy-six in the year 430.

In a sense, he was the last of the great Christian thinkers in the West. Augustine was one of the truly great doctors of the Church who was referenced the most during the Middle Ages.[379] Augustine provided a synthesis of universal history derived from his theory of human nature as well as from his theology of creation and grace. Thus, he connected a rational theory of the nature of society and law with social living in correlation to ethics.[380]

Essentially, the Greeks had the suppositions of society and a political philosophy while lacking a philosophy of history. It was more cosmological oriented than historical oriented since time did not have the same level of significance. Time was considered a "number of movement" with a regularity contingent on the influences of the heavenly bodies. While the Christian at this age had a basis or theory of history without the Hellenic notion of society and philosophy. In fact, the Christian faith was rooted in a sacred history, the revelation of a divine plan for all people. Moreover, the coming of Christ marks the very turning point of history and fulfillment of a divine purpose.[381]

It was John of Constantinople, who was consecrated bishop in 398, who utilized the Antiochene style of exegesis to promote the Christian faith. Essentially, the Antiochene tradition expanded on the scriptures by emphasizing the historical and literal meaning.[382] John, who later generations would refer to as Chrysostom (golden mouth), was born in Antioch. Syria Circa 350 A.D. Actually, the church of Antioch was founded by Paul and visited by Peter. Antioch had a population of approximately 300,000, mostly Greeks but various other ethnic groups such as Syrians, Phoenicians, Roman, and Jews?[383]

John's father died while John was still an infant and his mother, Anthusa was a devout Christian. At the age of twenty, John began his catechumenate and was baptized three years later by Bishop Meletius of Antioch.[384] John's teacher was a well-known rhetorician, Libanius who was asked who would succeed him. Libanius indicated that "John, but the Christians have laid claim on him".[385] John's mother did not want him to become a monk while she was still living. In response to his mother, John made their home like a monastery with three friends. After the death of his mother, John took to the ascetic life with the monks in the Syrian mountains. Under the tutelage of an old Syrian monk for about four years, John spent two more years in an isolated cave in full solitude.[386] After living the monastic life for six years, John had returned to Antioch where he was ordained a deacon and then a presbyter.

It was when a vacancy in the bishopric of Constantinople occurred, the emperor ordered that John fill the capacity of bishop as a result of the death of Nectarius in 397. After twenty years serving the church of Antioch, John became bishop in early 398.[387,388] The emperor Theodosius died, and his sons Honorius and Arcadius succeeded him. Essentially, Arcadius ruled the East. However, the palace chamberlain had enormous influence and used his power in a self-serving fashion. The empress Eudoxia, Arcadius wife was responsible for John's selection as bishop. Actually, the Patriarch Theophilus of Alexandria had preferred Alexandrine instead of John for bishop.[389]

The wealthy people of Constantinople lived a very luxurious lifestyle contrary to the gospel message. However, John first sought to reform the lifestyle of the clergy. Many Clergymen had "spiritual sisters" in their homes which was the impetus for scandal. Some clergymen had accumulated considerable wealth while the Church finances were not in good shape.[390] Essentially, John demanded that these women leave the homes of priests. Moreover, he straightened out the financial disarray of the church by selling various items of luxury in the bishop's palace in order to feed the poor. Also, John developed a financial system with oversight and openness. By and large, he catered to the poor and working class while harshly addressing the well to do from the pulpit.[391] John was well and wide y accepted by the common man. However, his powerful enemies included prelates, courtiers, and, most importantly, the empress Eudoxia.[392]

Moreover, the Patriarch of Alexandria Theophilus, who wanted someone else as bishop, brought many false charges against John before a group of bishops. Initially, John ignored these untruthful claims. However, Theophilus and others found John guilty as charged and collaborated with Eudoxia who convinced the emperor Arcadius to expel John into exile. Although John had many faithful supporters among the people and clergymen, John decided to surrender and leave without any resistance. Afterwards, an earthquake ensued which Eudoxia took as a sign from God. Thus, Eudoxia strongly requested that John return to the church of Saint Sophia and John concurred with her plea. John was greeted very warmly in the city, especially his church at Hagia Sophia.[393] In only a few months, John was again required to be exiled. Again, he had passively surrendered, not listening to his supporters who urged him to resist.

Essentially, it was not a quiet removal due to serious rioting of the people. Public buildings were set on fire and many of John's supporters were tortured. John had been exile to Cucusus, a faraway place without a pupil to preach. Thus, John began to write and Cucusus, a small village, received much attention. Pope Innocent put together a Latin delegation with a letter to Arcadius attention. This determined delegation experienced a "Babylonian treatment" upon arrival. This treatment included imprisonment, torture, and an offering of a three-thousand gold bribe. After refusing to take the bribe, the Latin delegation was brought to a ship which was designed to sink in the water. However, the delegation found a way to return to Rome. Moreover, John was exiled once again to a cold area around the Black Sea. John became very ill during the travel and died in a small church at his request to receive Holy Communion and preach a sermon.

His last and shortest homily was simply, "In all things, Glory to God Amen."[394] John died September 14, 407. John had preached many sermons during his priesthood in Antioch. His famous sermons on the parable of Lazarus and the rich man beginning in the year 388 or 389 set the tone for his priestly ministry.[395] John's church in Constantinople Saint Sophia was built initially per order of Constantine and completed under Constantins.

During the fourth century, the Christian presence and population grew in Constantinople. The bodies of Timothy, Luke, and Andrew were brought to the shrine of the Holy Apostles due to Constantius. In fact, this is the first time that relics were taken from the original resting place. Constantinople became a significant repository for relics.[396] In Edessa East of Antioch, a semitic type of Christian faith evolved which differed from the Greek and Latin Christianity around the Mediterranean. Ephrem

(d. 373) the Syriac poet had composed spiritual hymns which became part of the Syriac Liturgy.[397] He spent his final years in Edessa which became Christian during the tenure of King Abgarus LX (179-216). A legend existed that Jesus had written a letter and dispatched Thaddeus to Edessa to meet with King Abgarus V, a leper. When reading the letter, Abgarus was healed of leprosy?[398] In Adiabene, not far from Edessa, there is evidence of a Christian community residing there in the early second century. Moreover, Armenia was a buffer country between Persia and Rome. It served Rome's interests to Keep Armenia an independent entity so that it functioned as a protective area on the Eastern borders.[399]

Gregory Lusavorich, the Illuminator was converted in Caesarea of Cappadocia while in exile in the Roman Empire. His relative King Tradt III who was exiled as well would eventually be returned to die throne. Essentially, Gregory made his way back to Armenia and converted Tradt and baptized him on January 6, 303, the Epiphany. Gregory endured many trials and sufferings in order to convert Tradt. However, this resulted in mass conversions to Christianity in Armenia. Even the scriptures were translated into the Armenian language.[400] Gregory was made bishop via the metropolitan of Caesarea in Cappadocia and died in 328.[401] Actually, Armenia is the first country to convert to the Christian faith after the baptism of its ruler.[402]

John of Constantinople wrote a letter to Maron, a Christian ascetic who sought solitude on a mountain south of Cyrrhus and northwest of Aleppo, in 406 while in exile a year prior to his death. John indicated "Maron, priest and solitary that he is "joined to [him] in the bonds of charity and affection." Moreover, John of Constantinople (Chrysostom), who knows of the holy life of prayer led by Maron, requests Maron's prayers.[403] A Chalcedonian community called the Maronites were named after Maron who died in the early fifth century.[404] It is through the writing of Theodoret and John of Constantinople (Chrysostom) that the life of Maron was known to be the years 350 to 410 although Maron may have lived to 423.[405]

Essentially, Maron followed the way of the hermit Zebinas who spent his entire day in prayer. Theodoret, the bishop of Cyrrhus (393-466), had indicated in his writings, a religious history of Syriac asceticism, that Maron chose a mountain which had been a pagan temple. Moreover, Maron changed it into a Christian Church dedicated to the "true God".[406]

Basically, Maron lived a very austere life sleeping mostly in the open air although he had a small tent. He prayed and fasted most of the time. According to Theodoret, "He cured not only infirmities of the body, but applied suitable treatment to soul as well, healing this man's greed that man's anger, to this man supplying teaching in self-control and to that providing lessons in justice, correcting this man s intemperance and shaking up another man's sloth."[407]

After Maron's death, villagers took his body and built a church over it. Also, a monastery was put together at Qalauat al Modeeq near Apameus in Maron's honors. Thus, the Monastery of Maron (Bet Maroun) became well known and significant number of monks inhabited it. In fact, the Arab historian Abu Al-Fida indicated that the Emperor Marcian wanted to support the doctrine posited by the council of Chalcedon by permitting a hundred monks living in Bet Maroun.[408] Actually, both the Maronites and the Melkites were very strong defenders of the true doctrines of the council of Chalcedon. The leader of Bet Maroun, the monastery, Alexander sent a letter to the bishops of the region in support of the true doctrine. Essentially, this letter found its way in the year 553 in the acts of the Fifth Ecumenical council of Constantinople.[409]

During the fifth century, various controversies tended to divide Christians in the east. Essentially, Middle East Christians who mainly spoke Syriac and in communion with the emperor in Constantinople were the Melkites. The Copts in Egypt who had a patriarch together with the west Syrians residing near Antioch became Known as the Jacobites.[410]

The bishop of Edessa (543-578) Jacob Baradcus moved about consecrating bishops and making a separate independent hierarchy in Syria. Thus, the creation of non-Chalcedonians or miaphysites which included the Copts, had formed in the sixth century. Nestorians, Syriac-speaking Christians in the Sasanid Persian Empire were opposed to the Council of Ephesus in 431 where Nestorius, the disposed bishop of Constantinople claimed that Jesus had two personalities or two distinctly different persons.[411] Basically, he believed that Jesus, the Christ, could not be both God and man at the same time. Thus, Nestorius maintained that Christ not God was born in Bethlehem and that Christ not God who actually died on the cross.[412]

After the Councils of Ephesus (431) and Chalcedon (451), the majority of Persian Christians were against the decision germane to this notion of Nestorius. Thus, they were regarded as "Monophysite" since they believed that Jesus the Christ had one nature. His humanity absorbed into the divine nature.[413] In the Eastern Church, there were two schools of thought, the Antiochene and the Alexandrine. Essentially, both schools of thought were in

agreement that the divine was immutable and eternal. Thus, both schools of thought believed that Jesus, the Christ was divine and human. The Alexandrines were well-grounded in Clement and Origen of the early years, meaning that Jesus was the teacher of the divine truth. While the Antiochenes stressed that Jesus must be fully human since he was the savior of humans.[414] Basically, the Antiochene thinking was that divinity and humanity are not combined as one while the Alexandrine belief was that the divinity overcomes the humanity.

In the Western Church, the decline of the Roman Empire with Germanic invasions had more pressing issues. However, the church filled the void and ecclesiastical leaders obtained political influence and power.[415]

Basically, the Latin West rested upon the formulary of Tertullian meaning in Christ there were two natures in one person. It was Apollinaris of Laodicea who proposed that Jesus the Word of God fulfilled the role of the rational soul. Thus, Jesus would not have a human intellect although He had a physical body. Essentially, the Word of God was the rational soul or intellect. This theory was rejected by the Antiochenes since Jesus must be fully human. The Alexandrines found Apollinaris' supposition to be very palliable to them, Gregory of Nazianzuz indicated Jesus saved actually that which He "joined" to His divinity.[416]

When Nestorius, who was from the Antiochene school of thought became patriarch of Constantinople in 428, a confrontation would ensue with the Alexandrines. Bishop Cyril of Alexandria gained support from the Western Church as well as of emperors Valentinian III and Theodosius

II prior to the Council of Ephesus in 431. Since Constantinople became the capital of the Eastern Empire, the bishop of Constantinople was thought to have the authority in the east as that of the Bishop of Rome's authority in the west.[417]

John of Antioch, a proponent of Nestorius, had arrived two weeks late to the convening of the council. Both sides condemned each other and as a result Theodosius H declared the councils null and void. Moreover, he had Cyril and John arrested which subsequently led to a certain "formula of union". Thus, Cyril and John concurred in this compromise in 433. Nestorius was exiled to Antioch in a monastery. However, he ultimately would reside in Petra.[418]

Eutyches, a monk in Constantinople, proposed that Jesus was "of one substance (homoousios) with the Father." However, Jesus was not one substance with us. His hypothesis was that Jesus had two natures prior to the union and one nature afterwards. Eutyches were officially condemned by Flavian, Patriarch of Constantinople.[419]

Cyril successor Dioscorus blew this conflict out of proportion and the Emperor Theodosius II called another council at Ephesus in 449: Dioscorus dominated the proceedings as the officially appointed chairman by the emperor, Representatives of Pope. Leo was not permitted to read his letter publicly thus became known as Leo's Tome. In just a few days, Flavian died after being beat up. The two natures notion were determined to be heretical. Pope Leo referred to the Council as the "Robber Synod".[420]

It is believed that Theodosius II was the recipient of a significant sum of gold from Alexandria. When Theodosius' had broken his neck as the result of an accident on his horse, his sister Pulcheria took command. She called yet another council on behalf of Pope Leo of Rome. The council assembled at Chalcedon in 451 which condemned Dioscorus and Eutyches although forgiving others who had participated. Pope Leo's letter was read to all and was essentially a restatement of Tertullian's "two natures in one person." Thus, a definition of faith was constructed which served as a confirmation of past councils such as Nicea (325), Constantinople (381), and Ephesus (431).[421]

It is as follows: "Following, then , the holy Fathers, we all with one voice teach that it is to be confessed that our Lord Jesus Christ is one and the same God, perfect in divinity, and perfect in humanity, true God and true human, with a rational soul and body, of one substance with the Father in his divinity, and of one substance with using his humanity, in every way like us, with the only exception of sin, begotten of the Father before all time in his divinity, and also begotten in the latter days, in his humanity, of Mary the Virgin bearer of God. This is one and the same Christ, son, Lord, Only-begotten, manifested in two natures without any confusion, change, division or separation. The union does not destroy the difference of the two natures, but on the contrary the properties of each are kept, and both are joined in one person and hypostasis. They are not divided into two persons, but belong to the one Only begotten Son, die Word of God, the Lord Jesus Christ. All this, as the prophets of old said of him, and as he himself has taught us, and as the Creed of the Fathers has passed on to us."[422]

Certainly, die Council of Chalcedon became a turning point for Christianity. Essentially, the Monophysites (one nature) were prevalent in Armenia, Western Syria, Egypt, Nubia, and Ethiopia, while die Dyophysites (two natures) were connected with the theological school of Antioch as well as the teachings of Theodore of Mopsuestia and Nestorius. '

Moreover, the Persian Church also became known as the Nestorian Church. Thus, the Monophysite and Dyophysite theological positions were none Chalcedonian while the churches of the Latin west and Greek East supported the definition of faith, known as the definition of chalcedon.[423]

In 489, the well-known school in Edessa closed as a result of favoring Nestorianism.[424] Since the city of Edessa, Syria became part of the Roman Empire, it was incumbent on the school to conform to Constantinople's doctrinal beliefs. Moreover, the emperor Zeno pushed the teachers and students out. Thus, they went northeast to Nisibis, a Syriac-speaking city in Persia.[425] Narsai, the former director of the school in Edessa, became the first premier teacher as well as provided a significant mission theology to Nisibis. Unequivocally, it grew into "the most famous center of learning in all Asia outside China."[426]

In a strict setting, the school focused on the study of the scriptures. However, medical studies and Greek philosophy were salient parts of their curriculum. [427] By the conclusion of the fifth century, an independent national church of Persia with the appointment of a patriarch being confirmed by the shah was realized.[428] The purpose of the school of Nisibis was moral formation via an understanding of the scriptures. Faculty and students participated in prayer, meditation, and worship. The reading and recitation of scriptures was ritualistic and chant like.[429]

Essentially, overtime the Syriac-speaking Christians in the Sasanid Empire gained their own identity. However, when the Sasanids defeated the Parthians, Zoroastrianism became the official religion. Thus, persecution of Christians became a reality.[430] Actually, the Emperor Constantine's letter to Shapur H, then Sasanid King, hurt more than helped the cause of Christians living in Persia. Thus, the Sasanids called Christianity the "religion of Caesar" and the Sasanids doubled the taxes on the "Nazarenes". When the Christian leadership protested the tax increase, they were killed. Persecution was spurred by two variables, the notion that Christians were loyal to Rome and Zoroastrianism's re-emergence.

This Iranian religion had begun with Zoroaster (Zorathusra) in the second millennium B.C. According to the Sasanid King, "These Christians destroy our Holy Teaching, and teach men to serve one God, and not to honor the Sun or Fire. They defile water by their ablutions, they refrain from marriage and the propagation of children, and refuse to go to war with the King of Kings [the sasanid ruler]. They have no rules about the slaughter and eating of animals; they bury the corpses of men in the earth. They attribute the origin of snakes and creeping things to a good God. They despise many servants of the King and teach witchcraft".[431]

There were thousands of martyrs starting in 341 until the death of King Shapur in 379. The Persian Church was then able to gain its identity and become connected in faith with the western church of Rome.[432] The council of bishops in Seleucia-Ctesiphon in 410 was led by bishop Izhaq. They accepted the creed and canons of Nicaea and Constantinople and subsequently in 424 declared themselves as self-governing body. Thus, the bishops of Persia would no longer defer decision-making to the church of the West. Basically, the "Catholicos of the East" assumed the title of patriarch by the conclusion of the sixth century.[433]

Perhaps the etiology of this separation was mainly due to resentment against Constantinople's government which imposed taxes in the provinces as well as cultural and ethnic differences. Emperors would tend to create theological decisions to appease both sides of an argument in an effort to compromise and maintain loyalty. Thus, these theological compromises fostered controversy.[434] For example, Basilisens called for a council in 476 rejecting the decisions of Chalcedon. When Zeno regained power, he prevented a council from meeting and issued an Edict of Union (Henotikon) in 482.

Although Pope Felix ITT opposed Zeno's authority in regard to theological matters, Zeno was backed by Acacius, Patriarch of Constantinople. Thus, this schism of Acacius fueled a division between the church of the East from the church of the West until the year 519.[435] An agreement between the Emperor Justin and Pope Hormisdas approved the decisions of Chalcedon. Essentially Justinian, the nephew of Justin, became emperor and believed that there were simply semantic differences between the Chalcedonians and Monophysites. Thus, Justinian brought back Monophysite bishops as well as invited them as special guests at the emperor's palace.[436]

An important caveat between the churches of the East and West was the issue of celibacy. Although celibacy was an absolute in the monastic life, it was not a requirement for the clergy. In 486, a council met under Acacius who was still the catholicos and the bishops of Persia approved the marriage of bishops. Essentially, clergy (priest) or bishops were not permitted to marry after ordination. Celibacy was interpreted as an affront to Persian Culture.[437]

The scriptural foundation utilized by bishops of Persia was Paul's letter to Timothy (I Timothy 3: 1-2): "If anyone aspires to the office of Bishop, he desires a noble task. Now a bishop must be above reproach, married only once...." As well as Paul's letter to the Corinthians stating that "It is better to marry than to burn" (I Corinthians 7:9).[438] Essentially, the Church of the East was situated in the lowlands and hillsides on the East side of the Tigris River extending further Easterly.

The monks and bishops brought the gospel message to India, China, and Ceylon which is present day Sri Lanka.[439] By and large Latin-speaking monks spread Christianity to northern Europe while Greek-speaking monks brought the gospel to the Slavs and the Syriac-speaking monk continued Eastward. Certainly, the Silk Road which began at Antioch and went thru the Middle East to Persia via Sogdiana and Kyrgyzstan to the Turpan oasis in the Western part of China all the way to the Great Wall of China was the main path to the Far East. Of course, merchants brought silk, spices, jewels, perfumes, and glass but more importantly, culture and religion such as the Christian faith. Christian merchants, monks, and clergy in unique fashion spread Christianity, particularly Syriac-speaking ones to Merv which was positioned twelve hundred miles East of Syria. Thus, Merv became a base of operations for missionary work to the Turkish tribes East of the Oxus River and ultimately China.[440]

The religion of Islam founded by Muhammad would originate in Arabia in the seventh century. Moreover, Islam would extend from India to Spain within a century. Essentially, the Muslin Arab rule would split the Christian world by the year 750. Basically, under the auspices of Muslim rule, Christians were regarded as a unit politically according to a certain category, namely dhimmi. By and large, Christians were enticed to convert to Islam via a tax levied specifically upon Christian adult men. The tax was very severe, and some Christians succumbed to the wishes of the Muslims. However, Christianity actually grew in number despite the adversity. Since the Christians were educated, they remained valuable in fields such as education, medicine, trade, and administration. Thus, Christians were able to witness for Christ via their respective occupations overall within society.[441']

Essentially, East Syrian Christians were in the minority within a very strong interreligious milieu. Basically, Christians found Zoroastrians, Muslims Buddhist, and Manichaean Communities along the trade routes into northeastern Persia and across central Asia.[442] Moreover, Christians would encounter a wide variety of traditional religious practiced by the Turks, Huns and Mongols. Certainly, Christians found Taoist and Confucian religious beliefs in China and Hinduism in India.[443]

The East Syrian missionary, Alopen was present in the Chinese capital of Chang'an in 635. He was ordered to translate the scriptures into the Chinese language.[444] Altogether, there were twenty-one Christian Persian monks in China by the year 638, at this time the emperor financed the building of the first Christian church in China. More specifically, the church was built in Chang'an which was the largest city in the world at that time.[445]

The Emperor Tai-tsung (626-649) of the Tang Dynasty (618 - 907) had issued an official decree stating, "The Persian monk A-lo-pen has come from afar bringing scriptures and teaching .... The meaning of the teaching has been carefully examined; it is mysterious, wonderful, calm; it fixes the essentials of life and perfection; it is the salvation of living beings; it is the wealth of man. It is right that it should spread through the empire. Therefore, let the local officials build a monastery in the I-ning quarter with twenty-one regular monks."[446]

It is believed that Alopen had written four Chinese Christian treatises, the first one named Jesus-messiah Sutra while the others entitled, Discourses on Monotheism. Essentially, these works may possibly be previously written and then translated in whole or in part from earlier texts in Syriac. However, these works may have been written to address specific questions raised by Chinese scholars germane to Christian teachings.[447]

Basically, Christians experienced a relatively short period of persecution from 638 to 712 due to a regime change. However, a time of recovery from 712 to 781 had followed. In essence, East Syrian Christianity during this era was correlated with political connections and noted scholarship. Due to the Muslim Arab invasion of Persia, the Persian crown prince and some of his court vent to Chang'an joining East Syrian Monks and Persian Business traders.[448]

Certainly, a bishop named Adam whose Chinese name was Ching Ching, was "so famed for his knowledge of Chinese language and literature that even Buddhist missionaries came to him for help in translating their own sacred books."[449]

Prajna, a Buddhist, had requested assistance of Adam and they collaborated in translating seven volumes of Buddhist sutras to Chinese. Interestingly enough, Prajna resided with two of the most famous men of Japanese Buddhism who were founders of the Shingon sect of tantric Buddhism and the Lotus school of Japanese Buddhism. Thus, it is logical and apparent that "for the purpose of communicating the Christian Message, and for the deepening of their own faith-life in the Messiah, they employed Buddhist terms, expressions, and symbols".[450]

Evidence suggests that T'ang Dynasty Christianity was not on heretically Nestorian. Moreover, it was not "fatally syncretistic". Basically, Christianity was accepted by the T'ang dynasty which favored religious liberty. However, the Christian faith dissipated soon after the conclusion of the T'ang Dynasty in 907.[451] Unequivocally, the best evidence of Christianity in ancient China is a huge stone monument located on the precincts of a temple in Sian-fii near Xi'an. The black limestone monument is ten feet high and three and a half feet wide composed of seventeen hundred Chinese characters showing how to pronounce the words. The Syrian text identifies its author as "Adam, priest and bishop of the Countryside and spiritual master of Zinistan [China]".[452]

The construction of the monument was to honor a monk named I-ssu. Moreover, a historical account of Alopen from Persia contained within a history of the "luminous religion". The text indicates that there are twenty-seven books of Scriptures referencing baptism, worship, keeping the Sabbath, and certain rules for the monks. More specially, the text germane to Syriac-speaking monks:"Purification is made perfect by solitude and meditation; self-restraint grows strong by silence and watching."[453] It is important to note that aside from official Chinese records, a cache of various Christian documents were uncovered in a walled-up chapel in Tunhuang during the early nineteenth century.

Many works written in Chinese and some translated writings from Syriac with original documents were discovered. A hymn in adoration of the "Transfiguration of our Lord," a work entitled Jesus Messiah Sutra, a Discourse on the Oneness of the Rules of the Universe, and finally another one germane to almsgiving were found.[454']

According to an Arab writer in Baghdad in 987, he indicated that a monk who was a missionary to China had returned to Baghdad. The monk told this Arab writer that most Christians died, and their churches were destroyed. In fact, the monk could not find anyone to minister to. Thus, he came back home.

Essentially, there is no evidence of a continuous history of the Christian faith in China.[455] Turning to the mission of the African Christian church, there exists a continual line much longer than Christianity has in Scotland. In a sense African Christians can trace their Christian roots back almost to the apostolic age.[456] It was Tatian the Assyrian who is closely correlated with the initial stage of a monastic movement in Syria during the second century. Certainly, the life of Antony, a desert hermit who in 273 started his eremitical life.

During the fourth century, Pachomius, the Egyptian ascetic constructed a rule for communal monasticism. However, it did not end at this point but served as a catalyst for tens of thousands of men and women ascetic for many decades living according to his rules.[457] Two very ancient monastic traditions held to different approaches. While the Egyptian monastics emphasized stability and basically withdrew from the world, Syria monastics stressed movement and became wanderers. Egyptian monasticism had a very staunch nationalistic character. Moreover, it had spread across various nations and cultures in a variety of forms and thus evolved into the primary means of mission in both the Greek East and Latin West, Basil of Caesarea, Martin of Jours, Melania the Younger, Patrick of Ireland, and Benedict of Nursia were significant in fostering the missions.[458]

Moreover, the many desert fathers and mothers of Egypt are included in this vision of spirituality and ministry. Although Ethiopia can trace its Christian roots to the Ethiopian eunuch and the apostle Matthew, the king and royal court of Axum during the fourth century accepted Christianity. Frumentius, a young Syrian man was sold into slavery to the king of Axum. He rose through the ranks in the royal court and traveled to Alexandria to spread the Christian faith. Ironically, Frumentius became a bishop and missionary to Ethiopia. Basically, Frumentius converted the royal court to Christianity and translated scripture into the Ethiopian language of Ge'ez. Moreover, monks of Syria in the fifth century who followed the rule of Pachomius were missionaries to Ethiopia.[459]

Nubia (modern Sudan) was located between Egypt and Ethiopia. A though there were Christians present there during the fifth century, it was in the sixth century via the efforts of Theodora, the wife of the East Roman emperor Justinian by which a missionary made his way to a northern Nubian Kingdom. Julian, a priest in Constantinople who espoused to a non-Chalcedonian theological perspective, was an effective missionary. Not only did the royal family accept the Christian faith but also three other Nubian Kingdoms would follow suit by the conclusion of the sixth century.[460]

Interestingly, the Christian church of Nubia would over time develop a far better connection with the church of Egypt than the Church of Constantinople. However, the advent of Islam and its expansion just sixty years after Muhammad's death had an enormous impact on Christianity in Africa. Essentially, Muslim rule extended into al Maghrib (Arabic for "the place of sunset') which formerly had been Roman North Africa. Overtime, the Arabs and converted Muslims called Berbers (Barbarians formed a coalition).

Certainly, by the conclusion of the tenth century, there existed but a few scattered Christian groups along the coastal areas of the Maghrib. Even some members of the court of the King of Ghana became Muslims.[461] Since Arabs were welcome in Egypt by those who were dissatisfied with Constantinople's political, economic, and ecclesiastical (the Chalcedonian position) power, the relationship between Muslim and Coptic Christians was good.

However, by the eight centuries with the rise of Arabic as the official language and the demise of the Coptic language with usage only in the Coptic liturgy, the relationship eroded. Essentially, Coptics were not permitted to build new churches although near monasteries emerged in isolated desert areas.[462] However, the United Kingdom of Nubia provided the Muslim forces its first defeat. But, continued military attacks from Islamic forces lead to a treaty with the King of Nubia. Under certain terms, Nubia kept political and religious independence. However, a Nubian payment of three hundred slaves annually was required.

From the seventh to the tenth century, Nubia remained Christian, but the moving sands of the Sahara Desert took its toll on the Churches and villages. Since Ethiopians were helpful to Muslim refugees during the time of Muhammad, the Muslim force did not attack Ethiopia at this time.[463] However, Muslim rule greatly restricted the spread of Christianity ceasing missionary efforts especially east of Ethiopia.

Certainly, by the twelfth century Christianity in Nubia had dissipated. Moreover, the Arabic language had superseded the Nubian language by the fifteenth century.[464] It is important to note certain differences between Nubia and Egypt. Essentially, Egypt was more oriented in the Mediterranean world and the Middle East rather than Africa. However, Nubia which was South of Egypt was more of a land of dark- skinned people. Christianity was present in Egypt toward the end of the first century while in Nubia, Christianity first appeared in the fifth century, and it was not until the sixth century that the ruling family had converted.[465]

It was Theodora, Justinian's shrewd wife, who was an ardent miaphysite who pushed her husband to send a mission to Nubia. However, Justinian had firmly supported the council of Chalcedon. Basically, Theodora had temporarily suppressed her husband's ambassadors to give time for her miaphysite priest or presbyter to arrive first in Nubia. Justinian had written to a pro-Chalcedon bishop in the Thebaid in upper Egypt with Certain directives to go to Nubia. Furthermore, Justinian had stated in his letter that he was dispatching ambassadors "with gold and baptismal robes and gifts of honor" for the Nubian King.[466] Thus, these representatives of the emperor Justinian were roundly rejected by the Nubian King, Silko. Moreover, King Silko conquered the southern people on the eastern side of the Nile River and the miaphysite type Christianity was transmitted and adopted by them.[467]

Not only was the traditional culture supplanted by the new faith of Christianity, an old temple at Qase Ibrim was made a Christian church within a relatively short period of time. The old ways of buying a person with grave goods with the body had ceased. Certainly, over a few decades, the Christian faith found its way as far south as Ethiopoa.[468]

In a sense, Ethiopia has had a long continuous history for more than two thousand years. In fact, the Ethiopian eunuch baptized by the apostle Deacon Philip (Acts 8;26-40) was in reality from the Kingdom of Kush in ancient Nubia between Egypt and Ethiopia. This suggests that the Christian gospel message made its way to Ethiopia during apostolic times. It is noteworthy, that the Ethiopians utilized certain and various Jewish practices. Thus, ancient Israel played a role in Ethiopia which provides the Ethiopians a special uniqueness among Christian countries.[469]

The patriarch of Alexandria in Egypt, Athanasius consecrated the bishop of Aksum. It would not be until recently that the bishop would be other than Egyptian. Thus, the close ties to Egypt would be a reasonable supposition to why the Ethiopian church did not partake in disputing the person of Jesus Christ during the fifth century. The conversion of Ethiopia was mostly top down as opposed to the ground up process of the first three centuries in Roman world.[470]

This type of cultural shift is evidenced in coins minted by Ethiopian kings In fact, Ethiopia was the initial African country to issue gold coins which was rare for any kingdom in that age. Prior to the advent of Christianity, the coins had an image of a king and a crescent, divine symbols located over his head. After the conversion of King Ezana, the coins have a cross above the king's head. Moreover, inscriptions such as, "In the faith of God and the power of the Father and the son and the Holy Spirit" were placed on the coins.[471]

Finally, there was one particular coin made in the latter part of the fourth century which depicts the king with a cross above his head as well as a cross on the contralateral side with a small center of gold encompassed by a beaded circle inscription read, "By this a cross you shall conquer."[472]

A group of monks referred to as the Nine Saints hailed from the Roman Empire who were likely opponents of the doctrinal decree of the council of Chalcedon spread Christianity to the villagers. Moreover, they started monasteries using the rule of Pachomius in Ethiopia.[473] The Nine Saints had translated the scriptures from Greek into Geez, the Ethiopian language. This marks a significant path of missionaries of the East, nearly using the vernacular, the people's language for scripture and the liturgy. Conversely, the missionaries of the West taught Latin to recent converts.[474]

Certainly, evidence exists of Christianity in the Arabian Peninsula in the third century. It was through the effort of monks that Christianity had spread in the Arabic-speaking tribes in the fourth century. Various ancient and valid sources indicate a particular monk named Moses had resided among the Arab tribe by which Arabs were converted to Christianity. Prior to Islam, the most convincing evidence of Arabic-speaking Christians comes from Yemen. There existed a full array of ecclesiastical organization including a bishop, presbyters, deacons, and even deaconesses.[475] Certainly, the Arabian Peninsula served as a buffer between the Persians and Byzantines. More importantly, it provided protection to Arabic-speaking Christians. However, the rise of Islam decreased Christianity in the Arabian Peninsula.[476] It is noteworthy that Ethiopia was very strongly Christian and differed from Syria and Egypt in terms of being immune from the rising tide of Islam. Ethiopia was not taken over by the Muslims; perhaps, it was due to an Ethiopian King who showed mercy to Muhammad and his family.

This occurred at a time that the disciples of Muhammad were under attack by their fellow Arabs. In 615 Muhammad friends and family arrived across the strait of Babel-Mandeb to Ethiopia. There was approximately one hundred in this group that the Ethiopian king provided safety. Muhammad's son-in-law Uthman Ibn Affan, his daughter Rugayya, and two of his wives to be where part of this group.[477] The Ethiopians or Abyssinians whose brand of Christianity contained various traces of Judaic features not found in Christianity of the East, was left alone by Muslim invaders. The Bible used by Ethiopian Christians had an expanded version of the canon of scriptural books including not only wisdom, Sirach, Judith, Susanah, one and two Esdras, four books of Maccabees but also Enoch, Jubilees, and the Ascension of Isaiah.* Moreover, some of these ancient Jewish books only became known via the Ethiopian language.[478,479] Interestingly, two of the pseudepigrapha (from Greek: pseudo "false" tepigraphein "to inscribe") in particular, one Enoch and Jubilees, were certainly read as authoritative scripture at Qumran as well as the Ethiopian Christian Church.[480] Moreover, the canon of New Testament books which includes both the Shepherd of Hermas as well as one and two Clement in the Ethiopian language. Although it is conceivable that Ethiopian Christians became aware of these customs from Jews residing in Ethiopia or the Arabian Peninsula. However, it is truly unknown.[481]

Eusebius the historian starts his world history with Abraham and Augustine's work the "City of God" contains biblical history. However, Ethiopia has no doubt created a past indicating a direct correlation of descent from King Solomon to Ethiopian kings. Thus, Ethiopia was the "New Israel" in the strict sense. According to the Ethiopian tradition one of their first churches, namely Our Lady of Zion, was to have the Ark of the Covenant. Moreover, replicas of the Ark were a distinctive feature of the Ethiopian churches. Notwithstanding, the influence of Egyptian Christianity in particular, Ethiopia had its own distinct Christian culture or "micro-Christendom".[482]

A controversy had arisen with several Byzantine emperors concerning the use of images. During the eight century, byzantine emperors took specific measures to stop the usage of images. Emperor Leo IH who ruled in 717 to 741, had a statue of Jesus destroyed. Moreover, Constantine V who was Leo's son and successor did not allow the use of images and even condemned people who defended images in Christianity.[483]

Two major divisions would emerge in the Church namely, iconoclasts (destroyers of images) and iconodules (worshipers of images). Essentially, John of Damascus, who actually had lived under Muslim rule, was a major proponent of the iconodules. It is believed that Islam's strong teaching against images was a factor in this issue. John's "Exposition of the Orthodox Faith" expounded on eastern orthodox doctrine as well as a written response to Islam. In reality John's writings were the first significant reactions to Islam. In essence the iconodules' position was regarded as a corollary of Christological orthodoxy.[484] The Seventh Ecumenical Council met at Nicea in 787 and made a decision that a lesser form of veneration, namely dulia was appropriate for images. Latria is a greater form of worship reserved for God. Semantic differences in Latin for latria and dulia were problematic. However, Christians accepted the use of images in Church.[485]

Western belief that the Eastern Church was merely a puppet was due to the lengthy controversy concerning the use of images. The Photian Schism in 887 occurred when the Patriarch Ignatius was supplanted by Photius. Pope Nicholas supported Ignatius and as a result Photius claimed that the Western church was heretical. Photius indicated that the Nicene Creed was contaminated by the word Filioque (and from the Son). Basically, the old creed stated that the Holy Spirit proceeds "from the father" and by including "and from the son" had actually changed the creed as well as the old way of understanding the Trinity.[486] It is believed that this modification happened first in Spain and afterwords was found in France. During Charlemagne's time, the creed was read in the royal chapel at Aachen which had included the Filioque. In the Orthodox Easter Church, they demanded to know why Frankish monks who were visiting the East changed the wording of the ancient Creed. There existed a continuing increase in distrust between the East and the West. The old Roman Creed, referred to as the Apostle's Creed was promoted by the pope in a diplomatic effort not to offend either side, Byzantines nor Franks.[487]

Thus, in the west the usage of the Apostles' Creed became prevalent instead of using the Nicene Creed. With the winds of political change in Constantinople, Ignatius again became patriarch with the understanding that Photius would follow next as patriarch.[488]

The ingredients of a far more serious and final schism were present. Thus, in the eleventh century when Leo of Ochrid, the Bulgarian archbishop indicated that the Western Church was in error since it made celibacy a universal rule for priests as well as celebrating Holy Communion with unleavened bread. Pope Leo IX dispatched Cardinal Humbert as his legate to meet with Patriarch Michael Cerulerius to discuss this issue. However, on June 16, 1054, Cardinal Humbert went to the cathedral of Hagia Sophia and approached the altar during mass and; thus, in the name of the Pope placed a sentence of excommunication against "heretic Michael Cerularius and his followers".

Moreover, Cardinal Humbert simply left and went back to Rome.[489] Therefore, the East and West Christian Churches were separated. The Western Catholic Europeans emphasizing the core of the poor and fate of the soul brought these notions to Greenland. Thorstein the son of Eric the Red, the first European settler to become Christian, told his wife while on his deathbed, "He bade her beware of marrying a Greenlander and then he urged her to bestow their money upon the church or to give it to the poor; and then he sank back for the last time".[490]

Although the Christian Church of the west had become privileged due to Constantine's conversion in 312, the western church was not wealthy. At that time most of the upper-class Romans kept to a tradition to show generosity to their cities rather than the church or the poor. '

However, during the end of the fourth century more of the wealthy converted to the Christian faith. In fact, they had often become bishops and Christian writers.[491] However, giving was not restricted to the wealthy and elite. Essentially, all believers of Christ of all the socio-economic levels were encouraged to give to the church and the poor. Basically, to give to the poor was very different than past practices and it reached an immense and silent group. Writings and preaching of Ambrose, Jerome, Augustine, Paulinus of Nola, and the supporters of Pelagius touched on the subject of wealth.[492] The church moved to an age of affluence and were in the midst of a generally impoverished world.

Essentially, the collapse of the various old aristocracies left the church in a certain and unique position. The popes of Rome and various well-known figures including Gregory of tours to up-and-coming clergy from as far as Merida, Pavia, and Metz managed resources very well. Exceptional administration and building of luminous shrines were their trademark.

Certainly, this new collective wealth coupled with the significant support of lay donors drawn from every level of society exerted pressure, albeit somewhat discreetly on the churches of the Latin West (around 600AD). It concluded the ancient world and brought the church to the Middle Ages led by a clergy made different from themselves in culture. Moreover, the laity sought various and newer ways to place their money beyond the grave for salvation of their souls".[493]

Christianity had spread to Ireland via various ways. Patrick, who as young boy had been captured in Great Britain by Irish raiders, had escaped his captors and had a vision calling him to ministry. Monasteries would spring up over time and was spared of barbarian invasions. Thus, these monasteries would serve as a source of classical literature and information for Rome and others.[494]

During the Middle Ages, it was the Crusades whose hope was to defeat Islam in order to protect the Byzantine Empire and Constantinople. Moreover, it may facilitate bringing together the eastern and western churches as well as the regain the Holy Land. Essentially, the Crusades had dramatic and contradictory qualities. The Muslims would suffer initial defeats due to its own division.[495] Constantinople would make it to the fifteenth century before being invaded by the Ottoman Turks. By and large, the eastern and western churches did reunite via force due to the Fourth Crusade. However, this forced reunion was a Band-aid which cast suspicion and hatred in the long run between the churches. Basically, the Holy Land belonged to the crusaders for approximately a century before Islam re-entered.[496]

"Pope Urban II's statement provided the impetus; I say it to those who are present. I command that it be said to those who are absent. Christ commands it. All who got hither and lost their lives, be it on the road or on the sea, or in the fight against the pagans, will be granted immediate forgiveness for their sins. This I grant to all who will march, by virtue of the great gift which God has given me."[497]

Certainly, medieval Christianity reached its apex at the conclusion of the crusades. Pope Innocent HI proclaimed the following: "Just as God established two great luminaries in the heavens, the greater to preside over days and the lesser to preside over nights, so did he establish two luminaries in the heavens of the universal Church.... The greater to preside over souls over days, and the lesser to preside over bodies as over nights. These are pontifical authority and royal power."[498]

Finally, it is important to mention the Franciscan movement. Essentially, Francis (1181-1226) belonged to the merchant class. His real name was Giovanni, being Italian, however his mother was French. His father had good trade relations with France, and he liked the songs of the French troubadours. Thus, Giovanni was called Francesco (the little Frenchman) by his friends in his native Assisi. Basically, Francis had experienced a very religious and spiritual awakening. This experience brought Francis to embrace a life of poverty. I 1209, Francis listened to the reading of the Gospel, specifically Matthew 107 10, where Jesus had sent his disciples to preach taking neither gold nor silver with them.[499]

Thus, Francis had realized that poverty and preaching go together. Francis had returned to Assisi to preach. He found a few who would join him, and they went to visit Pope Innocent III." Essentially, the pope tested Francis by stating that Francis looked like a pig, and he should go and be among pigs. Francis did so and returned to the pope covered with mud. Francis had mentioned the following, "Father, I have done as you ordered; now, will you do as I request?"[500] Therefore the pope provided approval to Francis, and he again returned to Assisi with papal backing. The Friars Minor, order of lesser brothers was founded as well as Clarisses or Poor Clares with the help of Clare, a spiritual friend. Essentially, Francis made a will which was designed to forbid his followers to possess anything in order to keep the "Rule" which he had given them.[501] In fact, Francis relinquished his leadership role at the general chapter of the order in 1220. Francis died on October 3,1226 at the Portiuncula, the chapel which he had rebuilt in his youth. His final words included, "I have done my duty. Now, may Christ let you know yours. Welcome, sister Death'."[502]

CATHOLICISM IN THE UNITED STATES OF AMERICA

The first colonial power to enter what is currently regarded as United States territory was Spain. Certainly, the discovery of Puerto Rico by Columbus during a second voyage in 1493 and the establishment of a church in Sanjuan in1511 was the beginning of Catholicism in the territory. Bishop Alonso Manso had arrived in 1513, and Bartolome De Las Casas who on his ordination.to the priesthood in 1512 was the first priest ordained in the New World.[503, 504]

Essentially, Bartolome de Las Casas was born in 1474 to a family associated with Columbus' second voyage. He had gone to the island of Hispanic a in 1502. Since De Las Casas was a landowner, he became a slave owner. After his ordination, De Las Casa experienced a conversion of mind and soul. Thus, he believed that it was morally wrong to own Indian slaves. In fact, Father Bartolome De Las Casas became an advocate for the Indians, speaking before the Council of the Indies on the immorality of Indian slavery. Ultimately, Father De Las Casa entered the Dominican Order since they too were abhorrent to the slavery of Indians. De Las Casa wrote a well known treatise on the history of the Indies emphasizing various injustices inflicted on the Indians by the Spaniards.[505] Once De Las Casa became the Bishop of Chiapas (Currently Southern Mexico) in 1544, he ordered priests not to give absolution for the sins of slave-owners unless they would give their solemn word of honor to grant freedom and make restitution to slaves?[506] Bishop De las Casa was forced to leave his post when a riot ensued during Easter of 1545. Most Spaniards had not truly fulfilled their Easter duty since they would not agree to the terms of absolution. In fact, he had faced opposition not only from Spaniards but also priests. Thus, De Las Casas had no recourse but to return to Spain and resign his see in 1547.[507] It is important to point out that Pope Paul III had issued a Papal bull namely Sublimis Deus which denounced the enslavement of Indians in 1537. However, this letter was ineffective in preventing slavery.[508]

Finally, De Las Casa debated a famous priest, Juan Gines de Sepulveda germane to the use of force against the Indians. In essence, Father Sepulveda believed that the warfare used against the Indians was a just war while Father De Las Casa contended that all people are one. Sepulveda's supposition that some people are naturally born slaves based on their writings of Aristotle in order to support his argument of a just war.[509]

Essentially, there existed much poverty in Florida. Around one hundred Spaniards had died during the first winter since most food was sent from Cuba and Mexico. In fact, mass could not be celebrated due to the lack of bread and wine. The only crop was maize (Indian corn). However, the first parish founded in continental United States territory was Nombre de Dios with a secular priest and pastor Francisco Lopez de Mendoza Grajales.[510] The first hospital, La Soledad at St. Augustine (1598), and the first school (1605), a Franciscan seminary, were founded.

In 1606, the first bishop was Juan de la Cabezas de Altamirano of Santiago, Cuba. He had ordained about twenty men to the priesthood.[511] Basically, the very first mission of the Jesuits, the Society of Jesus, in North America was Florida. A Jesuit was killed by Indians on Sanjuan

Island in 1566. Moreover, eight Jesuits led by Juan Segura landed at Ajacan (modern Virginia) in 1570. Essentially, all eight Jesuits were killed by Indians there (between the York and James River). In just two years, the Jesuit mission in Florida was halted.[512] Thus, the Franciscan Friars stepped into Florida within a year. In 1587, Alonso Reinoso brought in a number of Franciscans. However, within a five-year span, only five Franciscans remained in Florida.

In 1595, Francisco Marron had orchestrated a significant mission and thus, various stations were opened along the Florida coast and northward. In 1635, the Franciscan provincial superior had indicated the following to the King of Spain: "The friars suffer greatly in this mission field. They must walk barefoot in this cold land when going about from mission to mission. The Indians are widely scattered bout in forty-four missions. For this great number there are only thirty-five religious. Many times, it is necessary for a missionary to walk eight or ten leagues [twenty-four to thirty miles] to hear a confession. All of these suffering is augmented by the fact that missionaries get very little aid in the form of assistants who might lighten some of their burdens. Some of the priests, being so overburdened with work and seeing so many Indians without hope of converting them, become discouraged and return to Spain."[513]

It was difficult to convert the Indians in Florida. During the Jesuit tenure in 1561-1571, the priests had declined an offer from Menendez to provide a number of soldiers. Thus, the Jesuits depended on a young Indian convert renamed "Luis de Velasco" after the viceroy who served as his godfather.[514] However, this young Indian convert who had previously been to Spain to meet the king and other high-ranking officials, turned against the Jesuits. Luis de Velasco had deserted the Jesuits, rejoining his people. It was in February of 1571 that De Velasco led a brutal and surprise attack upon the Jesuits, killing all eight priests and destroying their chapel. Essentially, only a young Spanish boy was spared.[515] It was during the 1590s and early 1600s that the Franciscan friars had founded a set of missions along the Atlantic coast north San Agustin into Guale (Georgia), in north-central Florida (Timucua) as well as to the west in the Florida Panhandle.[516]

Essentially in 1698, it was both Franciscans and Augustinians who had served the Indians. Again, it was apparent that Florida Indians were difficult to convert. Francisco Marron, who led a major effort in the missions in 1595, is considered the first great Franciscan leader in Florida. It is noteworthy to mention that Pareja, a 1595 arrival, worked with the coastal Timucuans. Francisco had written a grammar and dictionary as we as a Catechism and devotional books in Timacuan.[517] However, it was the Indian culture and customs, which included polygamy, wooden idols, and the traditional ball game, were hurdles for conversion. Priests had encouraged and tried to enforce Christian morality requiring marriage, monogamy and clothing that covered female breasts. Essentially, some Timucuans rebelled and indicated that "they enjoyed their vice and therefore it must not be evil but good and just."[518]

By and large, Franciscan friars had built their missions besides the major Indian villages. Basically, the principal village had storehouses, a large council house, and a circular public plaza. Moreover, the friars built a church, a cookhouse, residences for the missionaries, and a Christian cemetery?[519] Since the Friars were depended upon the Spanish government for financial assistance, a commixture of the sacred and secular resulted in conflicts. The main issue was Indian enslavement by civil authorities.[520]

In 1656 the Timucuans and Apalaches had revolted only to be put down by Governor Diego de Rebolledo. He had eleven chiefs publicly strangled. Thus, the friars had protested this behavior and as a result the governor was removed from office.[521] The friar's position with the Indians rose for about twenty-five years and in 1675, there are forty friars who ministered to approximately twenty thousand Indian native converts who were in thirty-six churches. [522,523] Essentially, the Friars had founded fifty missions, spread throughout the Rio Grande Valley as well as the adjoining Pecos Valley, by 1628.

The Franciscan friar's strategy was to isolate their Indian converts from the Hispanic colonists in New Mexico. The track record of the colonists was not good. Thus, the Franciscan friars did not want the Indian converts corrupted by the poor example of the colonist. By and large, the friars made considerable progress although they had required much from converts. The friars wanted the Indians to act like Spaniards in how they dressed and prepared and ate food.[524] Essentially, friars wanted the Indians to observe chastity prior to marriage as well as to practice monogamy within the sacrament of marriage. Moreover, the Franciscan friars required Indian women converts to cover themselves from neck to ankles in clothing?[525]

The Franciscans were respected since they had made sacrifices and endured many severe hardships in spreading the faith. Of course, the Franciscans embraced chastity, and they did not rape Indian women as other Spaniards would violate women. Moreover, Franciscans lived in poverty and some accepted martyrdom. They displayed their vestments, music, paintings, and sacred images all combined into processions and the celebration of the Eucharist during mass.[526]

However, the deadly epidemics bringing new diseases to the Indians worked mostly against efforts to convert the Indians. Basically, many Indians associated the diseases with the friars in their belief that the friars practiced a deadly sorcery. In particular, an Indian had forewarned his people that the Franciscans, "were nothing but impostors and that they should not allow them to sprinkle water on their heads because they would be certain to die from it."[527] However, the very tall and thick walls of the missions made them quite formidable citadels that served as protection against nomadic warrior tribes such as the Apache and Ute.

The Pueblo Indian population dropped from 40,000 in 1638 to 17,000 by 1680 due to disease, famine, and violence. Essentially, a severe and prolonged drought in the late 1660s lasting throughout the 1670s reduced many Pueblo Indians to starvation. According to a Franciscan, in 1669 after around three years of failed harvests, "a great many Indians perished of hunger lying dead along the roads, in the ravines, and in their huts." [528] Moreover, the Franciscans felt threatened when Governor Mendizabel defended and encouraged the ceremonial tribal dances as harmless and meaningless. However, the Franciscans were cognizant of the spiritual underpinnings of the traditional dances which posed a threat to Franciscan authority and the conversion process and missionary efforts.[529]

There existed a certain compartmentalized faith which merged the old ways with the new belief in Jesus. Basically, most Pueblo Indians attempted to retain their identity and culture of their ancestors while incorporating the Christian faith. In a sense, it provided a "back door" for the pueblo Indian to return to their ancient spirits and belief system?[530] Moreover, governors had utilized Pueblo Indians in the slave raids. As a result, the nomadic tribes perceived the Pueblo Indians as allies to the Spanish. Furthermore, nomadic tribes would seek revenge on the Pueblo Indians. Even some Pueblo Indians fled and joined the Apache tribe. According to one Franciscan friar, these Indian runaways, "gone over to the heathen, believing that they enjoy greater happiness with them since they live according to their whims, and in complete freedom."[531]

Essentially, the Franciscans often appealed to the viceroys in Mexico City, to recall corrupt governors. This resulted in governors seeking revenge toward the Franciscans by imprisoning and humiliating them. Moreover, Franciscans would excommunicate offending governors. Once, the Franciscans removed a church pew reserved for the governor. Franciscans even appealed to soldiers for help against an evil and corrupt governor. In particular, Governor Rosas disagreed with the homily by a Franciscan priest and stated the following: "Shut up, Father, what you say is a lie! [532]

In August 1680, a major well-coordinated rebellion strongly encouraged by a shaman named Pope was widespread over several hundred miles included the majority of the seventeen thousand Pueblo Indians as well as some Apache bands. They destroyed Catholic churches, altars, crosses, and images. This rebellion led to the murdering of approximately two hundred of die one thousand Hispanic colonists in New Mexico, including twenty-one of the forty Franciscan priests. Pope advocated restoring their former native names and to reverse their baptisms via jumping into the Rio Grande. Moreover, Pope dissolved Catholic marriages and fostered polygamy.[533] However, the Pueblo Indians revived their feuding among themselves, and the Apache took advantage of this feud and resumed their raiding. Pope had lost face and credibility, and he died in obscurity around 1690.

Governor Diego de Vargas invaded and reclaimed New Mexico in around 1692-93. In 1696, a smaller rebellion had occurred which resulted in the deaths of five priests and twenty-one colonists and soldiers. Thus, the rebellions of 1680 and 1696 taught the Pueblo Indians and Spanish colonists to compromise and respect each other.[534]

The Pueblos are the oldest Native American members of the Catholic Church since the merging of Spanish and Indian races and cultures in New Mexico (La Raza). There were altogether 18, 344 Christian Indians in 1776.[535] By and large, the Pueblo Indians of the Rio Grande had accepted the Catholic sacramental and seasonal liturgical cycle while keeping their Kivas traditional ceremonies very quietly. Franciscans had looked the other way, respecting then customs. Certainly, the Hispanic and Pueblo Indians relied on each other for mutual protection against the nomadic warrior raids from the Great Plains and the Rocky Mountains.[536]

Basically, society was feudal under the control of prestigious families with slaves being Apaches and Comanches. The Church was isolated from the outside world and mostly abandoned the Catholics of New Mexico. By 1810, there were approximately thirty-five thousand Spaniards and people of Spanish Indian ancestry as well as the thousand Pueblo Indians.[537'] Moreover, there existed various brotherhoods of the Sangre de Cristo such as Los Hermanos de los Penitentes which emanated from the third order Franciscans

Essentially, the sole major non-Franciscan Spanish mission was that of the Primerfa Alta in northern Sonora and Arizona south of Gila River Jesuits from the Mexican Sierra Madre to Sonora went to where Tucson is currently located. San Xavier del Bac was founded as a mission there in 1700. Eusebio Hino, Tyrolese Jesuit, had personally baptized in excess of four thousand Indians. He was a cattle rancher, explorer, and geographer. Eusebio traveled thousands of miles and determined without doubt that California was not an island.[538]

It is important to note that the expulsion of Jesuits in Spain in 1768 had an adverse effect in the new world. As a result, there were three missions which were given to the Franciscans. The first Spanish presidio was founded at Tucson in 1776. Francisco Garces, a well-known Franciscan, tried to convert the nomadic Yuma. However, he was killed in 1781.[539] Basically, Mexican independence led to the abandonment of missions with the last Franciscans leaving in 1828. Thus, the Catholic spiritual life was lacking until the establishment of the vicariate apostolic of Arizona in 1868. Essentially, in the southern part of Arizona, contiguous with the Mexican state of Sonora, exists survivors of the Jesuit mission period. Namely, the Yaqui and the Sonora Catholics who have a commixture of eighteenth-century Catholicism and their own Indian religion.[540]

In 1741, the Russians ventured south from Alaska to hunt sea-otters down the coast. Seventy years later, the Russians built Fort Ross in what is today, Sonoma County. In 1825, the Russian American Fur Company became restricted to the Russian Alaska colony.[541] Basically, it was Inspector-General Jose de Galvez and Junipero Serra, president of the Franciscan Mission in California, who planned as expedition as both missionary and military in San Diego, Monterey, and Santa Barbara. Moreover, a total of five missions emerged including San Diego, San Carlos (Carmel), San Gabriel, San Antonio, and San Luis Obispo.

Friar Junipero Serra (1713-1784) founded nine missions and is one of the best-known missionaries at this time. [542,543] Serra, a future American saint, had moved the San Carlos mission about five miles south (present day Carmel) in order to insulate the Indians from the soldiers who lassoed Indian women and introduced veneral and other diseases to them.[544] By 1814, about seventy-five percent of Indian infants died within a year of life. Although ninety-eight thousand Indians were baptized during this mission era, by 1832, which was the end of this mission period of time, the Indian population had decreased significantly. In fact by 1880, there were only twenty thousand five hundred Indians in California. About fifty people inhabited Yerba Buena (San Francisco). In 1800, there were approximately one thousand two hundred Europeans in California which rose to around four thousand by 1846.

The Mexican Period was 1821 to 1846 and California evolved into a place of exiles for Cholos brought from Mexican prisons.[545] Thus, Mexican independence effectively concluded the California mission era. There were many rebellions after 1828. Basically, the Spanish friars had left since they were not willing to swear allegiance to the new republic. The secularization of the missions finally came to fruition in 1834. Local politicians stole and partitioned millions of acres of land for themselves.[546]

Essentially, the Indians and Cholo herded cattle on large ranches for work. The Californios lived a lazy life and participated in brutal blood sports. There existed no school nor newspapers and the populace were illiterate. Government and Catholic religion had diminished. Actually, there were only thirteen priests in California. When the last of the Mexican fighting forces had surrender to the United States in 1847, Catholicism in California was virtually nill and disordered. However, Catholic church history would take a turn for the better after James W. Marshall discovered gold in 1848.[547]

Turning to Louisiana which was the most cosmopolitan and heterogeneous area composed of the towns along the Mississippi, the gulf coast, and vast hinterland. In fact, the United States would virtually double in size with the Louisiana Purchase in 1803.[548] Basically, this land controlled by France from 1699-1766 and Spain form 1766-1803 but via a secret Treaty of San Ildefonso in 1800, Napoleon regained Louisiana for France only to be sold to the United States for fifteen million. A church-state issue would emerge as a result of this sale. Sister Therese Farjon, the superior of the Ursuline convent at New Orleans, inquired how the American system of government under the Articles of Confederation as well as the new Federal Constitution would affect them.

According to President Thomas Jefferson on May 15, 1804: "The principles of the constitution and government of the United States are a sure guarantee to you that [the property] will be preserved to you sacred and inviolate, and that your institution will be permitted to govern itself according to its own voluntary rules, without interference from civil authority..."[549]

Moreover, President Jefferson had indicated that "whatever diversity of shade" which "may appear in the religious opinions of our fellow citizens" Thus, they would not be indifferent to the "charitable objects" as well as the "wholesome purposes" of the nuns and their school. Essentially, President Jefferson had conveyed to Sister Therese that his office would provide their school "with all the protection" possible.[550]

However, in Louisiana, the problems in the Catholic community were truly internal ones. It was in September 1805 that Bishop John Carroll of Baltimore would become in charge of the diocese of Louisiana and the "Two Floridas". Basically, Pope Pius VI in 1793 had established the diocese of Louisiana as well as the Floridas, centered in New Orleans which made it the third in seniority in America after Sanjuan (1511) and Baltimore (1789). Luis de Penalver y Cardenas who arrived from Cuba in 1795 and remained until 1802, wrote the following to Spain: "The Inhabitants do not listen to, or, if they do, disregard all exhortations to maintain in its orthodoxy the Catholic faith, and to preserve innocence of life." [551]

Other variables such as Pinckney's Treaty of 1795 gave Americans the right to use the Mississippi as a trade route. However, in 1797, a new Spanish governor denied most religious toleration. Thus, Protestant ministers were not permitted in Louisiana. A Capuchin friar, Antonio de Sedella, had arrived in 1781 in Louisiana. He was known as Pare Antoine and became superior to the Capuchins, vicar general, and pastor of St. Louis Cathedral?[552]

Essentially, he was on a mission to rid of "the American heresy". Although Pere Antoine was deported from the United States in 1790, he came back in five years with a royal warrant which ordered his restoration as pastor. Pere Antoine with his supporters attempted to gain an appointment as bishop via the Emperor Napoleon. A group of lay people known as the marguilliers (church wardens) tried to gain control at least partially of Church administration. Thus, Bishop John Carroll had talked with the Secretary of State James Madison germane to this situation.

In fact, Madison had consulted with President Jefferson. Basically, Madison had sent an official letter and a private one to Bishop Carroll. The private letter was strongly written and indicated that Madison found Pere Antoine and the marguilliers' attempt to obtain foreign support to gain power by way of the Capuchin's nomination for the top spot, "manifestly reprehensible."[553]

In summary, the bishop's seat was empty until 1815 when Sulpician William DuBourg became bishop. Firstly, DuBourg went to St. Louis and took his time about two years later arrived in New Orleans. He did not live there until 1823 and would resign the See three years later, returning to France. Pere Antoine remained untouched as pastor of St. Louis Cathedral in New Orleans when he died in 1829. Interestingly enough, Pere Antoine was buried with Masonic rites.[554] Overall, French America was not the economic answer which it had hoped. Basically, New France and Louisiana had cost the crown or emperor more to administer than they were able to gain in fur and deerskin trades. The heavy costs were to maintain forts and to provide gifts to the Indians. However, over time the Indians had become highly dependent on French trade. Thus, the Indians became impoverished and hungry being denied access to European goods.

According to a Cherokee Chief named Skiagunsta in 1753: "The Clothes we wear, we cannot make ourselves, they are made [for] us. We use their ammunition with which we kill deer. We cannot make our Guns. Every necessary Thing in Life we must have from the white People."[555]

The British had command of the seas and New France had about sixty thousand while the British Colonies had approximately one and a quarter million people living along the Atlantic Ocean at this time.[556] On September 13, 1759 General James Wolfe, the British commander, led the Siege of Quebec and had disguised himself as a common ordinary soldier in order to reconnoiter the fortress city. Thus, General Wolfe located the best place for his troops to mount an attack. Wolfe had become mortally wounded at the time of victory in a battle which lasted less than an hour. Within a year of the fall of Quebec City, Montreal would too fall which removed the French threat and ended the need of British protection. The Seven Years War in Europe (The French and Indian War in America) ended with a treaty called the Peace of Paris, which was signed in 1763.[557]

According to Benjamin Franklin in a letter to an English friend, "No one can rejoice more sincerely than I do on the Reduction of Canada: and this, not merely as I am a Colonist, but as I am a Briton. I have long been of Opinion that the Foundations of the future Grandeur and Stability of the British Empire lie in America."[558]

Certainly, Benjamin Franklin had written what was the prevailing attitude of Americans at that time. Thus, there was an expectation of greater autonomy in the aftermath of the French and Indian War. Basically, Franklin had experienced the failure of the Albany Plan of Union, he was elected in 1754 to present a plan at Albany, New York to advocate a notion of colonial union under British administration. However, jealousies of colonial legislatures stood in the way of this plan.[559] Thus, a caveat existed in Franklin's thinking, "When I say such a union is impossible, I mean without the most grievous tyranny and oppression".[560] Although the 1763 Treaty of Paris had concluded the Anglo- French rivalry, it was about a decade later that most of the Atlantic colonies had broken their ties with England.

There were approximately twenty to twenty-five thousand Catholics in the thirteen colonies. In 1773 on July 21st in Rome, Pope Clement XVI effectively removed the Jesuit Order from official Catholic Status.[561] According to Joseph Mosley, who virtually lived by himself for seventeen years on the Eastern shore of Maryland seeing his closet priest neighbor maybe once a year, "What part of our labors can we cut off, without neglecting our duty? Must I refuse when the sick wants me? Must I neglect my Sunday church exercise to ease myself by staying at home? Must I, when at the Chapel, refuse to hear half that present themselves? Must I, if call Must I, if call'd to the sick in the night, sleep till morning, and thus let the sick die without assistance? Must I, if call'd to a dying man in the rain, stay till it's fair weather."[562]

Moreover, after the faithful Jesuit Joseph Mosley received word of the abolition of his order, he stated that: "When I see so many worthy, saintly, pious, learned, laborious Missioners dead and alive have been members, through the last two ages, I know no fault we have been guilty of. I am convinced that our labors are pure, upright and sincere, for God's honor and our neighbors good. What our Supreme Judge on Earth [the Pope] may think of our labors is a mystery to me. He has hurt his own cause, not us It's true he has stigmatized us thro' the world with infamy, and declared us unfit for our business, on his service. Our Dissolution in Known thro' the world; it's in every newspaper, which makes me ashamed to show my face..."[563]

Although Joseph Mosley had thoughts of retirement to England. He had decided to stay on and continue his ministry. He had stated to his sister, "discontent or not, I see that I am a very necessary hand in my situation, and our Gentlemen here [his fellow former Jesuits] won't hear of my departure."[564] All seven of the English missionaries had remained as well. In fact, all of the other priests from Europe stayed in America. Essentially, the twenty-one Jesuits in Maryland and Pennsylvania were confident in the leadership skills of John Carroll who would be the first American bishop in May, 1789.[565]

Basically, Father John Carroll who indicated "our so long persecuted, and, I must add, holy society is no more," sought to return home to Maryland after being away for twenty-five years. It was at Bobby Brent's Landing that John Carroll had first stopped on his return from Europe in 1774. His oldest sister was Anne Brent, her husband Robert was a school fellow of his at Bohemia Manor. Moreover, another sister, Eleanor, was married to William Brent whose part of the family was historically both tory and Catholic?[566] Essentially the colonial Maryland form of Catholicism was according to the English Catholic pattern.

However, in Virginia it was the Brents, who patented about eleven thousand acres of land between 1651 and 1660, who were the major Catholic force. It was a Quaker, William Penn in 1681, who had basically chartered Pennsylvania. William Penn's group in 1682 were composed of English and Welsh Quakers as well as Irish Catholic Servants. Thus, William Penn's colony held to religious toleration, but Roman Catholics were not allowed to hold any public office.[567]

In 1741, Father Henry Neale had written to Sir John James, Bart., of Bury St. Edmunds about the Pennsylvania missions, "We have at present all the liberty imaginable in ye exercise of our business, and are not only esteemed, but reverenced."[568] It was Father Greaton who was the resident priest of Philadelphia. He had a permanent chapel in 1733-34 in the meadowland off Walnut Street, near to the Friends' almshouse. St. Joseph's became the first urban Catholic church in the thirteen colonies. By and large, Roman Catholics received good treatment in Philadelphia, with some exceptions. In 1755, the arrival of Acadians in Philadelphia did foster fears of a papist upheaval which prompted a census of Roman Catholics. Essentially, there were 692 males and 673 females over the age of twelve. They were composed of seventy percent German and thirty percent were English-speaking. Overall, Germans were in the majority by 228 to 150.[569The] French were Catholic who attended St. Joseph's church in Willings Alley. It is important to note that Roman Catholics were not permitted to bear arms in 1757.[570] Since a great deal of trade in Philadelphia was with Spain, Portugal, and France, English and Irish Catholics who were well connected with them, had become parishioners of St. Joseph's and later at St. Mary's.

In 1753, Father Robert Harding took over for Father Greaton as pastor. Father Harding eased into polite society and became a subscriber to the drive for Benjamin Franklin's hospital. The Irish group formed the Friendly Sons of St. Patrick while their pastor was, in fact, a founding member of the Sons of St. George.[571] Basically, Father Neale who was an assistant priest to Greaton as well as responsible for outlying stations, had indicated that "the necessaries of life were as dear, and several dearer, than at London itself... among other expenses I must of necessity keep a horse in order to assist poor people up and down ye country. Some twenty miles, some sixty, some farther off."[572]

Certainly, Father Neale's letter writing to Sir John had influenced him to bequest his fortune to Bishop Challoner in London. Although bequests to Catholic charities were illegal under English law, the bequest figured as "salary from London" became a source of funding for the missionaries. A portion which was to remain in England to support two priests in London who worked for the poor with the rest of the money for the missions in Pennsylvania found its way in the sum of 4000 pounds invested in East India annuities as well as the French East India Company. Monies found a way to support the missionaries who had various ways of support.

Farm income, ground rents, and in Philadelphia solely regular contributions from good parishioners supplemented the missions in Pennsylvania?[573] Father Neale indicated that: "Little or nothing can be expected from the country Catholics, who, tho' very numerous, are most of them servants or poor tradesmen, and more in need often times of charity themselves, than capable of assisting others".[574] When German priests, Theodor Schneider and Wilhelm Wappeler had sailed the Susquehanna in July 1741 and stayed with a certain Catholic Hiberian, Thomas Doyle" at Neustatt (Lancaster), Father Neale wrote that: "Their presence is very much wanted, My heart had yearned when I've met with some poor Germans desirous of performing their duties, but whom I have not been able to assist for want of language.[575]

Basically, Father Wappeler served the Susquehanna region with places at Conewago and York. Father Schneider served at Goshenhoppen particularly the Schuylkill and Delaware valleys while visiting German glass workers at Salem. However, Wappeler had no choice but to return to Europe due to poor health in 1748. Afterwards, many German missionaries including the Swabian Ferdinand Steinmeyer known as Ferdinand Farmer in America had arrived firstly in Lancaster. He became the first German pastor in Philadelphia during the years 1756 to 1786. Moreover, Father Farmer founded the first permanent Catholic Parish in New York City.[576]

It is important to point out that the Jesuit farms actually became "the hub" of Catholic life, changing from areas for mission Catholic action into parishes. Both Fathers Wappeler and Schneider landed at Jesuit farms. [577,578] In the strictest sense, the Catholic Church in America was under the authority of the vicar apostolic of London. It was after the American Revolution that John Carroll and others urged for a Church authority independent of England. Carroll perceived America now as a country not as a mission, but as a Church with "regular clergy" and not under the government of Propaganda Fide's authority.[579]

According to Carroll, in correspondence with Ferdinand Farmer in Pennsylvania, "We form not a fluctuating body of labourers in Christ's vineyard, sent hitcher and removable at the will of a Superior; but a permanent body of national clergy, with sufficient powers to form our own system of internal government, and I think to chuge [sic] our own superior, and a very just claim to have all necessary spiritual authority communicated to him, on his being presented as regularly and canonically chosen by us."[580]

Certainly, Father Farmer was not the first Jesuit in Manhattan. Rather, Isaac Jogues who found refuse there until Governor William Kieft made arrangement for Jogues a way home to France. However, it was forty years later that the Catholic Irishman, Thomas Dongan who became Governor in 1683. Essentially, New York did not have a representative assembly and there was a very delicate situation with the Iroquois as well as a dislike of the French. In order to satisfy the puritans from the Long Island ridings, Dongan established an elected assembly.[581]

Religious freedom was supported by two-thirds of the voters. The assembly's charter of liberties and privileges including the following: "Noe person or persons, which profess faith in God by Jesus Christ, shall at any time be any ways molested, punished, disquieted, or called in question for any difference in opinion or matter of religious concernment, who do not actually disturb the civil peace of the Province... All and every such person or persons [should] from time, and at all times freely have and fully enjoy his or their judgments or consciences in matters of religion throughout all the province, they are behaving themselves peacefully and quietly, and not using this liberty to licentiousness, nor to the civil injury or outward disturbance of others."[582]

When the dominion of New England, which at this time had included New York, was basically put together via King James in 1688, Thomas Dongan left the governorship. In 1686, King James annulled the charter. However, he did not touch the free exercise of religious clause. It was Jacob Leisler's rebellion in 1689 which halted religious liberty in New York until 1806. In August 1687 Thomas Dongan met with the Chiefs of the Iroquois at Albany he promised to replace French Jesuits with English ones. This resulted in the Duke of York who had talked with the English Jesuits who conferred with Rome that Father Thomas Harvey would be assigned to New York, "a respectable city, fit for the foundation of a collage".[583]

The overthrow of King James's government in 1689 proved to disperse the English Jesuits. In October 1791 the French Sulpicians started a seminary in Baltimore. In fact, Gabriel Richards (1767-1832), a Sulpician emigre from France, had arrived and was assigned to work in Detroit, upper Michigan, and Wisconsin. Not only a missionary, but he also became a pioneer in education, a publisher, and a member of the US Congress in 1823.[584]

Actually, the first overseas Catholic mission emanating from the United States was under the tutelage of John Carroll who inherited the Virgin Islands in 1804. Bishop Carroll had two priests of the Congregation of the Holy Ghost, namely Fathers Henry Kendal and Matthew Herard who had been in the Islands since 1793. Subsequently, they became prefect and vice prefect respectively.[585]

Historically, John Carroll was somewhat of a reluctant diplomat. He was very sensitive of the line between priesthood and politics. According to John Carroll who indicated: "I hope I may be allowed to add, that tho I have little regard to my personal safety amidst the present distress of my country, yet I cannot help feeling some for my character: and I have observed that when the ministers of Religion leave their duties of their profession to take a busy part in political matter, they generally fall into contempt & sometimes even bring discredit to the cause, in whose service they are engaged."[586]

Although in the tidewater states as well as on the frontiers, Catholics were involved on both sides in the American Revolution; however, a committee of Catholic religious had written the following to Rome in 1783: ...in these United States, our religious system has undergone a revolution, if possible, more extraordinary, than our political one. In all of them free toleration is allowed to Christians of every denomination, and particularly in the States of Pennsylvania Delaware, Maryland, and Virginia, a communication of all civil rights, without distinction or diminution, is extended to those of our Religion."[587]

Making no apologies for the role of Catholics during the American Revolution. John Carrol, being adamant about a general religious freedom, had indicated to "The Columbian Magazine or ^Monthly Miscellany": "Thanks to the genuine spirit of Christianity! The United States have banished intolerance from their systems of government, and many of them have done the justice to every denomination of Christians, which ought to be done to them in all, of placing them on the same footing of citizenship, and conferring an equal right of participation in national privileges."[588]

On October 19, 1781, Lord Cornwallis had surrendered unconditionally via his second-in-command General Charles O'Hara who offered his sword. He attempted to provide his sword to General Rochambeau. However, General Washington had indicated that it was only appropriate for his second-in-command General Benjamin Lincoln to receive the sword.[589] Essentially, negotiations of the Paris peace talks took many months. The provisional treaty was signed on November 30, 1782 however the final peace treaty was official on September 3, 1783.[590]

John Carroll began to develop a plan for organizing the clergy. He had indicated the following: "The Clergymen here continue to live in the old form: it is the effect of habit, and if they could promise themselves immortality it would be well enough. But I regret that indolence prevents any form of administration being adopted which tend to secure to posterity a succession of Catholic Clergymen, and secure to these a comfortable subsistence."[591]

Essentially, the "Constitution of the Clergy" was composed of financial parts delineating control of physical and financial assets. Moreover, it included a rule of life for priests as well as spiritual authority vested in a bishop. The main issue was simply that Catholics in the United States preferred an American bishop. According to Carroll, "No authority derived from the Propaganda will ever be admitted here".[592]

The pope's nuncio at Versailles, Cardinal Leonardo Antonelli for the Propagation of the Faith approached the American Minister Benjamin Franklin on this issue. Franklin had deferred to congress in Philadelphia. "Resolved, that Doctor Franklin be desired to notify to the Apostolical Nuncio at Versailles, that congress will always be pledged to testify their respect to his sovereign and state, but that the subject of his application to Doctor Franklin, being purely spiritual, it is without the jurisdiction and powers of Congress who have no authority to permit or refuse it, these powers being reserved to the general states individually."[593]

However, it was in the summer of 1784 that John Carroll was officially named the superior of the Mission m their thirteen United States of America Basically, Cardinal Antonelli expressed to Carroll the reasoning beneath his appointment, "it is known that your appointment will please and gratify many members of that republic, and especially Mr. Franklin."[594] Moreover, a notation found in Benjamin Franklin's personal journal written in Paris: "The Pope's Nuncio called, and acquainted me that the Pope had, on my Recommendation, appointed Mr. John Carroll, Superior of the Catholic Clergy in America."[595] Although Carroll was not pleased on how he acquired his new title technically offered in November, he formally accepted on February 27th of 1785. Moreover, Carroll had prepared a report about the statues of the Roman Catholic Church in America. His report consisted of three main parts: (1) an estimation of the population of Catholics. (2) a qualitative assessment of Catholic religious practice; and finally, (3) the clergy and vocations to the priesthood.[596] It was the Most Rev. John Ireland who recounted the dogma of the Catholic faith germane to church and State in 1913. He had indicated that there is no need for discord or contradiction. Church and State cover separate and distinct zones of thought and action: the Church busies itself with the spiritual, the State with the temporal. The Church and the State are built for different purposes: the Church for heaven, the State for earth. The line of demarcations between the two jurisdictions was traced by the unerring finger of Him who is the master of both: the law of God is ¾ "Render to Caesar the things that are Caesar's and to God the things that are God's."[597]

Although John Carroll was slow to respond in accepting his new role, he did not hesitate to initiate his plan. Certainly, prior to the summer's conclusion, he had traveled to the Maryland and Virginia missions. In the fall, Carroll went north to Pennsylvania and New York. It is important to note that the anti-priest Statue of New York was repealed in in 1784.[598] Carroll's assessment of Catholicism in America was that mostly mass and a homily were offered monthly. Moreover, religious practice and education in the faith was mostly poor. Essentially Carroll recognized the need to promote vocations to priesthood.[599]

The various nuances of the Catholic church in America were complex. Although the Maryland missions continued mostly as they have had for about one hundred fifty years, a new church in Baltimore on a lot purchased by the Charles Carroll family in 1764 now existed. Parishioners consisted of French Neutrals" who were the descendants of the Acadian exiles. Newer French arrivals were business traders in Baltimore who had no regard for religion and were a bad influence on the Acadians.[600]

In 1786, there were three priests who died in a short period of time. Ferdinand Farmer of Philadelphia was included as one of the priests who passed away. John Carroll had indicated that "this year proves fateful to our most excellent and incomparable German Brethren."[601] In 1776, when John Caroll had traveled to Canada, he had described New York City as "almost a desert".[602] It was on the fourth of December 1783 that General George Washington gave an emotional farewell to three hundred of his officers at Fraunces Tavern where he had resided that week. Washington had stated the following: "With a heart full of love and gratitude, I now take leave of you and now most devantly wish that your later days be as prosperous in your future lives as your former ones have been glorious and honorable.... I cannot come to each of you but shall feel obliged if each of you will come and take me by the hand."[603]

After greeting the officers present individually, Washington had traveled to Philadelphia the next day where he was honored very graciously. Finally, Washington made his way to the Maryland State House in Annapolis where Congress had relocated on a temporary basis.[604] Washington had stated the following: "Having finished the work assigned me, I retire from the great theater of action. And bidding an affectionate farewell to this august body under whose orders I have so long acted I hereby offer my commission and take my leave from all my employments of public life."[605]

However, on April 30, 1789, George Washington would return to New York where he would be sworn in as the first president of the United States. His inauguration took place on the balcony of Federal Hall on the corner of Broad and Wall Streets. In fact, Washington's left hand was placed on a Bible specifically upon a passage in Genesis.[606-607]

New York was changed forever, it had repealed the anti-priest law, and the first resident priest was Charles Maurice Whelan, an Irish Capuchin friar. John Carroll had estimated that there are approximately fifteen hundred Catholics in New York.[608]

Whelan saw immigrants from all over the world. According to Whelan: The Catholics in these parts are very poor, but very zealous. For the greater part they are Irish. As such they would not be able to build a church nor even to rent a place for saying mass. However, a Portuguese gentleman has given them a part of his house for that purpose, and I hope that divine Providence will provide us with another place by next May, since said gentleman cannot let us use his house any longer... In this country it is necessary for a priest to know at least the Irish, English, French and Dutch languages, because our congregation is composed of these nationalities, as well also as of Portuguese and Spaniards."[609]

Essentially, New York Catholics met at Vauxhall Gardens near the North River and then relocated to Barclay Street. With the help of King Charles m of Spain and Don Diego de Gardoqui, the Spanish minister, Saint Peter's Church was built and had opened its doors on

November 4,1786 actually on Saint Charles' Day.[610] John Carroll had made very clear to Whelan that it is not proper to accepted money for the administration of the sacraments. Moreover, Carroll was critical of Whelan's ability to preach. However, another Irish Capuchin, Andrew Nugent, was an accomplished orator.[611]

Whelan had made many enemies who sought to expel him. Since the diocesan and partial structure was still in its infancy in the United States, Carrollwas unable to name a pastor. Rather, he made the two friars, "joint chaplains".[612] When Whelan had retired to his brother's home in Johnstown, New York, Nugent had by default became solely in charge of the Church. This did not last for long since, the trustees made charges of personal nature against Nugent. As a result, Carroll had revoked Nugent's faculties and suspended him.[613]

In western Pennsylvania, the son of a Russian prince and of Counteos Amilia von Schettau, Dimitri Gallitzin was the first Roman Catholic priest to complete all of his studies in the United States. In 1799, which is currently Loretto, Pennsylvania, Dimitri was provided two hundred acres and a good horse as well as an annual contribution to be their priest. According to Carroll, "This place is about 40 miles distant from the Standing Stone. A great number of Catholics scattered thru this and the neighboring settlement."[614] Essentially, Kentucky was part of a second major Catholic effort to go westward.

Basically, the Nelson and Scott counties would contain eight Catholic settlements. Although no priest was available until 1787, Charles Maurice Whelan who had confronted Nugent in New York had relocated there. This pleased Carroll, who requested Whelan's superior in Dublin for another priest to assist Whelan. However, Whelan would last in Kentucky for only two and one-half years. It would be a refugee from the French Revolution, Stephen Badin, the first priest ordained in the United States who would fill this void There were two women's religious communities, the sisters of Loretto founded by schoolteachers and the sisters of Charity of Nazareth who served this catholic populace.[615]

In 1791, the Holy See determined that Baltimore's jurisdiction included the United States as a whole. Thus, Carroll was able to regularize the life of the church, even in the borderlands out west. Carroll had promptly authorized three priests who were refugee French Sulpicians to take charge of the western missions in 1792.[616] It is important to note that Philadelphia with its St. Mary's Church and the smaller St. Joseph's Chapel was still the main Catholic center. Certainly, Matthew Carey, the onetime Irish revolutionary, was a very prominent publisher had resided in Philadelphia. He had edited the Pennsylvania Herald, Columbian Magazine, and The American Museum, die most influential news magazine.

The "Carey Bible" was the first American edition of the Douai-Rheims version. The "Carey Bible" was first published in December of 1789 and the following year he published the Bible as a whole. The total cost was six dollars to subscribers who included both prominent Protestants and Catholics. Certainly, Carroll promoted the subscription to not only priests but the laity as well.[617]

Carroll had often responded in writing to anti-Catholic attacks. The Columbian Magazine and the Gazette of the United States published articles against the Roman Catholic church. Basically, Carroll believed in the rights of a national church. Thus, he wanted "a permanent body of national Clergy". Carroll saw the Catholic Church in the United States with no European "metro political" connection and thus there were not the "ecclesiological constructs" as in the European culture.[618] Carroll thought that the Catholic Church would be better served by "an ordinary national bishop contrary to a Vicar apostolic". His notion was a local church in communion with the Pope and the Holy See of Rome. In response to the papul bull Ex Hac Apostolicae by which he was appointed Bishop of Baltimore, Carroll had expounded in the following:

"The pope, according to the pretensions, which these of Rome has always supported, says he will nominate here after. But I conceive that The Clergy will have as good right to say, that the election shall be held by members of their own body, & that they never can or will admit any Bishop who is not so constituted... As to the investing of the Bp with the administration [of church property], I never conceived it as anything more than the expression of those claims which Rome has always kept up, tho universally disregarded; viz- that the pope is the universal administrator, some even have said, Dominos of all ecclesiastical property..."[619]

Carroll's main thrust was a Catholic education for priests, lay men and women. Certainly, a seminary was the sine qua non of this concept which became reality when St. Mary's Seminary was founded in 1790. Moreover, the academy at Georgetown opened in 1791. Carroll believed that the education of men and women should be "cultivated by the Church".[620] Although, the first nuns to arrive in the United States were the Carmelites, it was Alice Lalor who put together the Georgetown visitation convent which became the first Catholic women's school in the United States. However, John Carroll's plan for the development of the Catholic church did not occur as he thought. Actually, an economic recession around the War of 1812 had detrimental effects.[621]

In 1811, the Democratic-Republican controlled Congress did not recharter the Bank of the United States which was indeed the main source of loans for about the past twenty years to fund the U.S. Government's activities. This was due to bank restrictions on lending which effected the "boom-era" venture capitalists. Essentially, too many of the bank's bonds were held in England. Thus, the thinking was to have state banks which would allow a vast expansion of credit.[622]

However, American Catholicism had primarily internal issues. Basically, Carroll was unable to obtain effective Episcopal collaborators. Although he chose a very qualified gentleman, Lorenz Graess, as a coadjutor bishop. Un fortunately, he tragically died of yellow fever while ministering to the sick in Philadelphia.[623]

However, the following choice became unfavorable, an ex-Jesuit and missionary in Guyana, Leonard Neale. Certainly, he was a holy man who was indifferent in His teaching, preaching, and writing. Neale was the president of Georgetown College from 1799 to 1806 with a disciplinary approach which did not fit well at the college. Moreover, Neale was the regional bishop for Washington, Maryland, and Virginia. He was archbishop of Baltimore at the age of sixty-eighth although he was semi-retired at the Georgetown visitation Convent.[624]

Interestingly, Georgetown college's first student, William Gaston, was elected to Congress and became an associate justice of the North Carolina Supreme Court at a later time. Essentially, Gaston in 1835 became a staunch advocate for repeal of the state law, denying Catholics the franchise. However, it was Maryland's Roger Brooke Taney who was formerly a Federalist then subsequently became a "Jacksonian Democrat" who emerged as United States Attorney General and afterwards secretary of the Treasury. Overall, Taney's tenure of constitutional interpretations were prudent during the years of 1836 to 1864. However, the exception was his legal opinion of die Dred Scott case which dampered his extraordinary career as a Chief Justice.[625]

In summary, Dred Scott was a slave owned by army surgeon John Emerson, who took Scott from Missouri to posts in Illinois and Fort Snelling where Scott married a slave mutually owned by Emerson. However, it was after the death of Emerson that white friends encouraged Scott in 1846 to sue for his freedom since he had secured prolonged residence in a free state. Basically, the Missouri compromise of 1820 did not allow slavery west of Missouri and north of 36°30' latitude.

Taney indicated that blacks "had for more than a century before been regarded as beings of an inferior order... so for inferior, that they had no rights which a white man was bound to respect."[626] However more than thirty years earlier, Taney freed his own slaves with the exception of two slaves who were too old. These two, "I supported in comfort as long as they lived."[627]

According to Archbishop John Carroll in a letter written in the last year of his life to Archbishop John Troy of Dublin, "Since the great stir raised in England about Slavery, my Brethren being anxious to suppress censure, which some are always glad to affix to the priesthood, have begun some years ago, and are gradually, proceeding to emancipate the old population on their estates to proceed at once to make it a general measure, would not be either humanity towards the Individuals, nor doing justice to the trust, under which the estates have been transmitted and received."[628]

Jesuit Brother Joseph Mobberley wrote an essay on slavery, supporting the practice based upon scripture. Although his writings justified slavery, Mobberley actually advocated the abolition of it on the Jesuit farms. Essentially, some slaves of Jesuits in Maryland were dispatched to Missouri in 1823 to initiate missionary work for the Indians. Other slaves were sold, and some went to Louisiana in 183 8.[629]. It is important to note that the practice of slavery was common in religious institutions in southern and border states. Nazareth in Kentucky had freed its last thirty slaves which included children on January 1, 1865.[630]

Maryland had the most free blacks in the union. Moreover, the Sulpicians of Saint Mary's Seminary not only made available their basement chapel to black Santo Domingo refugees, but Sulpician James Joubert played a major part in the founding of the Oblate Sisters of Providence. By and large, their Saint Francis academy became the hub of worship for black Catholics. [631]

It was a Redemptorist, Taddeus Anwander, who had sponsored a black seminarian, William a. Williams, who studied at Urban College in Rome from 1855 to 1862. At first, he was discouraged from serving as a priest in the United States due to prejudice that Williams would encounter. However, Williams would work with Peter Miller and retired Bishop Michael O'Connor who were Jesuits in Baltimore. Essentially, a chapel for black people was destined to emerge as the first all-black Catholic church in the United States, named Saint Francis Xavier Church.[632] Moreover, Williams published a journal, the Truth Communicator, in post-Civil War years aimed at the needs of freed slaves.[633]

Gregory XVI in 1839 indicated the following: "We} do... admonish and adjure in the Lord all believers in Christ, of whatsoever condition, conditions, that no one hereafter may dare unjustly to molest Indians, Negroes, or other men of this sort; or to spoil them of their goods; or to reduce them to slavery'; or to extend help or favour to others who perpetrate such things against them; or to exercise that in human trade by which Negroes, as if they were not men, but mere animals. Howsoever reduced into slavery, are, without any distinction, contrary to the laws of justice and humanity, bought, sold, and doomed sometimes to the most severe and exhausting labours."[634]

The Holy Father, Pope Gregory XVI, clearly had forbidden any religious or Catholic layperson from defending or promoting the slave trade When the Holy Father was a cardinal, he had served as prefect of the Congregation of the Propagation of the Faith. It was likely that he had acquired experience of the new world and the various issues as slavery. Unequivocally, Pope Gregory regarded slavery as an evil and he was the foremost opponent of it during this era. [635]

According to Bishop John England in a correspondence with Van Buren's Secretary of State John Forsyth in 1840, England made a distinction between the pope being against the slave trade and the existence of domestic slavery in the United States. Essentially, Secretary Forsyth's utilization of the pope's letter for political purposes mainly to attack the whig presidential candidate, served as a catalyst for England to defend slavery via exegesis of scripture and Judeo-Christian Tradition.[636] This was contrary to England's behavior toward blacks and not consistent with his previous writings. Basically, England not only opened a school for black children in Charleston, but England wrote that "he was not friendly to the existence or continuation of slavery".[637]

However, it was Bishop Francis P. Kenrick of Philadelphia who was widely acknowledge as a brilliant theologian, in his moral theology textbook expressed "regret" that there were many slaves whose liberty was denied. Moreover, he maintained that the law of the land must be adhered to in order to avoid chaos.[638]

Kenrick's reference on law, he wrote the following: "What must one think about that domestic slavery which flourishes in most or our southern states the descendants of those abducted from Africa and still subject to the yoke [of servitude}? Indeed, in this fullness of freedom, in which we all take pride, it must be regretted that there are the teaching of reading and which impede greatly the exercise of religion at any place so that one must take care from any undertakings [contrary to the laws]. Since, for the rest, such is the state of affairs, nothing against the law must be attempted, neither anything by which the slaves might be set free, nor must anything be done or said that would make them bear the take with difficulty. But the prudence and the charity of the sacred ministers must be shown in this, so that the slaves informed by Christian morals, might show service to their masters, venerating always God, the supreme Master of us all; so that in turn the masters might show themselves gentle and evenhanded and might lighten the condition of their slaves with humanity and with zeal from their salvation."[639]

Basically, Kenrick promoted the tranquility of civil society, the good of the Catholic slave holders, and the general well-being of slaves.[640] He died on July 3, 1863, while the battle of Gettysburg was concluding. In a letter written to Eliza Allen Starr, Kenrick indicated that "from my heart I wish that secession had never been thought of."[641] Catholic newspapers held various views. The Catholic Miscellany of Charleston printed articles about states' rights. The Catholic Advocate of Louisville had opposed abolition. In fact, a reward notice in the classified section germane to the return of runaway slaves included the following note, "as they are Catholics, I would prefer selling them to a person of that persuasion," or "I would prefer selling them to a Catholic."[642]

According to Courtney Jenkins of the Catholic Mirror in Baltimore, 'there was not a happier people on earth than the slaves" and moreover, the freedom of slaves would be "fatal".[643] Patrick Donahue of the Boston Pilot believes that abolitionism was a Protestant crusade which is splitting the United States.[644] However, it was Jeremiah Cummings who was pastor of Saint Stephen's Church in New York who had normally contributed articles to the Brownson's Quarterly Review, indicated the following: "undeniable that no religious body in the country stands so generally committed to slavery and the rebellion" as Catholics.[645]

During the war between the States, Cummings pushed for an end to slavery without indemnity. In fact, Archbishop John B. Purcell publically called for the emancipation of slaves in August 1862 which was actually five months prior to President Lincoln's official proclamation.[646] According to the Archbishop Purcell's brother, Father Edward Purcell, editor of the Catholic Telegraph, "slavery and the Catholic Church could never get along well together".[647]

Unequivocally, Father Edward Purcell was the foremost supporter of the Union's cause. Interestingly, archbishop John Hughes maintained a long-time friendship with President James Buchanan since 1846 and the Mexican War. However, Hughes mentioned that "I cannot imagine a descendant of the Buchanans that I knew in Ireland who, knowing or believing himself to be right, would ever give way," he had written in March, 1858.[648] Moreover, Hughes wrote to another friend William H. Seward on June 18,1861: I pray you for heaven's sake not to allow it to be a half battle, but one in which whatever the consequences may be, the South will be taught that it is incapable of coping with the North."[649]

Although Hughes was a staunch and loyal Unionist, he wrote the following to Secretary of War Simon Cameron in October 1861: The Catholics so far as I know, whether of native or foreign birth are willing to fight to the death for the support of the constitution, the Government, and the laws of the country But if it should be understood that, with or without knowing it, they are to fight for the abolition of slavery, then, indeed, they will turn away in disgust from the discharge of what would otherwise be a patriotic duty."[650]

Essentially, Archbishop Hughes had the national flag m plain view at his cathedral and promoted Catholics to serve their country. "Let volunteers continue and the draft be made."[651] Hughes sent letters about secession to Bishop Patrick N. Lynch of Charleston, an old friend. His correspondence and return Otters from Lynch written in the summer of 1861 became public knowledge in September of 1861 in the Metropolitan record.[652]

Afterwards, President Lincoln sent both Hughes and Tharlow Weed, a politician, on an "unofficial" diplomatic mission to, Paris, where they forwarded the Union cause to Napoleon III and Eugenie. Moreover, they talked to Vatican papal officials and met with a "chilly" attitude.[653] By and large, Hughes found papal officials not amenable to the northern cause. Although Hughes had proposed to meet with Alexander II at Saint Petersburg, this request was denied by the state department. Essentially, Hughes remained in Rome until June, his final report fell short of expectations.

He indicated the following: "There is no love for the United States on the other side of the water. Generally speaking on the other side of the Atlantic the United States are ignored, if not despised—treated in conversation in the same contemptuous language as we might employ towards the inhabitants of the Sandwich Island, or the Washington territory, or Vancouvers Island, or the Settlement of the Red River or of the Hudson's Bay Territory."[654] Hughes died on January 3, 1864 after he had interceded in the Irish riot of July 13 to 16 in response to the draft.

Hughes address to the rioters began: "They call you rioters, but I cannot see a rioter's face among you.. ."[655]

Bishop Martin J. Spalding published his anonymous "Dissertation on the American Civil War" in the papal newspaper *Osservatore Romano* in October of 1863. Spalding described slavery of being a social evil with "the legacy of American's Protestant heritage".[656] Spalding indicated that die war's etiology was based on inequitable tariff structures revolving around an agrarian South and an industrial North. Moreover, he faulted Lincoln's war policies which was to exterminate the South. Interestingly, it was just six months later that Spalding would become the next Archbishop of Baltimore succeeding Peter Richard Kenrick.[657] When John Wilkes Booth shot Abraham Lincoln on April 14, 1865, Spalding released a public statement, "A deed of blood has been perpetrated, which has caused every heart to shudder, and which calls for the execration of every citizen..."[658]

Actually, it was at 10:15 pm that Booth shot Lincoln at Ford's Theatre. Major Henry Reed Rathbone responded to the sound of gunfire turning around while Booth used a knife downward onto Rathbone. When Booth jumped over the railing, he landed on the stage, fracturing the fibula of his lower left leg. However, the limping Booth managed to escape he theater with knife in hand, swinging it and forcing his way pass the set carpenter, Jake Ritterspaugh and a boy "Peanut John" out the theater onto his horse.[659]

General Hardie had sent a message which encouraged that crepe be hung on all Catholic church properties and buildings. Since the conspirators had planned Lincoln's assassination at Mary Surratt's boarding house, it became an issue for Catholics.[660] Essentially, Mary Surratt was a Catholic who was an active Confederate sympathizer involved with spying and smuggling weapons. Moreover, she had a pro-Confederate tavern in Surrattsville, Maryland where she and her late husband had owned a tobacco farm.[661] Basically, Pumphrey's stable and Surratt's boarding house on sixth and H streets provided Boothe, Lewis Powell, John Surratt, David Herold, and George Atzerodt, an opportunity to plan the assassinations of Lincoln, Johnson, and Secretary of State William Seward. In essence, Seward survived an attack in his bed by Lewis Powell, a former Confederate spy.[662]

In fact, if General Grant attended the theater with Lincoln, then Boothe would have had a possibility to kill Grant as well. Vice President Andrew Johnson who resided at a nearby hotel who was unguarded was at risk. Thus, Boothe and his cospirators had attempted to overthrow the government of the United States.[663] However, it was Thomas Jones, a smuggler who transported secret agent, diplomats and others across the Potomac River to the South routinely as his livelihood, who facilitated an escape route for Booth and Herold.[664] Finally, Dr. Samuel Mudd, a Catholic, who tended to the broken leg of John Wilkes Booth. However, Mudd would not loan his personal carriage to Booth and Herold.[665] Although Mudd tried to fabricate a story to his cousin George who was a devoted Union sympathizer and again provide false information to Lieutenant Alexander Lovett, it actually served to implicate himself. When Mudd's wife Sarah presented a razor and a boot, the name J. Wikes is clearly evident. Then, Dr. Samuel Mudd was arrested, and he spent the rest of his life in a remote penitentiary of Fort Jefferson in the Gulf of Mexico.[666]

In summary, a nine-member jury found Mary Surratt, Lewis Powell George Atzerodt, and David Herold guilty as charged. They were all hanged.[667] Although John Surratt was part of the plot, he had escaped and later found as a volunteer in the pope's own army (papal Zouaves). This aroused suspicions which fueled anti-papist prejudice.[668] Moreover, John Surrat was discovered and arrested. However, he temporarily escaped until uncovered in Alexandria, Egypt. Upon his return to the United States to be tried in Court, the jury was deadlocked, and he was freed. John Surrat died in 1916 of old age as a free man.[669]

On October 4, 1866, the second plenary council of the Roman Catholic church began with a procession of forty-five archbishops and bishops as well as two abbots. In fact, President Andrew Johnson had participated in a solemn session which concluded the two weeklong council. Spalding had presided over the first council of council of bishops in 1852 as well. The Roman Catholic church grew to a population of four million American Catholics and thus the number of churches and priests had doubled.[670] Basically, the council covered various theological topics including revelation, the Church, as custodian of Revolution the doctrine stating, "outside the church there is no salvation".

The nature and necessity of faith, Sacred Scripture, the mysteries of the Trinity, creation, redemption, sanctification, the future life, and veneration of the Blessed Virgin Mary.[671] Essentially, Pope Pius IX papal declaration of the Syllabus of Errors in 1864 influenced part of the five hundred thirty-four paged document of the American Catholic Council. However, the American Bishops had adopted a positive tone in their document. The notion of a collective episcopal authority which was articulated in a statement germane to the collegial role of all bishops:

"Bishops, therefore, who are the successors of the Apostles, and whom the Holy Spirit has placed to rule the Church of God. Which He acquired with His own blood, agreeing and judging together with its head on earth, the Roman pontiff, whether they are gathered in general councils, or dispersed throughout the world, are inspired from on high with the gift of inerrancy, so that their body or college can never fail nor define anything against doctrine revealed by God."[672]

However, the practical problems in America was addressed in the pastoral letter of 1866 as stated: "A large number of Catholics parents either appear to have no idea of the sanctity of the Christian family, and of the responsibility imposed on them of providing for the moral training offspring or fulfill their duty in a very imperfect manner."[673]

Peter Kenrick, the archbishop of St. Louis, was upset that issues which he had brought to the council were ignored. Basically, he proposed priest attire similar to the "tonsure oat" of the Irish. Moreover, he felt that lay people should hold title and thus, they would lease property to bishops.[674]

Pertaining to the pressing issue of evangelization of the four million black people who are now freed from slavery, a plan developed by Spalding which was suggested by the Vatican were somewhat reduced to local choice. Again, Kenrick fostered opposition to the plan indicating that "all that could be done was being done."

A plan to construct non-territorial missionary dioceses (prefectures-apostolic) for black people was made. This led to the council's legislation for religious communities to open schools as well as other institutions in order to minister to the black people. Due to the controversy, the council's pastoral letter had sent "mixed signals".

It read as follows: "We could have wished, that in accordance with the action of the Catholic Church in past ages, in regard to the serfs in Europe, a more gradual system of emancipation could have been adopted, so that they might have been in some measure to make a better use of their freedom, than they are likely to do now . Still the evils which must necessarily attend upon the sudden liberation of so large a multitude, with their peculiar dispositions and habits, only make the appeal to our Christian Charity and zeal, presented by their forlorn condition, the more forcible and imperative."[675]

Bishop Augustin Verot, who was pro-slavety prior to the war between the States, put together an extensive ministry for the black people. As a result of resident James Buchanan's declaration of a day of prayer and fasting on Friday January 4, 1861, Verot rendered a homily germane to slavery. In fact, Verot published his sermon as a booklet under the following title, "A Tract for the Times: Slavery and Abolitionism, being the Substance of a sermon, Preached in the in the Church of St. Augustine, Florida, on the 4th day of January 1861. Day of Public Humiliation, Fasting and prayer by the Right Kev. Verot, D.D., Vicar Apostolic of Florida."[676]

Although before the Civil War, Verot defended slavery, after the war he wrote a pastoral letter which indicated that people need "to put away all prejudice... against their former servants."[677] Certainly, Verot was m the minority at the council who had fully stood behind the Vatican's plan for a national approach and director of evangelization for the freed black people. Moreover, Verot firmly stated that "according to the mind of the Sacred Congregation something special for blacks was to be done."[678] Verot collected money in the amount of nine hundred dollars in the diocese of Eric, eight hundred dollars in Buffalo, and seven hundred dollars in Rochester. Moreover, he had requested the Sisters of Saint Joseph from Le Pay in France in order to offer a school for black people. Altogether, Verot had opened seven schools within ten years prior to his death.[679] Protestantism had an advantage over Catholicism in drawing the black people since the protestants exhibited emotionality in prayer meetings which resembled African dance. Another factor in being more attracted to Protestantism was that the black people had preferred their own Church.[680]

In 1886, Augustus Tolton, an ex-slave had finished his theological studies for the priesthood in Rome. Tolton was actually ordained on April 24, 1886 at the age of thirty-two in the Basilica of St. John Lateran.[681] Tolton was born a slave in Ralls County, Missouri in 1854. His mother, Martha Jane Chisley, was a slave in Mead County, Kentucky and arrived in 1849 as a dowry when Susan Manning had married Stephen Elliott who was an owner of a plantation in Ralls County. Essentially, Martha Chisley became married to Peter Paul Tolton who was a slave on the Hagan planation nearby. They were both Catholics who were married in a small parish near Hannibal, namely St. Peter's at Brush Creek. Augustus was the second of three children baptized at St. Peter's.[682] It is important to note that technically speaking, Missouri was a slave state which chose not to secede from the Union. However, it was split between two factions, pro-slavery and abolition. Basically, the Toltons left the Elliott plantation for Illinois which was a free state.

Augustus' pastor had broached the notion of a vocation to the priesthood for him. Tolton was a student at a Franciscan college. Quincy where he studied part time while teaching religious education in Sunday School for black children. Due to Father Michael Richardt's efforts, Augustus Tolton was sent to Urban College in Rome in March 1880 at age twenty-five.[683]*

Although Father Augustus Tolton was groomed to be a missionary to Africa, he had returned to the United States on July 6, 1886. He arrived in New York and five days later on July 11th, Father Tolton celebrated his second Mass in a new Catholic church in New York at St. Benedict the Moor on Bleeker Street. Actually, Tolton's first Mass was in Hoboken, New Jersey at Saint Mary's Hospital.[684]

At the first black Catholic congress in Washington in 1889, Tolton rendered a speech which included the following: "I heard the words of St. John "prepare the ways of the Lord and God gave me strength to persevere, for Rome had heard that no one of us could be found here to preach the Gospel. I rejoiced [sic] when I heard that I was [to] be sent to America. God is over us all, and he has many blessings for men of every race. When on the eve of going to St. John Lateran to be ordained, the word came expressing doubt whether I would be sent here. It was said that I would be the only priest of my race in America and would not be likely to succeed. All at once Cardinal simony (sic) said, "America has been called the most enlightened nation; we will see if it deserves that honor. If America has never seen a black priest. It has to see one now."[685]

Tolton had indicated that "the white people in this little Gem City of Quincy, Illinois, are really good-hearted, charitable, and non-prejudicial, no feelings of bitterness at all against a man on account of complexion."[686] The only problem was a German priest, Cather Michael Weiss, who did not like Tolton because many of Weiss" parishioners left his church in preference to Tolton. This situation had worsened when Weiss wrote to the bishop against Tolton. This disturbed Tolton considerably.

Mother Katherine Drexel was a source of moral and financial support to Tolton. According to Tolton: "In the whole History of the church in America we can't find a person that has sworn to layout their treasury for the sole benefit of the colored and Indians. As I stand alone as the first one to make such or sacrifice for the... downtrodden race."[687]

Tolton suffered from poor health partly due to stress from work. A letter written by Mary C. Elmer with the signature as Sister Angela de Mena, O.S.F, included the following: "Poor father - it seems strange after all the "gush" we read from week to week in the papers about the dear negro he is left to struggle on almost alone; in poverty and humility grappling with the giant task of founding a church and congregation in Chicago. We who come in contact with him in our labors, and are the witnesses of his ardent charity and self-denying zeal feel ourselves privileged to bow the knee for his saintly blessing."[688]

After working for seven years in Chicago, Tolton died on July 9, 1897. He had attended a retreat at Kankakee and returned by train. Tolton had collapsed walking from the train station to his rectory in over a hundred-degree temperature. Tolton was brought directly to the local hospital where he had died that day.[689] In a letter written by Father Slattery who led the Society of Saint Joseph, an offshoot of English Mill

Hill Missionaries, his correspondence to Walker Elliot, editor of Catholic World:

"Alas, there is fresh opposition to negro priests. The two already ordained have not been conspicuous success; one of them lost his health just as a bishop of the Diocese he lives in, had his impaired. The other gave a little trouble some years ago, nothing serious but enough to justify a hue and cry against negro priests."[690]

The second black priest was Charles Randolph Uncles, S.S J. He was ordained in 1891 via the efforts of Father John Richard Slattery in the Society of Saint Joseph. This was not the end of this emerging trend. Thus, others had followed including the society of St. Edmund, Spiritans, the society of African Missions, and the society of the Divine Word.[691] Essentially, the Society of Saint Joseph of Mill Hill was founded in England by Bishop Herbert Vaughan in 1866. It arrived five years later in the United States. In order to convert and minister to black people who were emancipated. Slattery, who was the son of a well to do New York family in the construction business, became the provincial until ousted in 1883.[692]*

Slattery's well-known homily "Dorsey sermon," which he gave at the ordination of Josephite John Dorsey, a black priest both educated and ordained in the United States, was a criticism of the American Catholic clergy. Priests in America were initially reluctant to encourage vocations to the priesthood among black Catholics. The *Catholic World* newspaper had published Slattery's speech in 1893 to the Columbian Catholic Congress germane to the identical theme of the "Dorsey Sermon". The title of the article and talk was "The Negro Race: Their Condition, Present, and Future".[693]

The college for black catechists was opened in 1900 in Montgomery, Alabama for the purpose of priestly vocations. Although Slattery believed that blacks would ultimately evangelize and receive a number of conversions in Africa, his model of mission was that of Charles Cardinal Lavigerie who was the founder of the Missionaries of Africa.[694] By and large, Slattery proposed industrial training for blacks as well as instilling various values and virtues. However, the notion of modernism in 1906 adversely affected bringing black men into the seminaries. Many of the

Black Catholic laity joined the Confraternity of the Rosary at Holy Trinity Church at St. Thomas Manor, Maryland.

The Journal of the Society of Colored People - The Holy Family Society in Baltimore was published by black Catholics. Daniel Rudd was the founder of the *American Catholic Tribune,* a black Catholic newspaper. Rudd, a former slave, was involved in the five Afro-American Congresses in 1889 to 1894. The primary issues were germane to injustices and discrimination experienced by black Catholics as well as the topic of evangelization of blacks.[695] Due to the Kulturkampf, a conflict between the Roman Catholic church and the German government, the Congregation of the Holy Ghost Fathers and Brothers fled to the United States in 1872. Not only did they develop a ministry for German Immigrants, but the African Americans as well.

Namely, the Divine Word missionaries ministered to Southern blacks. [696] Mother Katharine Drexel, who had founded the Sisters of the Blessed Sacrament for Indians and Colored people, had provided advice and financial assistance to the Divine Word missionaries. Written into Katharine Drexel's constitution for the community of the sisters was "to lead the Indian and Colored Races to the Knowledge and love of God and so make of them living temples of Our Lord's Divinity."[697] Actually, Katharine had donated much funds even prior to entering the convent. In fact, she had financed the construction of numerous mission schools for poor Indians and blacks. However, James O'Connor, Bishop of Omaha, had attempted to discourage and prevent Katharine's religious vocation due to her weak health and accustomed comfort. O'Connor had written in august of 1885 and indicated that, "the conclusion to which I have come in your case is, that your vocation is not to enter a religious order. "[698]

Her response in 1888 includes the following: "How I wish to spend my entire life entirely given to Him by the three vows which would consecrate me to Jesus Christ! it appears to me that the Lord gives me the right to choose the better part, and I shall try to draw as near to his heart as possible... Are you afraid to give me to Jesus Christ?"[699]

Thus, Katharine had taken her vows as the first member of the sisters of the Blessed Sacrament in February of 1891. Soon thirteen women would also take their vows and become postulants and novices with her. The sisters moved to Cornwell Heights in 1892. Katharine would serve as superior general for about forty-four years.[700]

When the sisters had purchased property for a school for black children in Nashville, Tennessee, the owner who originally, sold the land had attempted to buy back this property. When he discovered the sisters had planned to build for black children, the owner had changed his mind. But the property was already sold to the sisters. Even the town Council tried to obtain the property in order to prevent the building of a school for black children.

According to Katharine, who had remained steadfast: "It seems so appropriate for a Convert of the Blessed Sacrament- Christ dwelling with us-and the school of the Immaculate Mother to have people of the city [say that they] have no room for our precious Charge. They say, There is another place on the city's outskirts for our educational work. How truly was the Cave of Bethlehem the great educator of the world! This was indeed the school of the Immaculate Mother.... My God! How much light can be wasted when the darkness does not comprehend it!"[701]

Katharine had a heart attack in 193 5 and died twenty years later at the age of ninety-six. She was instrumental in the founding of fifty schools and her community was active in twenty - one states as well as the District of Columbia.[702] At the time of Katharine's death, her community was composed of approximately five hundred sisters.

When she had become ill and had stepped down as superior general, Katharine had written the following: "However high and holy our occupation, external activity has the power to distract, to cloud the soul. It is only by entering into oneself in prayer and meditation that the soul can be restored to its true poise, the mind clarified and the value of unimportant things be seen in its true light.[703]

Two major papal decrees in the nineteenth century include the definition of the Immaculate Conception in 1854 and the Syllabus of Errors via Pius IX in 1864. However, it was the Syllabus of Errors Statement which drew sharp criticisms in the United States. In New York, John McCloskey weighed in when he had written: "It is consoling to think and believe that our Holy Father has in all his official acts a light and guidance from on High- for according to all the rules of mere human prudence and wisdom the encyclical [Quanty Cura] with its annex of condemned propositions would be considered ill timed..."[704]

According to Martin Spalding, "a howl of indignation" was salient in the English and American press. Spalding had defended Pope Pius with a pastoral letter which indicated that the encyclical was aimed at "European radicals" rather than the American Constitution.[705] Other factors contributed to relief issues which had affected the American Catholic Church due to its connection with the Vatican. In 1866, there was a major collection taken at every parish in America for the pope.[706]

However, Robert Murphy, who was a banker in Paris, attempted to sell four million dollars in papal bonds. Essentially, this was met with resistance. Moreover, the Baltimore bank that Spalding had assigned the job of taking subscriptions for the loan, had failed.[707] James A. McMaster of the *Freeman's* Journal was recruiting people for the papal army of which Archbishop Parcell indicated, "Better trust to God, leaving in the scabbard a sword which never established a church." [708]

The eastern archbishops tried to prevent this effort. Since at this time priests could not be pastors, rather solely "rectors of missions" whom the bishops could do as they pleased. However, the proclamation of papal infallibility would continue to be an issue in the United States as well as the First Vatican Council. Pope Pius IV called for the council during the years 1869-1870.[709]

The pre-conciliar commission on doctrinal matters had met on December 30, 1868. Theologian James A. Corcoran of Charleston was part of these discussions. His main concern was that 'the fundamental principles of our (American and common-sense) political system" would be highly criticized. [710]

By and large, the First Vatican Council had mostly a European membership. There existed a preoccupation with nineteenth century problems in Europe. Certainly, the Enlightenment and French Revolution, Kant and Hegel, and European Liberalism were discussed. Most importantly, the Italian Risorgimento was the closet reality. Pope

Pius IX had officially convened the council on December 8, 1869, with pomp and circumstance in order to counter the threat to a thousand years of papal sovereign rule in Rome.[711] On July 18, 1870, the final significant meeting finished with the council fathers, Pio Nono support of the dogmas of papal jurisdictional primacy and infallibility. Moreover, a constitution on faith and reason already was firmly cemented.[712] Basically, eighty percent of the forty-nine American clergy felt that the infallibility piece of the documents was at the very least ill timed. Not only would the notion of the pope's infallibility renew a hostility toward the Roman Catholic Church in America. Also, there were historical and theological problems with it. Essentially, these clergymen did not believe this doctrine to be sound or rooted in church tradition.[713]

Other issues presented by Augustin Verot included the prayer-life of priests, reconciliation between the church and science, and the black and white races. Verot wanted a statement confirming that black people have souls.[714]

However, the predominate issue of papal infallibility had negative votes by bishops such as Bishop Edward Fitzgerald of Little Rock. Most bishops of America had already left for home so that they would not vote against infallibility in the presence of the Holy Father.[715] In the end, bishops of America had resigned to the fact that papal infallibility is now doctrine. However, the American Bishops brought much to the table in die First Vatican Council which would re-emerge in the second Vatican Council. Without doubt, the composition of membership in the Second Vatican Council would reflect far more diversity of culture.[716]

The one hundredth anniversary of the independence of die United States began on May 10, 1876 in Philadelphia.[717] On June 25, 1876, Lieutenant Colonel George Armstrong Custer and his younger brother, Tom Custer, and two other men were located on Crow's Nest perched above the Little Bighorn River in the Montana Territory. George Custer believed that he had found Sitting Bull and Crazy Horse when he sighted a very large Indian encampment. What was to be a surprise attack upon this Indian Village; however, Custer and his cavalry men were massacred.[718,719]

Certainly, every soldier was killed which numbered two hundred ten in all. There was not a white man to report as an eyewitness to this event. The Indians had mentioned varying accounts which were biased and contradictory.[720] "Custer's Last Stand," which was likely the worst defeat in American military history, made Custer a somewhat historical enigma. However, President Grant had indicated to the New York Herald, "I regard Custer's Massacre as a sacrifice of troops, brought on by Custer himself; that was wholly unnecessary- wholly unnecessary".[721]

In 1890, another massacre occurred however at Wounded Knee Creek, South Dakota, where two hundred Sionx Indian men, women, and children were killed.[722] It was the era of Manifest Destiny and the gospel of wealth promoted by American Protestantism. Moreover, Herbert Spencer's theory of Social Darwinism landed support to the notion of a socio-economic survival of the fittest.[723]

According to Historian Winthrop Hudson, "the most spectacular development in American religious life in the latter half of the nineteenth century was "the growth of the Roman Catholic Church".[724] Certainly, immigration was a major factor in this growth spur. Most immigrants who had entered the United States until about 1896 were from northern and western Europe, however, only 19.3 percent were of northern European countries and 80.7 percent from eastern and southern Europe by 1907. Between each decade starting in 1880 until 1920, over a million Catholic immigrants came to the United States. The period of 1901 to 1910 had increased to over two million Catholics seeking opportunity in the United States.[725] Eighty percent of New York City was composed of immigrants. Hostility and rejection towards Italian Catholics and Eastern Europeans were commonplace at this time.[726]

In 1889, Mother Frances Xavier Cabrini's Missionary Sisters of the Sacred Heart came to New York. There were seven sisters of the Salesian Missionaries of the Sacred Heart including Mother Cabrini, who arrived.[727,728] Originally, Mother Cabrini sought to evangelize in China. However, Pope Leo XIII had indicated, "Not to the Orient but to the West."[729]

Mother Cabrini who was the youngest of ten children, was born in 1885. She had poor health throughout her entire life. At the tender age of eighteen, Francesca Cabrini attained a degree and license to teach elementary school in Milan.[730] In 1881, her community's Rule was approved, and Mother Cabrini had designed a simple and very basic habit: a flat cap without a starched head-dress. [731] At the end of March 1889 when the sisters landed in New York to as-sist Italian immigrants, they made home visits and taught children the sacraments. Moreover, they provided English as a second language classes for adults.[732] The sisters had a pragmatic approach in helping poor families providing them with food, clothing and employment.[733] By the turn of the twentieth century, Mother Cabrini's sisters served in schools and orphanages in the dioceses of New York, Brooklyn, Newark, Scranton, Chicago, and New Or-leans. Moreover, they had branched out to Denver, Nesqually (Seattle), Los Angeles, and Philadelphia. The Columbus hospitals were started in Manhattan in 1892, Chicago in 1905, and Seattle in 1915 in part, founded by the sisters.[734] Interesting enough, Mother Cabrini would not become an American citizen until 1909 at the age of fifty-nine.[735]

Finally, Mother Cabrini would write to her sisters from a hospital bed in New York's Columbus Hospital during World War I: "You will have it [Jesus" peace] by accepting all that happens- great and small- as gifts of God and placing all your joy in pleasing Him. This fall conformity to the will of God, this abandonment of self in the bosom of the infinite bounty renders the soul a participant in two attributes of God: impeccability and infallibility. As two liquefy and become one, so the soul by conformity to the will of God becomes one with Him."[736]

Many Spanish-speaking Catholics assimilated into the United States as a result of the war with Mexico in the years 1846 to 1848.[737] Moreover, Porfirio Diaz, the dictator of Mexico from 1876 to 1911 promoted emigration to the United Sates. The effects of his land reforms had left about ninety-five percent of these Mexicans virtually without any land.[738] The United states' policy formulated the 1882 Chinese Exclusion Act and the 1907 "Gentlemen's Agreement with Japan fostered opportunity for Mexican immigrates. By and large, Mexicans composed approximately eighty percent of the farm workforce in the west.[739]

In 1850, the first French parish in new England since Poterie and Rousselet was founded in Burlington, Vermont.[740] However, the

Irish Catholics were not welcoming to them. It was likely because of a perception of an economic threat.[741] The French tended to work longer hours for less pay. However, the French Catholics were not use to contributing money to their parish. A Frenchman had stated that "it costs quite a bit to practice one's religion here".[742]

In 1886, Bishop Louis de Goesbriand of Burlington discovered "complete ignorance of religion" in reference to the immigrants. He claimed that they "knew not either confession or communion and many of whom have been invalidly married before Protestant ministers".[743] The solution to this dilemma was to import French speaking priests from Quebec. However, Louis La Fleche, bishop of Trois-Rivieres, had stated that New England's annexation to Quebec was likely.[744] This controversial statement in 1889 did not help the cause.

Ironically, immigrants who arrived in the latter part of the nineteenth century with roots to Maryland in 1634 as well as to Florida, Maine, and the southwest were still regarded as "foreign" newcomers.[745] By and large, Catholic immigrants remained in the cities and tended to be laborers. Since Catholic immigrants often live in poverty, they focused on elementary schools and works of charity.[746] Instead of building up their wealth, Catholics would contribute to the church. For example, a group of catholic laborers earning a dollar a day each made a pledge of fifty dollars to a Massachusetts parish.[747] In fact, the church became the center of their catholic and social life.

By the year 1880, there existed eleven archdioceses, forty-seven dioceses, six vicariates - apostolic run by missionary bishops, and only one prefecture apostolic with a priest as head. Archbishop John McCloskey of New York was the first American Cardinal in 1875, and Archbishop James Gibbons of Baltimore became a cardinal in 1886.[748] Most Catholics were devout praying the rosary and involved in their parish. Religious education was rosary and involved in their parish. Religious education was salient in parochial schools and in the absence of such a school. There were Sunday schools after 1885 with the "Baltimore Catechisms."[749]

However, the Catholic community had its issues according to Orestes Brownson, a convert, who had written to Isaac Hecker in August of 1870. Brownson had indicated that "the most lawless and rowdyish and even criminal portions of the population: are Catholics or their offspring".750 Brownson had joined the Presbyterian Church in October 1822, with the notion of becoming a missionary. However, Brownson became dismayed with the Presbyterian discipline and doctrine. Basically, he rejected Calvinism for its liberal Christianity. Then, Brownson became a Universalist at the age of twenty in 1824.751 Actually, he was ordained in June 1826 and preached as well as wrote as a universalist minister. Although he referred to himself as a Christian, he denied all divine revelation, the divinity of Christ, and a judgment time.752

Brownson exhibited much compassion with the laboring class. In essence, Brownson was not a believer, but he embraced the religion of humanity. He was a pastor of the Unitarian Church at Walpole, New Hampshire in 1832. Then in 1834, he became a pastor of the First Congregational Church at Canton. Massachusetts. 753 Moreover, he put together in Boston the Society for Christian Union and Progress when he preached in the Old Masonic Temple on Tremont Street in 1836.754

Brownson frequently published articles in various journals and he began his own journal, namely, *The Boston Quarterly Review in January 1838*.755 His essays germane to politics drew attention throughout the nation. Moreover, this political writing brought him in contact with the leaders of the Democratic Party.756 In July 1840, he forwarded the democratic principles to the utmost logical conclusion. Thus, he strongly promoted the abolition of Christianity. This was in reference to the only form of Christianity that he had known. Brownson had fully accepted the doctrine of Locke, Jefferson, Mirabean, Portalis, Kent, and Blackstone that basically the right to bequeath property was firmly rooted in statute not on natural law.757 Brownson had condemned the industrial system, in particular the way of labor at wages. Thus, he promoted the doctrine of European socialist and the Saint Simonians.758 This had adversely affected the Democratic Party and President Van Buren who sought a second term faulted Brownson for his defeat in election.759

It was in 1844 that he had converted to Catholicism. Moreover, he unveiled the new *Brownson Quarterly Review in January 1844*.760 Brownson had viewed Protestantism as pure materialism and Catholicism as spiritualism and exalts his "Church of the Future". His work, "The

Mediatorial Life of Jesus" (Boston, 1842) lead to his path to become Catholic,[761]

When Brownson had applied to the Bishop of Boston for admission to the Catholic church, the co-adjutor Bishop John B. Fitzpatrick made it official.[762] Since the majority of Catholics belonged to the laboring class, Brownson advocated for them. At a time when there was much prejudice against Catholicity and opposition to Catholics, Brownson became a Staunch defender of the Faith.[763] In fact, he had received a letter of approbation and encouragement from the bishops attending the Plenary council at Baltimore in May 1849. Moreover, Pope Pius IX sent a letter to Brownson in April 1854. Thanking him for his effort to defend the Faith.[764] Brownson was a prolific writer who wrote *The Spirit Rapper* published in Boston in 1854. This book was a novel and a biography linking spiritism with modern philanthropy, visionary reforms, socialism, revolutionisism in order to revive the Gospel age of faith.

In 1857, he had written another book, *The Convert; Leaves from my Experience,* in which Brownson recounted his entire religious life and the path to Catholicism.[765] During the war between the States, Brownson opposed secession as well as abolition of slavery. However, this belief had turned away many of his supporters both in the north and the south.[766] His two sons died in the summer of 1864. As a result, he decided to discontinue publishing his *Review* in October 1864.

Then in the following eight years, Brownson wrote *The American Republic; Its Constitution, Tendencies, and Destiny* in New York 1865.[767] Moreover, Brownson contributed articles to the *New York Tablet, The Ave Maria,* and *The Catholic World.* He had written a small book, *Conversations on Liberalism and the Church* in New York in 1869.[768] Finally, Brownson had revisited his *Brownson's Quarterly Review* in January 1873 which concluded in 1875. His final publication was an article which appeared in the *American Catholic Quarterly Review* in January 1876.[769']

His daughter Sarah had written many articles, stories, and poems published in Catholic magazines. Some of her writings include "Marian Elwood, or How Girls Live" (New York, 1863). "At Anchor; a story of the American Civil War" (New York, 1865), "Here more Brandon; or the Fortunes of a Newsboy" (1869) and "Life of Demetrius Augustine

Gallit Zin, Prince and Priest" in New York, 1873. Sarah married William J. Tenney of Elizabeth, New Jersey on November 26, 1873. She died on October 30, 1876, at Elizabeth, New Jersey. Orestes Brownson had died on April 17, 1876, in Detroit.[770]

Brownson did not originate in any system of philosophy and recognized his sources appropriately. Moreover, his daughter Sarah wrote novels which were interesting, genuine, and original. Her trademark demonstrated independent thinking, "with good sense and judgment, without undue bitterness, and with great benevolence towards the poor; and she scatters over her pages many excellent reflections."[771]

This was an era where various publications would emerge. Cardinal Gibbon's "Faith of Our Father" was published in 1876. The congregation of Holy Cross at Notre Dame created the *Ave Maria* magazine in 1865 while the Paulists published the *Catholic World* that same year. The following year the Jesuits published the *Messenger of the Sacred Heart*. In 1870, Isaac Hecker, a convert monthly paper, *The Young Catholic: An Illustrated Magazine for Young Folks*.[772] Actually, his sister-in-law Josephine Wentworth Hecker was the editor.

The Paulists had organized and sponsored the Catholic Publication Society which produced a number of books. However, Lawrence Kehoe, director of the Catholic Publication Society had indicated in 1886 that prayer books and religious instructional manuals were widely distributed and sold. But he expounded on this "the best books couldn't be counted on to sell a thousand".[773] It was Charles Constantine Pise's *Father Rowland* which was published in 1829 that was the first Catholic novel written in the United States. Fictitious novels had its place in various Catholics magazines throughout the nineteenth century.[774] The Freeman's Journal was edited by James McMaster from 1848 until his death in 1886. Patrick Ford was in charge of Irish World. The United States Catholic Historical Society was founded in 1884 with the well know Catholic historian John Gilmary Shea as its first president.[775]

The publication for the society began in 1899 which was called the *Historical Records and Studies*. It was Martin I.J. Griffin who founded the society and wrote considerably as well as edited the *American Catholic Historical Re-searches* from 1886 to 1912.[776]

During this era, various church groups and secret societies emerged such as the Knights of Columbus (1882), Knights of St. John (1886), and both the knights of Peter Claver as well as the Holy Name Society in 1909.[777] The Knights of Columbus was founded by Father Michael J. McGivney who believed in the commixture of Catholicism and American fraternalism.[778]

"From its origins to World War I, the Order's goals were most visibility expressed in its assertion of the social legitimacy and patriotic loyalty of Catholic immigrants. By accepting indeed, extolling- the religious and ethnic pluralism of American Society, by portraying Catholic citizenship as the highest form of American Citizenship, by promoting American- Catholic culture (symbolized by their strong support of the Catholic University of America),and by expressing a firm belief that the American Catholic experience has had a transforming effect upon Catholicism and upon American Society, the Knights generally reflected the optimism characteristic of several ecclesiastical leaders associated with the "Americanist" posture in American Catholicism."[779]

In 1881, Father McGivney, the curate at Saint Mary's church in New Haven, Connecticut was the chaplain for the Saint Joseph's Young Men of New Haven which was not related to the Knights of Columbus.[780] At first, Father McGivney mentioned to a group of Irishmen that the "Sons of Columbus" was a suitable name. However, they decided upon the Knights of Columbus as the name of their organization. "By adopting Columbus as their patron, this small group of New Haven Irish-American Catholics displayed their pride in America's Catholic heritage."[781]*

Father McGivney was born in Waterbury, Connecticut on August 12, 1852, and he had received his sacraments at the church of the Immaculate Conception, which was incorporated in 18 66.[782] Basically, the first rectory in Waterbury was on "the site of the old Immaculate church, brought on Nov. 11, 185 1".[783] Saint Peter's Church located on 110-118 East Main Street became the Immaculate Conception Church. It was Father Hendricken who was responsible for the building of the first Immaculate Conception Church on 101-103 East Main Street in 1857 and a rectory later in 1869-1870 at 97 East Main Street in Waterbury.[784] Hendrickens had mentored McGivney and supported him in initiating his seminary studies in Canada.[785] Father James Smyth (1837-1847) was part of the beginning of the first Immaculate Conception Church.[786]

The church consisted of red brick with a tall spire and its cost reached forty-five thousand dollars. "The building ranked among the most pretentious churches of the diocese (pretentious presumably having been meant as a compliment)."[787] The present location of the second Immaculate Conception Church is on West Main Street off the city's "Green". It was completed on August 15, 1926, and was granted recognition of a minor basilica via Pope

Benedict XVI on February 9, 2008, thru the efforts of Monsignor John Bevins, 788 Foreigners who were Catholic immigrants were mainly resented during the 1880s and 1890s. The third Plenary Council of Baltimore in 1884 was the church's demarcation concluding American Catholicism organizational era and entered a period of anti-immigrant and anti-Catholic opinion.[789]

The main thrust of the Council was that every Catholic parish would have a parochial school. In fact, by 1884, forty percent of the parishes in the United States had grammar or elementary school.[790] Gibbons, Ireland, and Keane had addressed the National Education association in 1889 and 1890 in order to promote Catholic elementary schools. However, they were careful not to attack public schools. Archbishop John Ireland of St. Paul who was referred as: "He is a Celtic American through and through... quite content with cata-combical public worship."[791] Essentially, Ireland foresaw difficulties in conducting Catholics parochial schools without state financial support. Ireland believed in public support or even allowing state control of Catholic school during the regular school day with church control of afterschool religious instruction. This was named the "Pough Keepsie plan" since it was in progress in that city under Archbishop of New York Corrigan's diocese.[792] It was in May 1893 that Pope Leo XIII encouraged Catholic schools. However, he favored having local bishop use their discretion in reference to Catholic children attendance at public schools.[793]

In 1880, there were about 2,246 Catholic elementary schools with approximately, 405,234 students in the United States. However, by 1900, there existed 3,811 Catholic schools with about 854,523 students.

This trend continued and by 1910, 4,845 Catholics schools had enrolled 1,237,251 students.[794]

Although Catholic high schools showed a slower pace, by 1900 there were sixty-three Catholic colleges. In 1889, Catholic University of America began as a graduate school of theology for priests.[795] Certainly, Saint Mary's seminary at Baltimore in 1822 and Georgetown college in 1833 were in existence. However, the schools were not at the university level. Various educational philosophies influenced the Catholic presence in education. However, the American Catholic school system had a prescribed curriculum. Paternalistic and authoritarian were salient features in Catholic schools.[796] It was Notre Dame of Maryland in 1899 where academic degrees were awarded to women. By and large, Catholic colleges were built via a concerted effort of religious and devoted laity.[797]

Pope Leo XTTT issued the Rerum Novarum in 1891. It was germane to the right of private property and upward mobility for Catholics. This prompted other papers such as the *Peace Memorial* which was distributed in twenty-five languages to leaders of nationals. Basically, this paper was a protest against the arms race by Christian nations and that "wars do not settle causes of disputes between nations on principles of right and justice, but upon the barbaric principle of the triumph of the strongest."[789] Another urgent issue in American Catholicism was the initial relationship between the Roman Latin Rite and the Eastern-Rite Catholics. Certainly, the gist of this issue was celibacy.[799] Archbishop Ireland did not truly welcome the Carpatho-Russians which led them to join the Russian Orthodoxy.[800]

In 1893, the archbishops in a meeting had indicated the following: "That the presence of married priests of the Greek rite in our midst is a constant menace to the chastity of our unmarried clergy, a source of scandal to the laity and therefore the sooner this point of discipline is abolished before the evils obtain large proportions, the better for religion..."[801]

Eastern-rite Catholics had a difficult time understanding the Latin-rite's persistence in this matter. The archbishop's stance: "The possible loss of a few souls of the Greek rite bears no proportion to the blessings resulting from uniformity of discipline".[802] However, there was resistance against "hibemarchy", the dominance of the Irish bishops in the American catholic milieu.[803] In 1886, the ethnic background of the bishops consisted of thirty-five Irishmen, fifteen Germans, eleven Frenchmen, five Englishmen, one Dutch, one Scot, and one Spaniard.

Father Peter M. Abbelen of Milwaukee brought a list of complaints to the Vatican that year which outlined mistreatment of German-American Catholics by the hierarchy in the Church in America.[804] There were approximately ten to twenty million Catholic immigrants who left the Church in America. Cardinal Gibbons did not like interference in the American Catholic Church by "officious gentlemen" in Europe.[805] In 1884, the "Pastoral Blatt" has stated that since 1842 the system made German as well as other "national churches" or parishes very dependent on "Irish" churches or parishes.[806] Moreover, Franciscan liturgist Innocent Wapelhorst had indicated that it was the influence of the public school system which caused many catholic immigrants to leave the Church.[807]

A response to John Jay's article about American identity in the Federalist Papers from the Buffalo Volksfreund included the following: "America is no nation, no race, no people like France, Italy or Germany. We have citizens of a republic, but no nation and, therefore, no national language outside the languages which the immigrated races speak in their families,"[808]

The Chicago Tribune had printed the following: "A contest between the supporters and enemies of the American free schools, between the right of Americans to make their own laws and the claims of an Italian priest living in Rome that he has the power to nullify them."[809]

Essentially, this issue had reached the United States Senate and President Benjamin Harrison met Cardinal Gibbons at Cape May, New Jersey. Pope Leo's Secretary of State, Cardinal Mariano Rampolla del Tindaro sent a letter to Gibbons indicating a rejection of demands. However, the letter urged the Bishops of the United States to attend to the various needs of immigrants.[810] Although Catholics had a long history in America, the perception was that Catholics were immigrant newcomers. By and large, there existed a deeply rooted conviction of the synergy of American democracy and Catholicism.

A belief shared by Protestants as well is that Americans are chosen people, the new Israel of God.[811] Pope Leo XIII issued an encyclical letter, Longinqua Oceani, which indicated "thanks are due to the equity of the laws which obtained in America and to the customs of the well- ordered republic". Moreover, the holy father was pleased that "unopposed by the Constitution and government of your nation, fettered by no hostile legislation, protested against violence by the common laws and the impartiality of the tribunals". Thus, Catholicism was "free to live and act without hindrance". However, the encyclical ended with a warning about the American form of separation of church and state would not be a model for other societies. The pope's belief that the church in America "would bring forth more abundant fruit if, in addition to liberty, she enjoyed the favor of the laws and the patronage of public authority".[812]

On August 11, 1913, John Ireland addressed the Twelfth Annual Convention of the Federation of American Catholic Societies where he stated the following: "No room is there for discord or contradiction. Church and State cover separate and distinct zones of thought and action: The Church busies itself with the spiritual, the State with the temporal, The Church and the State are built for different purposes, the Church for heaven, the State for earth. The line of demarcation between the two jurisdictions was traced by the unerring Finger of Him who is the master of both; the law of God is - "Render to Caesar the things that are Caesar's; and to God the things that are God's."[813]

In 1903, Cardinal Gibbons became the first American to vote in a papal election. Pope Pius X was chosen and in five years, the papal document, Sapienti Consilio had changed the status of the United States as being a mission. By and large, there were no new archdioceses but thirteen new dioceses in his tenure from 1903 to 1914.[814] The Catholic population had grown to 16,363,000 by 1910 and 19,828,000 by 1920. By this time about three and a half million more immigrants had entered the United States since 1900.[815]

The Catholic Encyclopedia was published from 1907 to 1914. The editors were composed of religious and laymen. The Jesuits initiated a weekly journal, America in 1909. Franciscan friars and sisters of the Atonement at Graymoor in Garrison, New York founded in 1898 as Episcopalian had become part of the Roman Catholic Church.

Edward Douglass White, a Catholic from Louisiana and a Confederate soldier at one time, had become the Chief Justice of the United States from 1910 to 1921,[816] Political power had belonged to the Irish. John F. Fitzgerald was elected as Boston's third Irish mayor in 1905, his grandson became the thirty-fifth president of the United States in 1961.[817] Essentially, conflicts be-tween Catholics of various ethnic backgrounds were centered around control of the parochial schools. Certainly, a high proportion of public-school teachers were Catholic.

However, the Catholic school system grew rapidly. In 1910, there were more children in Philadelphia Catholic schools than in the public schools of all but about a dozen American cities.[818] In 1908, the Catholic University started a department of education. In 1911, they began publication of the Catholic educational Review. In fact, the National Catholic Educational association suggested that high schools focus on an arts curriculum.[819] Moreover, the emergence of the United States as a global power provided a new role on the American Catholic church. Instead of being mostly on the receiving end of missionary work, American Catholics would become missionaries for other countries.[820]

The Catholic Foreign Mission Society, namely the Mary Knolls. was founded by James A. Walsh and Thomas Price. In 1911, this was the first American group who focused solely for work in foreign lands. In 1918, the first Mary Knolls traveled for Kwangtung Providence, China.[821] Various problems would emerge in Spanish American areas such as the Philippines where a native clergy would not develop. Moreover, the Catholic church in Puerto Rico had a chronic shortage of priests.

In 1908, the United States Supreme Court recognized and upheld church property titles from early Spanish times.[822] In Cuba, Bonaventure Broderick became the auxiliary bishop of Havana. In 1902, American troops left Cuba, but they had returned from 1906 to 1909. However, the American Catholic church did not truly maintain a visible presence.[823] In 1904 Gibbons expressed his desire for Filipino independence. However, in 1912 President Taft urged Gibbons to have bishops work against legislation for independence. Moreover, Cardinal Merry del Vai stated that Spain's former colony, the Philippines were not ready for independence.[824] In fact, the archbishop of Manila, Jeremiah

Harty indicated in confidence that Japan would take over an independent Philippines.[825]

Certainly, Roman Catholicism had a constituency of multi-ethnic origin by 1914. However, the age of immigration had ceased with the passage of the national Origins Act during the years 1921-1924.[826] When the dictator Porfirio Diaz was thrown from power, the clergy of Mexico were persecuted. In 1911, various restrictions on the Catholic church took place. In response, Gibbons worked with President Woodrow Wilson and his administration to cope with this situation.[827] In March 1915, Gibbons had publicly attacked President Venustiano and Francisco ("Pancho") Villa as well. President Wilson chose to recognize President Carranza's government in October 1915, which brought him much criticism from American archbishops.[828]

The advent of the first world war when Archduke Franz Ferdinand was killed at Sarajevo on June 28, 1914, had turned the Wilson administration away from Mexico.[829] Moreover, Pope Pius X had died on August 20, 1914, while Europe was at war. Cardinals O'Connell and Gibbons sailed on the S.S. *Canopic* to Rome. Cardinal Giacomo Della Chiesa became Pope Benedict XV.[830] Although the Italian-Americans were pro-Allies, the Irish-Americans tended to root for the Central powers due to their disdain for the British.[831] Moreover, advocates for Irish independence felt that their cause was not consistent with the goals of the Allies.[832] Thus, President Wilson was not pleased with "hyphenated" Americans with their "hearts" not in the right place.

At the Paris Peace Conference five years later, President Wilson had remarked the following when posed a question germane to the subject of Irish independence: "My first impulse was to tell the Irish to *go to* hell, but, feeling that this would not be the act of a statesman, I denied myself this personal satisfaction."[833]

Although the official position was neutrality, ethnic loyalties was the quintessential factor. Catholic German-Americans were fall of German pride, not recalling the Kulturkampf, policies designed to minimize the Catholic church in Germany.[834] They were pleased with editorials from the *America Magazine* by Tierney who favored the Central powers. However, Catholic German- Americans did not care for the Paulists of the *Catholic World* periodical. John Burke, C.S.P., the editor had written in 1915: "War is by no means a Christian tradition. Indeed, our very profession of Christian means that we are pacifists".[835]

Burke's "Recent Events" column was known to favor the Allies. There were only four Catholic conscientious objectors to serve in the first World War out of 3,989 Catholics.[836] Approximately, a million Catholics out of 4,791,172 people who served in the military at that time.[837] In fact, a Catholic convert, admiral William Shepherd Benson was not only the highest-ranking Catholic officer, but he was the first person to hold the position of Chief of Naval Operations.[838]

Congress had declared war on Germany on April 6, 1917, however the United States had officially severed diplomatic relations with Germany on February 3rd. This process began in 1916 when John J. Pershing led American troops to capture Pancho Vill who was backed by the Germans.[839] Actually, Arthur Zimmermann, the German foreign minister, believed that the Mexicans could possibly invade Texas as a result. Thus, he had signaled Germany's ambassador in Washington, communicating the notion of building an alliance with Mexico. Essentially, three different routes were utilized to send this message. America and Room 40 had intercepted all three communiques.[840']

Then, President Wilson had published the Zimmermann telegram in a way to protect 40 s secrecy. Basically, Room 40 of the Admiralty Old Building was staffed by academics rather than professional sailors. Certainly, the director of naval intelligence, Reginald 'Blinker' Hall who was a formidable interrogator of prisoners as well as an adapt runner of agents and spies. Room 40's secret work was aided by the German s belief and effort in the wireless provided by real-time communication and facilitated the concentration of military forces for them. However, their messages were largely intercepted by the English.[841]

President Wilson had addressed the American nation stating the following: "The right is more precious than peace, and we shall fight for the things which we have always carried nearest our hearts - for democracy, for the right of those who submit to authority to have a voice in their own governments, for the rights and liberties of small nations, for a universal dominion of right by such a concert of free peoples as shall bring peace and safety to all nations and make the world itself at last free."[842]

American Catholic bishops did support the "Preparedness Movement". Moreover, Gibbons provided a statement that "the Members of both houses of Congress are the instruments of God in guiding us in our civic duties"[843] The archbishops had collectively told President Wilson the following: "We are all true Americans, ready as our age, our ability, and our conditions will permit, to do whatsoever is in us to do, for the preservation, the progress and triumph of our beloved country."[844]

It was during Holy Week that the United States Senate voted 82 to 6 in favor of the Declaration of War against Germany. Moreover, the house voted for war by a wide margin 373 to 50 while the majority of the fifty votes against were cast by Congressmen from the German-American Midwest.[845]

In fact, George M. Cohan, an Irish- American composer, wrote the song which became the theme of the first World War:

"Over there, over there!

Send the word, send the word, over there!

That the Yanks are coming, the Yanks are coming,

The drums rum-tumming ev'rywhere!

So prepare, say a prayer, send the word.

Send the word to beware!" [846]

Although the American Catholic church had no national organization in 1917, the Knights of Columbus made a concerted effort with hats ("Everybody Welcome, Everything Free") consisting of recreational facilities, offices, and chapels at approximately two hundred fifty centers overseas as well as three hundred sixty in the States.[847] Moreover, there were about two thousand "secretaries" and around twenty-seven thousand volunteers credited to the Knights of Columbus.

It is important to point out that the last plenary council was held in 1884 and still there was not a permanent secretariat.[848] Thus, Gibbons called for a meeting at Washington, D.C. for August 11-12, 1917 with John J. Burke of the Catholic world, Lewis O' Hern, the bishops liaison with the government for appointment of chaplains, William Kerby, founder of the National Conference of Catholic Charities, and Charles P. Neill, for men U.S. Commissioner of Labor. Altogether, there were one hundred fifteen delegates from sixty-eight dioceses and twenty-seven societies who attended and chose Burke to be in charge of the National Catholic War Council (NCWC).[849]

This was the first time that the Roman Catholic church in America made an institutional commitment and political action. However, the Knights of Columbus did enjoy a degree of autonomy within this framework.[850] Pope Benedict desired to play a role in the peace process, but Gibbons was very slow to respond to the Holy Father's August 1, 1917, peace note. Essentially, Gibbons was relucent to broach President Wilson with this request. Moreover, Pope Benedict sent a cable to Gibbons to talk personally with Wilson.[851]

Certainly, the National Catholic War Council (NCWC) made an indelible mark on the American Catholic Church. The Knights of Columbus were the most salient Catholic group in the American Expeditionary Force and various army camps.[852] It was the cooperation between the organizations serving the troops which was unique. For instance, the YMCA and the Knights worked together for religious and social purposes.[853] In fact, the government and church funds were mingled and utilized indiscriminately without any public complaints. Basically, Catholics realized that unity was their strength. More-over, Catholics found a new sense of acceptance as a result of their efforts.[854]

On February 12,1919, John A. Ryan wrote the "Social Reconstruction: A General Review of the Problems and Survey of the. Remedies" which was issued via the auspices of the NCWC administrative committee.[855] Ryan had addressed reforms for the returning veteran germane to employment, housing, and maintenance of wage scales. He promoted vocational training, minimum wage laws, various forms of insurance as well as the issue of inflation and cost of living control. Within six years (1913-1919) inflation rose seventy-three percent. Lasdy, Ryan Strongly opposed child labor in which he stated, "this reproach to our country".[856] Finally, Ryan had indicated that "a reform in the spirit of both labor and capital" was required. The document ended with the statement: "This is the human and Christian, in Contrast to the purely commercial and pagan, ethics of industry."[857] It was at Gibbon's fiftieth anniversary as bishop that the pope's representative, Archbishop Bonaventura Cerretti pushed American bishops to work for a just and lasting peace. On April 10, 1919, Pope Benedict XV gave his stamp of approval and National Catholic Welfare Council was the result.[858] When Pop Benedict died on January 22, 1922, Pope Pius XI dissolved the NCWC. However, he rescinded his decree just four months later. [859]

There were revisions such as modifying "council" to "conference" making it non-conciliar, non-legislative. This was mainly due to Bishop Joseph Schrembs's effort to restore the NCWC. He went directly to the Vatican in order to preserve the organization. Essentially, Prohibition, woman suffrage, and child labor were the most pressing issues in America during this era.[860] Thus, the Nine-tenth Amendment was passed on June 5, 1919, and ratified on august 26, 1920. Essentially, women were permitted to vote at the ballot box. [861]

During the first World War in Germany, Edith Stein earned a doctorate in philosophy under the tutelage of her mentor Edmund Husserl. Stein, one of the first women in Germany to attain a doctorate, wrote her dissertation on the topic of "empathy".[862] She was born on Yom Kippur, the Day of Atonement, on October 12, 1891. Stein was raised in Breslau, Germany, the last of eleven children.[863] It is important to mention that the German city of Breslau is currently Wroclaw in Poland. Although she graduated summa cum laude in 1916 with a doctorate, Stein was Jewish and a woman, both limiting factors in Germany.[864]

In a letter written to Fritz Kaufmann (at the Front), on august 16, 1916 (Breslau), "I simply cannot miss school [as a teacher] such a short time before graduation, when there is no substitute to be had here'. Moreover, the letter states the following: "When I was in Freiburg for about a fortnight and the Master [E. Husserl] was still sulking because I was so cruel, forcing him to read my thesis, one evening I overheard him telling a lady he considered it necessary to have an assistant, just as Hilbert does... Then, timidly, I began to weigh the proposition: Should I offer my services to him? And I found the nerve to do so when, the next day, he confided that he was very satisfied with my thesis, and that, indeed, a good bit of it coincided with essential portions from Part II of Ideen. His delight at the thought of how having a person entirely at his disposal was apparent although, obviously, he has no clear idea as yet how we will actually work together."[865]

Stein would be Husserl's assistant in Freiburg from 1916 to 1918. A university appointment would not materialize for her although she made several inquiries over the next fifteen years. Stein taught at St. Magdalena, a Dominican Sister school in Speyer, Germany from 1923 to 1931.[866] Moreover, she published her dissertation, "On the Problem of Empathy" in 1917. However, Stein 's treatise "Concerning the State" was written before October 1920 and completed the summer of 1921 and prepared for publication and press by October, 1922. It was her last of four phenomenological works prior to conversion.[867] Stein was baptized on the first of January 1922.

Stein's conversion to Catholicism was a series of steps. Actually, in Stein's teenage years and well into her twenties, she avoided prayer and religions ways. [868] Stein loved to read Shakespeare and other works. She very much enjoyed studying and reading Latin. "It was as though I were learning my mother tongue. That it was the language of the Church and that later I should pray in this language never ever occurred to me at the time. "[869] Although her mother had encouraged her to study law, Fran Stein allotted Edith "Full freedom of Choice" in her career endeavors. In fact, Edith's mother had stated: "No one has a right to tell you what to do. After all, no one's making us a contribution towards it. Do whatever you think is right for you.'[870]

When Edith Stein would elect to pursue philosophy, most of her relatives had disapproved. Within a few years, Stein would be greatly affected by observing two women of faith. The first a grieving widow, the wife of her cousin Walter. During the funeral, once the Rabbi completed the final prayers, the young Christian widow knelt at the gravesite and loudly prayed the Lord's Prayer. Those who attended the funeral were very moved by this act of faith. Stein was profoundly touched by this unexpected prayer.[871] The other woman of faith was a complete stranger.

While walking with Pauline Reinach, the sister of Adolfo Reinach, Edith and Pauline went into the Frankfurt Cathedral: "...[while we looked around in respectful silence, a woman carrying a market basket came in and knelt down in one of the pews to pray briefly. This was something entirely new to me. To the synagogues or to the Protestant churches which I had visited, one went only for services."[872]

Edith had keenly observed this woman's behavior which greatly affected Edith's path in life. This stranger would serve as a witness of faith and silent prayer which would forever be etched into Edith's visual memory.

"[Here was someone interrupting her everyday shopping errands to come into this Church, although no other person was in it, as though she were for an intimate conversation. I could never forget that."[873]

The first woman's faith was overt in praying aloud while this second woman of faith was quiet and passive. However, it was the loss of her friend, Adolf Reinach, who died on the battlefield which would lead Edith to the liv-ing person of Jesus Christ.[874] Adolf Reinach was truly a beloved friend and teacher whose religious faith was deepening during his military service. His widow Anna had requested Edith to organize Adolfs philosophical papers.[875] Edith had discovered Anna to be a committed Christian who was suffering, but at peace.

"It was my first encounter with the Cross and the divine power that it bestows on those who carry it. For the first time, I was seeing with my very eyes the Church, born from her Redeemer's sufferings, triumphant over the sting of death. That was the moment my unbelief collapsed, and Christ shone forth— in the mystery of the Cross."[876]

According to Father Johannes Hirschmann in a letter dated May 3, 1950, to the Mother Superior at the Cologne Carmel: "Sister Teresa Benedicta herself distinguished between the cause of her conversion to Christianity and the cause of her entrance to the Catholic Church.... The most decisive reason for her conversion to Christianity was, as she told me, the way and manner in which her friend Mrs. Reinach made her offer in the power of the mystery of the Cross after her husband died at the front during the First World War."[877]

When Edith was fifteen years of age, she lost any belief in God which her family had imparted to her. At age twenty-four, she studied phenomenology whole-heartedly. It is interesting to note her peers were mostly Christian, as well as Husserl and Scheier. By 1920 at the age of twenty-nine, Edith was discerning her call to follow Jesus either as a Catholic or Lutheran.[878']

It was in 1918 that Edith had broken away from the role as Husserl's personal assistant. In a letter dated January 28, 1917, to Roman Ingarden, Edith wrote: "The master's latest prognosis for the production of Ideen: first of all, I am to stay with him until I marry; then I may only accept a man who will also become his assistant, and the same holds for the children. Highly unpropitious! Even apart from time, the requisite preconditions are absent. For if, in the long run, it is not entirely beyond the realm of the possible that someone could be found who would not shy away from an alliance with me (and vice versa), I deem it essentially impossible that a man could be his assistant. He is now busying himself with the constitution of nature (of course, without any review of the draft). In the meantime, I have continued working on that draft on my own authority, without running into any opposition about that, and am as for as "Person." The natural consequence of this is that we hardly talk together anymore. For me, this is very painful, because matters are very complicated and the material, I have at hand is altogether incomplete. However, I am working pretty independently now, and that is, of course, very enjoyable, but some exchange of ideas could be highly beneficial...[879,880]

In a letter dated February 19, 1918, to Roman In garden, Edith wrote: "When, the Master recently favored me with a list of instructions for die treatment of his manuscripts (in a friendly manner, of course, but at die same time, I cannot tolerate something like that), I explained (of course, also in a friendly manner) that the arrangement (1) basically, is impossible; (2) in general, insofar as it could be done, it could be best be done by him, for himself; (3) I would be especially unsuited for it and could endure it all only if I were able, in addition, to do some of my own work. I am curious what he will say about that. I offered to remain in Freiburg and help him with the editing of the Jahrbuch and some other work but not as his assistant at work, whose meaning is not clear to me. In principle, I just cannot bear the thought of being at someone's disposal. I can place myself in the service of a cause, and I can lovingly do all kinds of things for someone, but to be in service to someone in a word, to obey someone, is something I cannot do. And if Husser I cannot accustom himself to treating me as a collaborator for the cause, as I have always seen our relationship, and he also, in theory, then we will have to part ways. That would be sad to me because I believe there would then be even less hope of maintaining a connection between him and the 'youth'..."[881]

In a letter dated February 28,1918 to Roman Ingarden, Edith wrote: "The Master graciously approved my resignation. He wrote a very friendly letter, though not without a somewhat reproachful undertone. Thus, I am now free, and I think it is good even if, at the moment, I am not exactly happy... "[882]

Basically, it was a difficult year and a half working under Husserl. Since he did not make the effort to review Edith's work. Edith had described that her unbelief shattered" in 1917. However, she would not fully embrace the Catholic faith until 1921.[883]

Edith discovered the book *Spiritual Exercises of St. Ignatius* in a bookstore. She not only read the book but made her own thirty-day Ignatian retreat. Above Edith's desk at home hung a picture of St. Francis of Assisi by Cimabue, a well-known Italian artist of the thirteenth century. In essence, the parlor at home became Edith's office. Her sister Ema, a medical doctor, was married in the winter of 1920. Edith's health was suffering which she had attributed to spiritual conflicts unknown to others.[884] During the summer of 1921, Edith visited a fellow philosopher and student of Husserl's, Hedwig Conrad-Martius, who converted to Lutheranism. It was in her friend's private library that Edith found the "Autobiography of St. Teresa of Avila."[885] Edith read the volume in one night and he had stated, "This is the truth." Essentially, the reading of Saint Teresa's life showed Edith the mystery of a lived relationship with the Lord Jesus. The following day Edith had purchased both a missal and the Catholic Catechism.[886,887']

In a letter dated September 13,1925 to Fritz Kaufmann, Edith wrote: "... Now, I am to tell you something about myself. Where shall I begin, Herr Kaufmann, after 5 years? There is something I would like to comment on about the time just prior to those years. If I failed you, humanly speaking — and it was only much later that I realized fully just how much I did so, although even that summer of 1919 in Gottingen I was painfully and oppressively aware of it — then it was probably at least partially due to my being in such a pitiable state myself, almost as deplorable as yours. It occurred to me only a few days ago that, most likely, you never really knew about that and that it can explain a great deal to you. That [condition] began even earlier and, through many changes, lasted for years longer, until I found the place where there is rest and peace for all restless hearts. How that happened is something you will allow me to be silent about today. I am not reluctant to speak about it and, at the right time, will surely do so with you also, but it has to "come about"; It is not something about which I can "report." For all of three years now I have been living behind the sheltering walls of a convent, at heart — and this I may surely say without any presumption-like a real mm, even though I wear no veil and am not bound by vows or enclosure. Nor, for the present, may I think of contracting such a bond. That I am teaching at a college [belonging to Dominican nuns] you will probably have heard. Let me divulge something to you; I do not take myself too seriously as a teacher and still have to smile when I have to put it down anywhere as my profession. But that does not hinder me from taking my responsibilities seriously, and so, in Spirit and Soul, I am deeply absorbed by them. That is why the opportunity to do any scholarly work is still a problem. During the first two years, I only did a bit of translation besides my schoolwork; that was as far as it went. Then I wanted to get at something bigger, namely a critical examination of St. Thomas (Aquinas). I did make a start with the study of the Ouaestiones Disputatae but so far the necessary continuity has not been established, and I have to wait to see what comes of it."[888,889]

On January 1,1922 at the age of thirty Edith with a black dress and a white mantle·around her received baptism and her first Holy Communion from Father Eugen Breitling at the Church of St. Martin. Edith took the names of Theresia and Hedwig. Her sponsor was Hedwig Conrad- Martius.[890] In a letter written to Ema Hermann dated September 8, 1931 Edith wrote, "Certainly, you have no need to worry that anything may be done incorrectly. Everything is outlined very clearly in the ritual. At the time, II asked the priest who baptized me to lend me the book and I looked at the rite very carefully. I wore a black dress and had white mantle put around me.[891]

Edith had frequently mentioned that on the day of her baptism, she had decided to enter the order of Saint Teresa of Avila. It would be eleven years later that Edith would enter Carmel.

On February 2,1922, Edith was confirmed in the chapel of the bishop of Speyer, Bishop Ludwig Sebastian. Actually, Monsignor Josef Schwind, vican general of the diocese of Speyer who provided spiritual direction to Edith, had her wait entering Carmel "until it would become unmistakable evident that this was God's will for her."[892] Schwind became a friend and a father figure to Edith who was truly inspired by "his pure love of God."[893]

Edith had later made mention to a friend that one's vocation, "cannot be solved merely through self-examination plus a scrutiny of the available possibilities. One must pray for the answer ... and, in many cases, it must be sought by way of obedience." [894,895]

Moreover, Edith's mother was a concern since Fran Stein had such a difficult time accepting Edith's conversion. "[She]...would not be able to withstand this second blow for the time being. She would not die of it, but it would fill her with such bitterness that I could not take responsibility for that. I would have to wait patiently. My spiritual counselors assured me of this over and over."[896]

Edith was very insightful for she was cognizant that "one may not set a deadline for the Lord."[897] Her prudent advice to a new convert, Ruth Kanturowitz, in a letter dated October 4, 1934, Edith wrote:

That you're becoming a Catholic gave your dear father joy is a very special grace for you and for him. This joy is, after all, a sign that he himself a sign that he himself was very close to the Light and that he went into eternity in the friendship of God. Will you please help to pray for my mother, that her understanding, too, will be enlightened? Now regarding your questions. Before all else I would like to tell you to lay all care for the future, confidently, in God's hands, and allow yourself to be led by Him entirely, as a child would. Then you can be sure not to lose your way. Just as the Lord brought you into his church, so he will lead you to the place in tit that he wants you to have. Despite your 33 years, I would advise you to set aside, for the time being, the question of a religious vocation. God's will is not halted by any boundary of age. After all, I was accepted at 42 years of age, and many others even later. Naturally everything is easier when one enters while still young... For the moment I would say: remain patiently at your job as long as you do not receive a definite hint from above to undertake something else. Use your free time to get to know and to love God and the church better: the doctrines of the faith, the liturgy, our saints; but also the religious institutions and Catholic life in the present time, along, with its shadows, which will not remain concealed from you in the long run."[898]

Essentially, Edith's Road map at the initial stage of her Catholicism was studying Church history, Scripture, and the fives of the saints. Moreover, she attended daily Mass and spent time in prayer for long periods of time.[899] In a letter to Anneliese Lichtenberger dated August 17,1931, Edith wrote:

"God leads each of us on an individual way; one reaches the goal more easily and more quickly than another. We can do very little ourselves, compared to what is done to us. But that little bit we must do. Primarily, this consists before all else of persevering in prayer to find the right way, and of following without resistance the attraction of grace when we feel it. Whoever acts in this way and perseveres patiently will not be able to say that his efforts were in vain. But one may not set a deadline for the Lord... But the Lord is patient and full of mercy. In his household of grace he can use our faults, too, if we lay them on the altar for him. 'Corcontritum et humiliatum Deus non despicies' (A contrite and humbled heart, O God you will not scorn) (Ps.50)."[900']

Certainly, Edith provided prudent spiritual direction thru her letter writing to her circle of close friends. In a letter to Fritz Kaufmann dated January 6, 1927, Edith wrote:

"This letter [of yours] was an unexpected major achievement. I know how difficult it is for you to write, and therefore I thank your doubly for it. Why do you regret that you spoke openly with me then? You must have realized that all your misgivings could not touch me in the least. And if you gave me a glimpse of your innermost thoughts, then

I was only grateful for it. I always appreciate being able to see a person's distress at close range and very clearly, because then I am better able to know what I must ask on his behalf. I believe there is hardly anything else I can do for you right now. Arguments will be of no help to you. Were one able to free you from all argumentations, then you would be helped. And Advice? I have given you my advice: Become like a child and lay your life with all the searching and ruminating into the father's hand. If that cannot yet be achieved, then plead; plead with the unknown and doubted God for help in reaching it. Now you look at me in amazement that I do not hesitate to come to you with wisdom as simple as that of a child. It is wisdom because it is simple, and all mysteries are concealed in it. And it is a way that most certainly leads to the goal..."[901]

It was through Father Schwind's intervention that Edith obtained a teaching position at St. Magdalena's school in Speyer and a place of residence at the Dominican Convent. Edith indicated that "living behind the sheltering walls of a convent, at heart ...like a real nun, even though I wear no veil and am not bound by vows or enclosure."[902] Edith did not envision her role as a teacher. In this letter to Fritz Kaufmann dated September 13, 1925 Edith continued: "I do not take myself too seriously as a teacher and still have to smile when I have to put it down anywhere as my profession. But that does not hinder me from taking my responsibilities seriously, and so, in spirit and soul, I am deeply absorbed by them."[903]

However, Edith had translated the writings of John Henry Cardinal Newman from English into German as well as St. Thomas "Disputed Questions on Truth" from Latin into German.[904]

In a letter to Sr. Callista Kopf, OP dated February 12, 1928 Edith wrote:

"Of course, religion is not something to be relegated to a quiet corner or for a few festive hours, but rather, as you yourself perceive, it must be the root and basics of all life: and that, not merely for a few chosen ones, but for every true Christian (though of these there is still but a "little flock"). That it is possible to worship God by doing scholarly research is something I learned, actually, only when I was busy with [the translation of] St. Thomas [Aquinas' Quaesuones de Ventate from Latin into German], (in the little booklet that the sisters here use for the Thomas Sundays, there is a beautiful meditation about that.) Only thereafter could I decide to resume serious scholarly research. Immediately before, and for a good while after my conversion, I was of the opinion that to lead a religious life meant one had to give up all that was secular and to live totally immersed in thoughts of the Divine. But gradually I realized that something else is asked of us in this world and that, even in the contemplative life, one may not sever the connection with the world. I even believe that the deeper one is drawn into God, the more one must "go out of oneself"; that is, one must go to the world in order to carry the divine life into it. The only essential is that one finds, first of all, a quiet corner in which one can communicate with God as though there were nothing else, and that must be done daily. It seems to me the best time is in the early morning hours before we begin our daily work; furthermore, [it is also essential] that one accepts own choices. Finally, one is to consider oneself totally as an instrument, especially with regard to the abilities one uses to perform one's special tasks, in our case, e.g., intellectual ones, we are to see them as something used, not by us, but by God in us."[905]

Thus, Edith's faith was connected to everything about her and her work. It was the quintessence of her identity. She did not neglect her students. Rather, Edith spent time talking with her students and carefully listening to their problems. In fact, she provided a strong moral foundation which enabled them to enter the world with the "tools" needed including Christian virtue.[906]

"With very few words - just by her personality and everything that emanated from her - she set me on my way, not only in my studies, but in my whole life. With her you felt that you were in an atmosphere of everything noble, pure, and sublime that simply carried you up with it.[907]

It is noteworthy to mention that Edith had become a very popular speaker germane to Christian spirituality, especially on the vocation of women within a relatively short period of time, within six years of her conversion. Actually, one of her initial talks, "Ethos of Women's Professions" was not only well received but paved the way for numerous invitations to speak.[908]

"Edith went 'beyond sociology, psychology, and philosophy' in her treatment of the problems of our time, but she did so by ignoring these disciplines but by placing them with in the faith dimension in which she presented her suggested solution, "...She shared the fruits of both, her years of association with important thinkers, and her wide human experience; and she did this sharing in a heartfelt simple manner as one who had deep empathy for her hearers and their challenging situations. She awoke the conscience of teachers and parents, but did not leave them without the means for waging their own contest."[909]

Edith was a prolific writer who had written both anonymous and autographed works. Essentially, she wrote book reviews, chapters of her dissertation and published her lectures, letters, prayers, skits, and poems.[910] However, it is her personal letter to friends, former colleagues, fellow religious, and family members which depict an accurate picture of her life and legacy. It is important to note that her Carmelite Sisters felt compelled to destroy many of her correspondences due to fear of the Nazis.[911] Although Edith remained private about expounding on certain matters in particular about specifies of her own conversion, by and large, her writings cover a wide range of topics and themes. According to Edith Stein, "The formation of an unshakable bond with all whom life brings in my way a bond in no way dependent on day-today contact, is a significant element in my life."[912]

Edith kept in touch with Edmund Husserl. Four years after her Baptism, she visited Husserl in Freibug. Both his reception of Edith and their conversation that day were marked with depth and beauty that she never forgot. It occasioned, however, reflection on her part about the attitude to be taken toward others who do not share one's beliefs. Edith wrote to Sr. Adelgundis in February 1930, advising her to exercise care when discussing matters of religion, including the last things, with the ailing Husserl.[913]

Father Schwind had commented about Edith's preoccupation with discussing theology. It was Schwind who introduce Edith to the Jesuit philosopher theologian, Erich Praywara. Actually, it was Praywara who recommended that she translate Cardinal Newman's Letters and Journals as well as Aquinas' De Veritate.[914] When Father Schwind suffered a heart attack while listening to confessions, a friend who witnessed this occurrence sought Edith. She went at once to be at his side. However, Schwind had died. Edith prayed and *remained with* him as the medical personnel carried him from the cathedral.[915]

Edith had written his obituary so beautifully: . . He relied upon his deep knowledge of human beings and his years of apostolic experience, yet his penetration remained gentle through utter reverence before the workings of God's grace in the soul.[916]

Afterwards, Archabbot Raphael Walzer of the Benedictine Monastery of Beuron became Edith's spiritual director.'[917] The monastery had been a silent refuge for her own personal retreats. Edith regarded Walzer her religious superior because of her earlier private vows. However, Walzer rendered the same recommendation as Schwind had in spiritual advising. Thus, discouragement from entering a cloistered convent and encouragement for Edith to participate in international symposia was the emphasis.[918, 919] Edith had become one of the most outstanding lecturers throughout German-speaking Europe such as Switzerland, Austria, and Germany. In fact, she was the lone woman speaker at various general conventions of Catholic Academic Associations.[920]

One of her lectures, "The Spirit of St. Elizabeth as It Informed Her Life," Edith had stated: "Our Knowledge is piecemeal. When our will and action build on it alone, they cannot achieve a perfect structure... Nor can that knowledge, because it does not have complete power over the self and often collapses before reaching the goal. And so this inner shaping power that is in bondage strains toward a light that will guide more surely, and a power that will free it and give it space. This is the light and the power of divine grace."[921]

Edith had left her teaching position in Speyer in order to complete her work entitled, Potency and Act and allow her time to lecture in Europe. Edith spoke on education, social justice, women's roles in the church, and personal responsibility. [922] However, Edith did seek a professorship in Freiburg and at Kiel in January of 1931 but to no avail. In 1932, she was offered a teaching position at the German Institute for scientific pedagogy in Münster in the field of philosophy. In February, 1932, she moved to Münster. When she went there to teach, Edith lived with the Sisters of Our Lady at the Colle-gium Marianum. Actually, the

German Institute for Scientific Pedagogy was a catholic School; there were a large number of nuns from various orders who had studied at the Institute.[923] Edith taught there for two semesters but political changes in Germany such as Adolf Hitler's appointment as chancellor on January 30, 1933. Anti-Semitic laws ensued which banished Jewish employees of the state. The first concentration camp was opened in Dachau, near Munich.[924]

The administrator of the institute in April of 1933, Edith wrote:

"He considered it best if I would refrain from scheduling any lectures for [that] summer and just do some quiet research in the Marianum. By autumn the situation would settle down, perhaps the Church would take over the Institute. In that case nothing would prevent me from resuming my activities. I accepted this information very calmly... How I came to Cologne Carmen. I attached no importance to the hopes he held out."[925]

It seemed that a clear path was emerging for Edith to enter Carmel. She wrote:

"...Might not now the time be ripe to enter Carmel... For almost twelve years, Carmel had been my goal; since summer 1921, when the life of our Holy Mother Teresa had happened to fall into my hands and had put an end to my long search for the true faith."[926]

Edith submitted a request to archabbot Walzer near the end of April 1933 to enter the Carmelite Order. By mid-May of 1933, her prayers were answered. Thus, Walzer granted her permission to proceed.[927] Edith's friend Dr. Elisabeth Cosack made an appointment for her with the Discalced Carmelite nuns in Cologne. On May 20, Edith was invited to an interview with the Mother Prioress. While awaiting her interview that day with the princess, kneeling adjacent to the altar of Carmelite Saint Theresa of Lisieux, Edith indicted that she "experienced the serenity of someone who has reached her goal."[928] Edith was formally accepted for admission on June 19, 1933. After spending time between July 16 and August 15 in the convent's external quarters in order to become oriented to the nuns' horarium or daily schedule, Edith made her final visit with her family.[929] Meeting with the Mother Prioress, Sister Mary Josepha of the Blessed Sacrament was actually the initial step. It was after meeting the vicar for religious who expressed reservations. However, the vicar gave Edith a positive impression. Edith soon received a telegram which stated, "Joyful assent, Regards, Carmel".[930]

Edith went to church to thank the Lord Jesus. She prayed for strength as well. Only her sister, Rosa, was aware of Edith's path to join the Carmelites within Edith's family circle. At the cathedral of tier after meeting with her Spiritual director on August 10, she prayed before the Holy [Robe].[931]

Edith was waiting for the right place and time to reveal her intentions to her mother. A priest friend had suggested that Edith write a book to counter caricatures of Judaism. Edith planned to utilize her mother's view. Thus, Edith and her mother had developed an even deeper bond thru the process of working on the book.[932] However, frau Stein posed the question to Edith, "What will you do with the sisters in Cologne?" When Edith had responded, "Live with them," her mother took the news very badly.[933]

...The great pain that I must be causing her and have before my eyes daily. You will help me, won't you, to beg that my mother will be given the strength to bear the leave-taking, and the light to understand it?"[934]

Moreover, with the exception of Rosa, family members felt abandoned by Edith at this time of persecution. When one of the Carmelite sisters, Sister Marianne came to supervise the founding of the new Carmel in Breslaw, Edith's mother met her. Frau Stein attempted to enlist Sister Marianne's assistance in discouraging Edith from entering the Carmelite order. Edith wrote, "...The decision was so difficult that no one could tell me with certainty which was the right path. Good reasons could be cited for both alternatives. I had to take that step in the complete darkness of faith."[935]

Edith routinely attended daily Mass at St. Michael the Archangel near her home. One prior day of her leaving for Carmel, Edith went to Mass and then spend time at the synagogue with her mother for the Jewish Feast of Tabernacles. While returning home, they talked about religion.

"It was totally impossible to make my mother understand anything. Everything remained in all its starkness and incomprehensibility, and I was able to leave only by was able to leave only by placing a firm confidence in God's grace and by the strength of our prayer. That my mother, too, has faith, and, finally, that she still has great inner strength made it a little bit easier."[936]

The day Edith left home, her mother cried in sadness and could not eat her breakfast. Edith held her mother tightly until it was time to leave. This last image of her mother in grief had a deep effect on Edith. Her sister Else and Rosa walked with Edith to the train station. Typically, a family member would wave to the trolley from the parlor window if one of them was traveling. However, Edith did not find anyone waving from the house. This caused her pain. Edith would not see her family again, with the exception of Rosa who would later convert to Catholicism.[937]

Once Edith had arrived in Cologne, she would stay overnight at her close friend's home, Hedwig Spiegel. Edith and Hedwig joined the Sisters for vespers and subsequently met with Sister Teresa Renata, the Mistress of Novices. As they stepped to the entrance of the cloister, Edith had indicated, "At last it opened, and in deep peace I crossed the threshold into the House of the Lord."[938] Edith took the name of Teresa Benedicta of the Cross (Cruce) as a Discalced Carmelite. She was accepted as a Carmelite novice on April 15, 1934.

"...Only someone whose spiritual eyes have been opened to the supernatural correlations of world by events can desire suffering in expiation, and this is only possible for people in whom the spirit of Christ dwells, who as members [Glieder] are given life by the head, receive his power, his meaning, and his direction... because being one with him our happiness on earth, the love of the cross in no way contradicts being a joyful child of God. Helping Christ carry his cross fills one with a strong and pure joy, and those who may and can do so, the builders of God's Kingdom, are the most authentic children of God."[939]

Edith had taken her first vows on April 21,1935. Carmelites can repay God's love by their everyday lives in no other way than by carrying out their daily duties faithfully in every respect. "This is the 'little way', a bouquet of insignificant little blossoms that are daily placed before the

Almighty - perhaps a silent, life - long martyrdom that no one suspects and that is at the same time a source of deep peace and hearty Joyousness and a fountain of grace that bubbles over everything - we do not know where it goes, and the people whom it reaches do not know from whence it comes."[940]

Although Edith truly sought a full life of prayer, the prioress had requested that Edith complete her work, Potency and Act. She was bringing the philosophy of phenomenology in line with the Catholic tradition in this work of literature. Edith had written, Finite and Eternal Being in 1936.[941] However, Edith's mother died in September 1936. Within nearly three years of Edith's entrance to Carmel, her mother rarely wrote to Edith. Only she would include a few lines at the end part of Rosa's letters to Edith. However, Edith treasured those few lines which served as a consolation for Edith.[942] In a letter Edith wrote to her mother Petra Bruning:

"Every bulletin from Breslau reports worsening. I must be prepared to hear the worst any day. The 'Scimus, quoniam diligentibus Deum... 'We know that, for those who love him, God turns everything to the good' (Rom 8:28) will surely apply to my dear mother too, since she truly loved 'her' God (as she often said with emphasis). And, with confidence in him, she bore much that was painful and did much that was good. I also think these last months when her life was constantly in peril were particularly grace-filled days- above all, the days since she no longer troubles herself about anything in her external life. And no one but the Lord himself knows what is happening in her soul."[943]

Edith's mother had died of stomach cancer on September 14,1936, the feast of the Holy Cross. The Carmelite Sisters typically renew their vows on this feast day. Edith wrote, "As I was standing in my place in choir waiting to renew my vows my mother was beside me. I felt her presence quite distinctly."[944]

On October 25, 1936, the Rome-Berlin Axis was formed by Hitler and Mussolini.[945] When the Nazi came to power in 1933, Pious XI was favorable to Hitler's anti-communism. Cardinal Pacelli had negotiated a concordat which had effectively funded the church with annual tax revenues of five hundred million marks. The Pope did sign this concordat.[946] However, Pacelli had sent fifty-five notes which protested breaches to this agreement. Pacelli had stated, "Christianity has supposedly gathered together all races, whether negro or white, into a single, big family of God."[947] Moreover, Pacelli opposed the Nazis, "superstition of race and blood." The Nazi secret police had determined that Catholics are "ideologically un-teachable" in their support of Jewish merchants.[948] Pacelli urged Christians to "save the world" from pagan "false prophets" which was interpreted as a call to be against Hitler.[948]

The Propaganda Minister Joseph Goebbels had recorded: "4 March 1939 (Sunday). Midday with the Fuhrer. He is considering whether we should abrogate the Concordat with Rome in light of Pacelli's election as Pope. This surely happens when Pacelli undertakes his first hostile act.[949]

Munich Cardinal Michael Von Faulhaber had grave concerns which he had expressed as follows, "Their philosophy is a de facto religion... They had their own sacramental rituals for baptism and confirmation, marriage and funerals. They changed Ash Wednesday into Wotan's Day, Ascension Day into the Feast of Thor's Hammer. They crowned the Christmas tree not with a star, but with a swastika. The Nazis even made 'the blasphemous claim that Adolf Hitler is essentially as great as Christ.'"[950]

According to German-Jesuit Father Peter Gumpel, the Vatican was hardwired by Gugdielmo Marconi, inventor of the radio. He put together a telephone exchange, a radio station, and a short-wave link to the to the papal summer villa. Pope Pius XU (Pacelli) authorized this intervention in order to refute propaganda against him.[951] Marconi offered his services free of charge however, his marriage was annulled which permitted him to remarry. Moreover, there existed microphone-concealments throughout the Papal Library utilizing a system which operated "through a contrivance which made it possible to hear everything in the room next door."[952]

Essentially, the Nazis had banned Catholic organizations, censored its press, and fired teachers as well as closed Catholic schools.[953] Hitler stated in a Reichstag speech that, "The priest as political enemy of the Germans we shall destroy."[954] It was in March, 1938 that the Nazis took over Austria and about six months later, the Sudetenland, part of northern and western Bohemia as well as northern Moravia. In effect, the Nazis swallowed all of Czechoslovakia.[955]

On April 21, 1938, Edith made her perpetual vows as a Carmelite and received her black veil of a Discalced Carmelite Sister Her friend and "Master" (Mentor in philosophy) at Göttingen and Freiburg, Edmund Husserl passed away on April 27.[956] On November 9,1938 most synagogues across Germany and Austria were destroyed on Kristallnacht, the Night of Broken Glass. Basically, nearly every Jewish-owned store and business were broken into and robbed as well as many Jews were rounded up, arrested, and brought to con-centration camps.[957]

Edith's Carmelite superiors made plans for her to move to a Carmel in Echt, Holland although Edith requested the Holy Land. However, the British had for all practical purposes closed that route. [958,959] Edith's sister expressed her thankfulness to Edith for being a good role model for the family. Edith stated that, "It is I who must thank God for having allowed me to live with you."[960]

On January 1, 1939, when Edith had arrived in Echt, she indicated in a letter to Mother Petra Brüning written on April 16,1939:

"I would rejoice with all my heart if you were able to come here sometime.

You would come to love the Carmel of Echt as quickly as you did the one in Cologne. And the Sisters would be happy to tell you about Mother Paula, who is said to have been such a holy little Mother. I am allowed to send you the photos as a small Easter treat: Thanks, from the heart for the holy Mass and for the generous donation to Cologne. The printing is again stopped, and everything is in question once more. Naturally I am in touch with my brothers and sisters; there are prospects of Rosa's getting to Belgium, to a Tertiary of our Order. All this, however, I would rather tell you in person.... My basic attitude since I 've been here is one of gratitude - grateful that I may be here and that the house is as it is. At the same time, I always have a lively awareness that we do not have a lasting city here. I have no other desire than that God's will be done in me and through me. It is up to him how long he will leave me here and what is to come then. In minibus tuis sortes meae. < My days are in your hands. (Ps 31:15)> There everything is well cared for. I need not worry about anything. But much prayer is necessary in order to remain faithful in all situations. Especially [must we pray] for those who have heavier burdens to carry to carry than I have, and who are not so rooted in the Eternal. Therefore, I am sincerely grateful to all who help."[961-962]

On September 1, 1939, Germany conquered Poland. Then Great Britain and France declared war on Germany. A million Germans had invaded Poland and Hitler took a train to tour the front. Reinhard Heydrich, SS Spy Chief, had stated that, "the Catholic priests...must all be killed."[963] Hitler placed Hans Frank in charge of Poland. Hitler stated, "The task I give you, Frank, is a Satanic one."[964] Hitler watched his army destroy Warsaw "and his eyes nearly popped out of his head, and he became quite a different person. He was suddenly seized by a lust for blood. [965] Hitler made a decision to invade France; however, his generals "fought tooth and nail against the French Campaign."[966]

"Hundreds of priests were arrested and shot by the Germans during the first month, while Catholic intellectuals, clerics, or laity were arrested and sent to concentration camp Oranienburg near Berlin....The basis of this program was the elimination of the intellectual elite and the traditional influence of the clergy.[967]

Pacelli described Hitler as "not only an untrustworthy scoundrel but as a fundamentally wicked person."[968] The pope had decided to serve as a secret foreign agent for the resistance against Hitler. "Never in all history had a Pope engaged so delicately in a conspiracy to overthrow a tyrant by force."[969]

In summary, Pope Pius (Pacelli) was posed the question of what type of government that Germany should work toward, according to father Leber's notes, "Any government without Hitler".[970] By the conclusion of 1939, Germany and the Soviets had effectively taken Estonia, Latvia, and Lithuania. Moreover, Finland fell to the Germans and Soviets in March of 1940. Germany soon took Norwegian parts and all of Denmark. Orders were in place to establish concentration camps at Auschwitz, Poland which was the first of three altogether there. Thus, prior to the conclusion of the war, the Nazis set up over one hundred concentration camps including six death camps in Europe.[971] It was on May 10 that the

Germans went on the offensive against the Netherlands, Belgium, and France. By June 22, most of France was taken, which included Paris.[972]

In a letter written to Mother Johanna van Weersth, dated July 10,1940, Edith wrote:

"Last evening after 8 o'clock there were two sharp rings at the turn and soon thereafter the Sister Portresses recognized the vigorous voice of our Father Bishop. A few minutes later the domestic bell called all the Sisters together. Father Bishop most cordially greeted each one, individually, and exhorted us not to worry, to have great confidence, to sleep well, and to talk to one another more frequently since this would be good for us at a time like this. But above all else he urged us, of course, to untiring prayer and sacrifice and to fidelity to our vocation since we must now fight in the front line. You know that eight persons searched his house for hours. He told them off in no uncertain terms; one must, after all, tell those poor people the real truth for once. First Bolshevism had come from the east to fight against God, then National socialism [Nazis] came with the fight against the Church. But neither would be victorious, because in the end Christ would conquer. All of us would at sometime have to get on our knees. But first there would be a relentless battle between these philosophies of life. He continued; we had nothing against the people as individuals. But we have to be steadfast in our principles and may not surrender on any point. That was how Father Bishop had spoken to the people, and that was how we were to speak to them should they come to us. In conclusion he even gave them his pastoral letter of the previous year to take along; they should read it through thoroughly to understand his thinking Farther Bishop wants to be in Maastricht on August is in order to dedicate the entire diocese a new to the Mother of God in the basilica Sterre der Zee [Star of the sea]. Prior to that a triduum - [three days] of prayer and penance - is to be held in all the churches and chapels in the bishopric. Now we must pray that this plan does not prove impossible to carry out as happened currently with the Marian Congress. Father Bishop is, after all, prepared for a lot more. He will gladly accept being episcopus et martyr [bishop and Martyr]."[973]

The Nazis invaded Greece and Yugoslavia in April of 1941. In September, 1941, Edith and her sister Rosa were required to wear the yellow star of David and the word "Jude" (German for "Jew") was inscribed on it. Moreover, they had to go before occupation force magistrates in Maastricht and in Amsterdam.[974] Essentially, all non-Aryan Germans in Holland were considered as stateless and were required to report by December 15 for deportation.

"The Carmelite Nuns [in Echt] wrote to the French-speaking Carmel of Le Paquier m Switzerland; one of the novices there knew Edith from those long-ago days when she had lectured in Switzerland. A haven was sought for Rosa with a religious congregation not far from Le Paquier. But such correspondence was very slow-moving; and the official papers that had to be obtained in Holland, in Switzerland, and from Rome, since Edith was a professor religious, were so numerous and so reluctantly granted that the whole effort failed."[975]

Edith did finish an article for publication, "Symbolic Theology of Pseudo-Dionysius" for a journal of philosophy in the United States. Moreover, she continued to write, *The Science of the Cross*.[976] Edith had celebrated her fiftieth birthday on October 12, 1941, which would be her last one.

The sisters of Echt had put together their own skit of the patriarchs German to the book of Ecelesiasticus (Sirach) in her honor.[977] In a letter written to Hilde Verene Borsinger on December 31, 1941, Edith wrote:

"…Today it is three years that I've been in the Carmel of Echt. A short time ago, both chapters decided that the transfer should be a permanent one. The decision must be made after three years and may not be taken up sooner. Now, just in the days when this was being voted on, the Occupation Forces issued a decree that declared all non-Aryan Germans in the Netherlands as stateless and ordered them to report for emigration by December 15. We, i.e., my sister Rosa and I, complied because failing to do so would have incurred a severe penalty. But I immediately drafted a petition for us to be permitted to remain in the Carmel of Echt and to be taken off the list of emigrants; the petition is now being typed. But in case that fails we have to look for alternative possibilities. More than anything else, our Reverend Mother would like to put us up with the Carmelites of the Divine heart (the sisters of Sittard) in one of their Swiss convents, until such a time as a return will be possible(r). Their Mother General lives here in Limburg, and the petition to her convents in Switzerland could pass through her hands, from you, on the other hand, I would like to find out whether, provided we are accepted by a convent, we could obtain an entry permit and visa, and to whom we ought to apply for it. I do not know that Switzerland is Strictly closed to immigrants, but I could imagine that under these particular, circumstances an exception would be made.... My sister, who was baptized in Cologne at Christmas 1936, has been here since the 1ˢᵗ of July 1939, and is well established as an extern and outside sacristan, so that she will be sorely missed; She is also a Tertiary of our Order (Sister Rosa Maria of Jesus)."[978]

Hider's official plan concerning the Jewish people was deemed the Final Solution," the total extermination of Jews in Europe. On January 20, 1942, the Third Reich made this determination. According to available notes taken in their meeting:

"Europe is to be combed through from West to East in the course of the practical implementation of the final solution... The evacuated Jews will be taken, group by group, to the so-called transit shettos; in order to be transported further east from there. Their 'Final Solution' was the planned destruction of all eleven million Jews in the countries Germany already controlled and the ones they expected toconquer."[979]

On March 1, 1942, transport trains ran to Auschwitz. In a letter to Hilde Verene Borsinger dated April 9, 1942 Edith wrote:

"Now that, after years, I am out to pay my correspondence debts, I would also like to thank you sincerely for your kind note of January 23. Since I have had no further word from you, I take it that you have received [in Bern] the sane answer we had here from the Superior General of the Carmelite Sisters of the Divine Heart: that entering Switzerland is impossible. At the end of January we had to go to Maastricht about our affair and to Amsterdam at the end of March. We were assured that there could be no thought of emigrating before the end of the war. And we cannot possibly prepare today for what is going to happen then. So we continue to lead our lives calmly and leave the future to him who alone Knows anything about it."[980]

In July 1942, the Carmelite monastery at Le Pâquier became an option for Edith as well as a convent of Third order Carmelites for Rosa. On July 6, 1942, the Dutch bishops led by Archbishop Johannes de Jong and Bishop Lemmens had publicly opposed the Nazi persecution of the Jewish people. Moreover, on July 20, 1942, the bishops sent a pastoral letter to the commander of the German occupation forces in Holland which stated, "Contrary to the deepest conviction of the Dutch people and... to God's commands of justice and mercy."[981] However, the Nazis had reacted by arresting all non-Aryan Roman Catholics in Holland.

Moreover, the Commanding Officer of Security Police and the Public Security Administration had indicated: "Since the Catholic bishops have interfered in something that does not concern them, deportation of all Catholic Jews will be speeded up and completed within the coming week. No appeals for clemency shall be considered. On Sunday, August 2, General Kommissar Schmidt will publicly respond to the bishops intervention at the Party gathering in Limburg."[982]

Edith's brother Paul Stein and his wife Gertrude were part of approximately 1,100 Jews deported on July 27, 1942, to the concentration camp located at Theresienstadt. Edith's sister Elfriede "Frieda" Tworoger was deported as well to TheresienStadt.[983] On Sunday August 2, 1942, at 5:00 PM, both Edith and her sister Rosa were retrieved by the Gestapo and taken away. Edith said to Rosa, "Come, let us go for our people."[984] Essentially, Catholic Jews were transported by train to station in Amersfoort, then to the assembly then to the assembly camp of Westerbork which, was the central detention camp in the east of the Netherlands.[985] Actually, there existed eyewitness reports of Edith at Westerbork by survivors and others.

According to Fran Bromberg, the mother of a Dominican priest described the following:

"What distinguished Edith Stein from the rest of the sisters was her silence. Rather than seeming fearful, to me she appeared oppressed. Maybe the best way I can explain it is to say that she carried so much pain that it hurt to see her smile. She hardly ever spoke; but often she would look at her sister Rosa with sorrow beyond words. As I write it occurs to me that she probably understood what was awaiting them. She was, after all, the only one who had escaped from Germany as a refugee, and this would have given her a much better idea.... As I say, in my opinion, she was thinking about the suffering that lay ahead. Not her own suffering - she was too resigned for that -but the suffering that was in store for the others. Every time I think of her in the barracks, the same picture comes to mind: a Pieta without the Christ."[986]

Moreover, survivor and eyewitness, Julius Marcan of Cologne had stated:

"It was Edith Stein's complete calm and self- possession that marked her out from the rest of the prisoners. There was a spirit of indescribable misery in the camp; the new prisoners especially suffered from extreme anxiety. Edith Stein went among the women like an angel, comforting, helping, and consoling them. Many of the mothers were on the brink of insanity and had sat moaning for days, without giving any thought to their children. Edith Stein immediately set about taking care of these little ones. She washed them, combed their hair, and tried too make sure they were fed and cared for."[987]

Although a moot point, a letter from the Swiss Consulate dated August 3, 1942 had rejected Edith's and Rosa's request. Edith's captivity did not deter her from letter writing. In a letter written to Mother Ambrosia Antonia Engelmann from the Drente-Westerbork, Barracks 36 dated August 4, 1942, Edith wrote:

"During the past night we left the transit station A. < Amarsfoort> and landed here early this morning. We were given a very friendly reception here. They intend to do everything possible to enable us to be freed or at least that we may remain here. All the Catholics are together and, in our dormitory, we have all the nuns (two Trappistines, one Dominican), Ruth < Kantorowicz>, Alice <Reis>, Dr. [Lisamaria] Meirowsky, and others are here. Two Trappist Fathers from T. are also with us. In any case, it will be necessary for you to send us our personal credentials, our I.D. cards, and our ration cards. So far, we have lived entirely on the generosity of others. We hope you have found the address of the Consul and have been in touch with him. We have asked many people to relay news to you. The two dean children from Koning Bosch <Annemarie and Elfriede Goldschmidt> are with us. We are very calm and cheerful. So far there has been no Mass and Communion; maybe that will come later. Now we have a chance to experience a little how to live purely from within. Sincerest greetings to all. We will probably write again soon.... When you write, please do not mention that you got this."[988]

In a letter written to Mother Ambrosia Antonia Engelmann from Drente-Westerbork, Barracks 36 dated August 5,1942, Edith wrote:

"A.R.C. R.C. nurse from A. intends to speak today with the consul. Here, every petition [on behalf of fully Jewish Catholics has been for bidden since yesterday. Outside [the camp] an attempt can still be made, but with extremely little prospect. According to plans, transport will leave on Friday. Could you possibly write to Mére Clarie in Vento, Kaldenkereweg 185 [the Ursuline Convent] to ask for our [my] manuscript if they have not already sent it. We count on your prayers. There are so many people here who need some consolation, and they expect it from the sisters."[989]

In a letter to Mother Ambrosia Antonia Engelmann from Drente West-erbork, Barracks 36 dated August 6, 1942, Edith's final letter, she wrote:

"A mother Superior from one of the convents arrived last evening with suitcases for her child and now offers to take some short letters along. Early tomorrow transport leaves (Sibesia or Czechoslovakia??). What is most necessary: woolen stockings, two blankets. For Rosa all the warm underwear and whatever was in the laundry; for us both towels and wash clothes. Rosa also has no toothbrush, no cross and no rosary. I would like the next volume of the breviary (so far I have been able to pray gloriously). Our identity cards, registration cards [as Jews], and ration cards. A thousand thanks, greetings to all, Y.R.'s grateful child. "[990]

In conclusion, and entry was found in 1950 when the Dutch Gazotte published the names of all Jews who had been deported from Holland on August 7, 1942, which included number 44074: Edith Theresia Hedwigstein, Echt. Born October 12;1891, Breslau, Died - August 9, 1942.[991]

In the United States, the bishops' joint letter in 1942 stated the following, positive duty of a nation to wage war in the defense of life and right. Our nation now finds itself in such circumstances... [the] premeditated and systematic extermination of subjugated peoples like the Poles and declared their deep sense of revulsion against the cruel indignities heaped upon the Jews in conquered countries and upon defenseless people not of our faith."[992]

American Catholics represented approximately twenty-five to thirty-five percent of the armed forces during the war. Moreover, there were 3,036 military chaplains.[993] There were isolationist and pacifist including Dorothy Day who was the founder of the Catholic Worker Movement. In fact, the New York "Catholic Worker" had sponsored a Catholic conscientious objector camp at Stoddard, New Hampshire.[994] James Gillis and Fulton Sheen felt that the past sins of Europe were catching up with them. There was opposition to the arms embargo, the 1940 Selective Training and Service Act, and the 1941 Lend-Lease Act.[995] However, Alfred E. Smith gave a speech in order to reduce Irish prejudice against the British. Moreover, Archbishop Francis J. Spellman of New York stated that. 'We really cannot afford to be moles who can-not see, or ostriches who will not see.[996]

Bishop Fulton J. Sheen was on radio since the early 1930s, he believed that the war was, in reality, a theological based conflict against the "anti-Christ.' President Roosevelt signed the 'Servicemen's Readjustment Act", the "G.I. Bill of Rights" on June 22, 1944. By 1952 about 7,600,000 veterans of World War II had received education or training due to this act.[997]

The Catholic population practically doubled their population from twenty-one million in 1940 to forty-two million by 1960. Basically, the birth rate was high, immigrants became part of the church, and converts were numerous.[998] Fulton Sheen entered the realm of television and became a significant Catholic TV star. Moreover, he was a prolific writer who authored *Peace of Soul* (1949) and *Life is Worth Living* (1953-57).[999] From 1912 to 1963, the Catholic population in the United States grew from 15,015,569 to 43,851,538.

Hugh Nolan depicted an accurate picture: "The Catholics of that era were a Joyous group positive of their identity, proud of their church and of their priests and of their schools. There was a truly strong parish spirit. Most Catholics in a parish knew one another: the school pulled the parishioners close together as the children played and competed together on the various parish teams; parishioners often socialized together and, in many instances their children intermarried. Most parents wanted to give their children a better education than they themselves had, and greatly preferred the Catholic colleges..."[1000]

Catherine de Hueck Doherty (1896-1985) was born in Russia into the Russian Orthodox faith. Since her father's work required much travel, she went to Alexandria and Constantinople. It was at Alexandria that Catherine attended Catholic school run by Roman Catholic nuns.[1001] Catherine married her aristocratic cousin Boris de Hueck at the tender age of fifteen. In 1917 the Bolshevik Revolution forced them into poverty, and they emigrated to Canada in 1921 when their son was born.[1002] Catherine had converted to Catholicism in November 1919 in the diocese of Westminster.[1003] Within nine years, they separated and then divorced. The marriage was annulled. Catherine held various jobs as laundress, waitress, salesclerk, and public lecturer.[1004] Bishop McNeil of Toronto was very supportive for Catherine to initiate a new apostolate to the poor. Certainly, Archbishop McNeil served as a spiritual father to her, and she had consulted him on issues germane to her personal, spiritual, and apostolic life until his death in 1934.[1005]

Catherine founded the first Friendship House in the slums of Toronto. Other Friendship Houses were established in the 1930s and 1940s both in Canada and the United States. During the Second World War, Catherine worked as a journalist for various Catholic periodicals.[1006] She married Eddie Doherty, a well-known and highly paid journalist. In 1947, they moved to Combermere, Ontario since she was rejected by staff members of a Friendship House in the United States.[1007] Although she was broken-hearted, many people had desired to live and work for her in Combermere. Thus, the Madonna House apostolate emerged.[1008] Father Henry Carr, CSB was instrumental Catherine's early years of her Toronto apostolate. Father Carr was Catherine's spiritual director, and they communicated mostly via letter since Catherine was mostly in Ottawa's Friendship House.[1009]

Father Carr had significant influence on Catherine's spiritual development which somewhat correlates with her "Little Mandate". He imparted the spiritual doctrine of St. John of the Cross to her. Thus, via negativa as well as seeking and finding the Lord in the hidden parts of one's soul: "Take up your cross, My cross, and follow me. Be hidden".[1010] Moreover, St. Thérése of Lisieux (the little Flower): "Do little things exceedingly well for love of Me, Be childlike."[1011] Father Carr emphasis on trusting in divine providence and "Sell all you possess. Give it directly, personally to the poor. Be simple poor."[1012] Carr taught her to "Love, love, love, never counting the cost."[1013] Furthermore, he truly impressed upon Catherine to "Preach the Gospel with your life - without compromise."[1014]

Lastly, Carr recommended to Catherine to practice self-renunciation and truly offer herself as a victim to Christ for other under her care.[1015] Catherine's "Little Mandate" is a small text which is a road map for living the Gospel without compromise. Basically, it stresses the "Spirituality of Nazareth". Catherine had received words of the spirit or "words of command" during prayer. Her scripture reading, "Go, sell what you possess, and give to the poor" (Matthew 19:21) became the thrust of her ministry.[1016] Catherine had exhibited a spiritual motherhood or staritsa to those with spiritual problems. However, she did experience a time of significant trial during her apostolate at the Friendship House.

In a letter to Father Carr dated October 26, 1936, Catherine wrote:

"Is it cowardly to want some comfort, and encouragement? If it is, forgive me Father, for I am nothing really but a poor, week woman, a great sinner -who as yet cannot fully understand that God himself has taken her at her word, where she, in the enthusiastic youth of her spiritual life exclaimed, "I love you. I want to be with you unto the end", and here it is the end or the new beginnings - Gethsemane or Calvary. I wish it were the latter, for then all would be consummated soon. But if it is the former, then facing me is Herod, the court of the priests, Pilate, the way of the cross. Father, I need you to understand, don't you? Will you see me? Please."[1017]

In a letter to Father Carr dated March 4, 1937, Catherine wrote:

"Father, do not feel horrified that it comes to me. I am not giving in, but I wrestle with is as Jacob with the angel. Face to face, body to body, night after night, for it comes to me in the darkness. I know it is of Satan. He once came during my term of imprisonment by the Communists - it is suicide. I am, physically speaking, so tired of living. Since my marriage (1915) I have never had one year of peace or human happiness. I am an absolute failure, as a wife, a mother, a woman and how even as God's worker. I am weary and bruised and sick at heart: I am surrounded with enemies, and my loneliness is complete. My days are sort of a way of the cross inwardly and outwardly. There seems to be no hope, no future, no use to go on living such are the whisperings of Satan. It is now two months after they began that I have the courage to write to you about it. But if I cannot tell you the truth, to whom can I?"[1018]

Another priest who served as a spiritual director to Catherine was Father Paul Hanly Furfey of the Archdiocese of Washington and chairman of the sociology department at the Catholic University of America. He invited Catherine to lecture in his department in 1937.[1019] Catherine had started another Friendship House on February 14, 1938, in Harlem, New York,[1020] Furfey did contribute to this endeavor at the Friendship House as well as at the Madonna House at a later time.

"As Catherine's spiritual director he prayed much and was blessed with the gift of Counsel. His direction is clear, firm yet gentle and always presents her with a new challenge. He wants her to be a saint and constantly by calls her to heroism. At the same time, he reassures her that her vocation is from God and thus heals her of the wounds inflected by the Toronto experiment."[1021]

Essentially, Furfey made a major adjustment in his spiritual direction once he knew her better. Namely, Furfey felt that the Benedictine model - ora et labora - a combination of quiet prayer and apostolic activity had much better fit her as opposed to the former Ignatian approach. [1022] In a letter dated Good Friday, 1940:

"Nowhere comes the main point of my letter. As I read over your excellent and generous resolutions, it occurs to me that they are all in the Jesuit direction, whereas what you need is more emphasis in the Benedicitne direction. Did anyone who knew you ever call you lazy? Of course not! You're the unlaziest person in the world. You're energetic to the nth degree. And now when you get in the corner and go on retreat to extricate yourself, what is your solution? Characteristically enough, it is to whip yourself up to a still higher degree of energy. But perhaps that isn't quite fair. As I read your letters, I find that here and there you do remark that you need more tranquility. I do think you are on the right track there. Our Lord loves to have you rushing around hither and thither doing things for Him, but he also loves to have you relax now and then and be like Mary who sat beside His feet and listened to Him while Martha was so busy."[1023]

During the years 1946-1948, Catherine needed to leave the Friendship House and move to Combermere, Ontario. In a letter dated December 20, 1946, to Father Furfey, Catherine wrote:

"I guess He wants me to detach myself from the very thing [Friendship House] He once asked me to create with His grace. So be it. His will is mine. And I am ready to lift my anchor once more and set myself as a rift on the sea of life. I am not as young as I once was, but with His help I shall serve Him the best I can wherever I go. Friendship House comes first, and if my absence from it is for its best, I will absent myself. Amen."[1024]

Actually, Catherine and Father Furfey subsequent letter were germane to Friendship House matters as well as other pragmatic concerns. Catherine's second husband Eddie Doberty entitled Catherine's biography, Tunibleweed since Father Furfey had referred to her as God's tumbleweed "blowing through the world, wherever the breath of the Holy Ghost may send her." [1025] In Au-gust, 1948, the letter writing virtually came to a halt. Father Furfey was supportive of Catherine's new endeavor at the Madonna House.

In a letter dated May 19,1974, Furfey wrote: "Things turned out magnificently, didn't they? Everything I hear about Combermere is good. Your work speak for themselves. God has blessed your work abundantly. That seems to me to constitute unanswerable proof that your work is holy and blessed.

May God continue to bless you! Be assured, I admire you. There can be no doubt on that point."[1026]

In a letter dated January 17, 1979, Catherine wrote: "I didn't think you realize what you have meant in my life. You were one of my Spiritual Directors who really took me by the hand and, like St. John of the Cross, led me into the heart of God. My gratitude is beyond all telling, so is my love and constant prayers for you. I don't talk too much about my feelings, but I want you to know that I have loved you with a great love in the Lord since you took hold of my soul and shaped it according to God's will."[1027]

Catherine had requested Father John Callahan of the Diocese of Rochester, New York to be her spiritual director. Callahan would eventually go to Madonna House permanently to serve as the chaplain. However, the initial spiritual direction was via letters as well. Callahan brought about the "Total Consecration to Jesus through Mary of Saint Louis de Montfort" to Catherine and the Madonna House Apostolate.[1028] An expert in the Spiritual Diary No.37 dated December 3, 1953, states:

"Madonna House was a new beginning, and yet it seemed no beginning at all-because no one believed but me that it was to be anything at all but a nice place for me and Eddie to live off our writings. Then Mary's slavery- a growth overnight-phenomenal. Staff workers arrival. Growth in summer School, of everything physical, inward, outward like roses in June. Then the change inward Father Cal wants me to write about, and of which I can say so little. The discovery of a whole new horizon within myself. The life betwixt and between. Sights, sounds, gifts. Vows of poverty, obedience for life. Secrets of the heavenly King. A new life- and light, blinding, clear, on the apostolate, the truths of God; and love of Him and Mary that any minute seems to grow so big it must burn me up, annihilate me! But it never does or did."[1029]

According to Guglielmi, the Marian Consecration had a positive effect upon the Madonna House. It provided the Madonna House with its distinctive Marian Spirit. It brought Father Callahan to the Madonna House and many people came seeking spiritual guidance. Moreover, Catherine's spirituality grew to another dimension in terms of her interior life and spiritual maternity. Finally, Callahan believed that Our Blessed

Mother Mary began to form Catherine's spiritual motherhood via his direction.[1030]

In a letter written to Father Callahan, dated November 9, 1953, Catherine wrote:

"The night has come to stay. Where I abide there is no day. And yet I have a lamp, a light, that is darker than my dark night. Yet all the hidden ways, the heights, the depths, the endless plains stand all revealed through its dark light that shines so bright, and yet is darker than my night. There is no comeliness in me. I am a wounded thorn thing that has been given over to darkness and pain. Fiat, Fiat, Fiat is my only refrain."[1031]

Catherine and Eddie took private vows of poverty, chastity, and obedience within their marriage on October 30, 1955. In a letter written to Father Callahan, dated October 10, 1955, Catherine wrote: "There is in me a strange light. It is not mine. The "picture," the sensation, persists. A light, angels, archangels, powers, principalities, Our Lady, Christ, the Uncreated Trinity. I walk in the glory of the Lord. Our Lady is here, close, coming, and there is a light before her face; and in it a great role suddenly is given over to priests.

Now the last work he has for me is PRIESTS. There is something I must do, for, through priests, and it deals with motherhood, and something elusive. 'Arise my beloved; winter is over in our land.'"[1032]

One final point Catherine was able to blend Eastern spirituality she retained from Russian spiritual traditions with western spirituality into the Ma-donna House. She felt that love is the glue which held them together. In her words, "The longer I live, the clearer I see that the answer to our personal, collective, national, and international problems is bridge-making between human beings-not allowing any human being to be an island unto himself -but connecting each with the other, with bridges of love."[1033]

RITE OF CHRISTIAN IINITIATION OF ADULT (RCIA)

The promulgation of the Rite of Christian Initiation of Adults (Ordo Initiations is Christianac Adultorum) in 1972 by Pope Paul VI was a punctuated change in the way of initiating adults into the Catholic church. 1034 Essentially, the RCIA resulted from the second Vatican Council's restoration of the catechumenate. Vatican Council II had forty-three Americans involved in organizing the agenda. Moreover, another twenty-three had served on committees as well as at least sixty official periti.[1035] Cardinal Spellman had introduced 131 of the 341 oral and written American interventions during the Council.

Cardinals Spellman and Meyer were council presidents with Cardinal She-Hand who replaced Meyer who died in 1965.[1036] Official observers Sister Mary Lake Tobin, Catherine McCarthy who was president of the National Council of Catholic women and James J. Norris who was not only assistant executive director of Catholic Relief services but president of the International Catholic Migration Committee.[1037] The various items germane to a Commonweal series in 1962 included:

"...freedom of thought in the church; emphasis on its prophetic as well as priestly and institutional reality; the priesthood of the laity and the laity's role in development of doctrine; religious liberty and renunciation by the church of privileged status; consequences of human solidarity in Christ's Mystical Body; common responsibility for all the peoples of the world; Christian unity; dialogue and real communication between people and pastors; cultural adaptation of worship forms, including introduction of vernacular languages; diminution of pomp and pageantry; emphasis on bishops as informed teachers and witnesses of faith, rather than rules or administrators; confrontation with the "deinstitutionalized Catholic"; recognition that a serious gap existed between clergy and laity or birth control, with statistics showing Catholic practice not substantially different from that of other Americans."[1038]

Cardinal Cushing had indicated that "there is no Christian rationale neither theological nor historical - for any inequity, hatred or persecution of our Jewish brothers."[1039] However, religious liberty was the most important issue raised by American bishops during the council. In November 1964 a maneuver at the council's third session had obstructed the passage of the Declaration on Religious Liberty. However, Cardinal Meyer procured in excess of eight hundred signatures in order to have a protest petition with a half-hours' time to bring to Pope Paul.[1040] On September 21, 1965, the declaration was voted on and according to Robert Cushman of Duke university stated that day "a very ancient order of things - at least in principle - passed away. In principle, the era of Constantine - sixteen hundred years of it-passed away."[1041] Cardinals Spellman and McIntyre advocated for the retention of Latin as the language of the Mass. They felt that active participation of the laity was a distraction.

However, in 1963, the Constitution on the Sacred Liturgy (Sacrosanctum Concilium) states:

"...in the restoration and promotion of the sacred liturgy, full and active participation by all the people is the aim to be considered before all else.[1042] Christian people, 'the chosen race, the royal priesthood, the holy nation, the people of whom God has taken possession' (1Pt2,9; secc 2, 4-5). This full and active sharing on the part of the whole people is of paramount concern in the process of renewing the liturgy and helping it to grow, because such sharing is the first, and necessary, source from which believers can imbibe the true Christian spirit. Therefore, in all pastoral activities, those charged with responsibility must work strenuously towards this sharing by means of appropriate formation..."[1043]

Certainly, the Mass was celebrated in the vernacular language in 1964. Actually, this new rite was required in 1970. Moreover, the council's new openness to the orthodox as well as the deployment of its resources to promote both peace and justice, was decisive. [1044]" In reference to the Rite of Christian Initiation of adults (RCIA) which is a recapitulation of the ancient practice of the early church is contained in numbers 64and 66 of the Sacrosantum Con-cilium. Actually, RCIA is not regarded as a program such as convert class, but rather it is a sacramental process. Basically, conversion refers to the "whole person". Thus, it is via the Holy Spirit that liberation and redemption is attained through Jesus, the Christ.[1045] Conversions are not truly entirely sudden nor really planned as a personal project. Certainly, the Lord meets a soul at a crossroad in one's life. The Lord in some way which is not expected makes His real presence known.[1046]

According to Saint Teresa of Avila: "Although I abandoned you, Lord, you did not abandon me so completely as not to turn to raise me up by always holding out your hand to me. And often times, Lord, I did not want it; nor did I desire to understand how often you called me again."[1047]

According to Saint John of the Cross: "We live I the midst of so much danger and find it so hard to arrive at truth. The clearest and truest things are the darkest and most dubious to us, and consequently we flee from what most suits us. "[1048]

Father Donald Haggerty described the conversion as follows:

"At the heart of every conversion is an encounter with the mystery of God himself. We come to know that God is utterly personal and real in his mystery, with eyes of a secret penetration cast upon a soul. In a unique way for each person, he enters within our life to invite us to fix our gaze in the direction of his approach. If we allow ourselves to be drawn and step closer, a brief unmasking may take place. We know him then indisputably as our Lord and our God. All our prior reflection about God may seem at that hour unfocused and superficial, a chasing after shadows. For we perceive now that he possesses an exquisite personal quality beyond any previous idea we may have had. The certainty in faith of his presence in near proximity to our soul leads quite spontaneously to the prostration of our spirit before him. Every dramatic discovery of God in a conversion provokes us to our knees, ready now to pray from a deeper layer of soul, drawn to prayer often for the first time in our life. [1049]"

Certainly, conversion is the major theme throughout the whole initiation. There exist various periods or stages starting with evangelization and the pre-catechumenate and finishing with mystagog or postbaptismal catechesis. Without doubt, formation involves the parish community as well as teachers and sponsors who directly work with candidates. Thus, a reciprocal interaction between the candidate and parish member is evidenced. Typically, it has been found that members of the parish witness to their sense of "being ambassadors for God" and thus they tend to utilize God's gifts more fully. [1050]

"...the people of God, as represented by the local Church, should under-stand and show by their concern that the initiation of adults is the responsibility of all the baptized. Therefore, the community must always be fully prepared in the pursuit of its apostolic vocation to give help to those who are searching for Christ. In the various circumstances of daily life, even as in the apostolate, all the followers of Christ have the obligation of spreading the faith according to their abilities. Hence, the entire community must help the candidates and the catechumens throughout the process of initiation: during the period of the precatechumenate, the period of the catechumenate, the period of purification and enlightenment, and the period of postbaptismal catechesis or mystagogy. "[1051]

RCIA is a step by step gradual process by which candidates/ catechumens are aided by sponsors who can attest to the particular individual under their care Germane to moral character, faith, and intention. Although a different person other than one's original sponsor may stand on behalf of the candidate in the rite of acceptance and the period of the catechumenate, the godparent will be with the candidate on the day of election at the celebration of the sacraments of initiation such as baptism, confirmation, and the eucharist. The godparent guides the candidate, and it is via the god-parent's example of Christian practice that one bears true Christian witness to the candidate.[1052] The teachers or catechists are encouraged to play an active part in the rites. Certainly, teachers need to be "filled with the spirit of the Gospel, attuned to the liturgical signs and the particular church years' cycle as well as "suited to the needs of the catechumens"[1053] Typically, the rite of election (enrollment of names) occurs on the first Sunday of Lent while the scrutinies must take place on the third, fourth, and fifth Sundays of Lent.[1054]

The scrutinies are intended to purify the hearts and minds of catechumens. The purpose is to cultivate a spirit of repentance and a better understanding of sin. This is attained via exorcisms.[1055]

Basically, the Creed is covered during the week following the first scrutiny and the Lord's Prayer is introduced during the week after the third scrutiny.[1056] The elect is invited to this most treasured prayer and to reflect on the pattern of prayer which they have experienced in RCIA. It is important to memorize the Our Father and the Creed if possible. However, the key is to know them in one's heart and mind. The second scrutiny requires the elect to meditate and reflect sufficiently prior to moving to the third scrutiny. The first lectionary text from the third scrutiny utilizes Ezekiel 37:12-14 in order that the elect, names the graves of death and where they experience the Spirit.[1057]

"Therefore, prophesy and say to them: Thus says the Lord GOD: Look! I am going to open your graves; I will make you come up out of your graves, my people, and bring you back to the land of Israel. You shall know that I am the Lord, when I open your graves and make you come up out of them, my people! I will put my spirit in you that you may come to life, and I will settle you in your land. Then you shall know that I am the Lord. I have spoken; I will do it oracle of the Lord."[1058]

The second scriptural text (Ephesians 5: 8-14) from the second scrutiny is preparation for the third scrutiny. Essentially, it is a reflection on the "light in the Lord" as well as where their "darkness" is found.[1059]

"For you were once darkness, but now you are light in the Lord. Live as children of light, for light produces every kind of goodness and righteousness and truth. Try to learn what is pleasing to the Lord. Take no part in the fruit-less works of darkness; rather expose then, for it is shameful even to mention the things done by them in secret; but everything exposed by the light becomes visible, for everything that becomes visible is light. Therefore, it says: Awake, O sleeper, and arise from the dead, and Christ will give you light."[1060]

The three scrutinies are celebrated on Sundays and thus, they are reinforced by an exorcism exposing the elect about the mystery of sin for the purpose of salvation of their sins. The gospel message of the Samaritan woman is utilized in the first scrutiny, the gospel message of the man born blind is used in the second scrutiny, and the gospel message of Lazarus is employed in the third scrutiny.[1061] Essentially, the readings with their chants are germane to Sundays in the Lectionary for Mass, Year A. However, for various reasons when these ritual Masses cannot be celebrated on their proper Sunday, it is acceptable to utilize other Sundays of Lent or perhaps days during the week.[1062] Since the texts from Year A is a longtime tradition in the Church for preparation of Baptism, it is mandatory to use Year A (not B or C) with the exception only with the bishop's consent can one of the three scrutinies be left out.

It is important to point out that the scrutinies are celebrated with the unbaptized.[1063]

The presentations follow the scrutinies. For example, the first presentation is the creed and follows the fivot scrutiny. Likewise, the second presentation is the Lord's Prayer which follows the third scrutiny. Moreover, the elect will recite the Lord's Prayer in communal worship initially during the celebration of the sacraments of initiation.[1064] The focus of catechesis during the enlightenment period differs from that of the catechumenate. While scripture, doctrine, worship, community, and service is manifested in catechesis during the catechumenate, readiness, and complete immersion towards the goal of baptism is in a retreat mode in the purification and enlightenment phase.[1065] The Ephphatha Rite (Mark 7: 31-37) is a prayer for God to open the ears and mouth of the elect.[1066] In reference to the cure of the deaf mute: "Touching each of the elect on the right and left ear and on the closed mouth with his thumb, the celebrant say, 'Ephphetha: that is, be opened, that you may profess the Faith you hear, to the praise and glory of God."[1067]

Essentially, at the core of this rite is that the ability to ear and respond to the word of God is via grace. Thus, to open the ears of the elect to hear God's word and to open the mouths of the elect to proclaim it can happen only by the grace of God, [1068]

Although RCIA does not specify any directives about Holy Thursday and Good Friday, the celebration of the full Triduum is vital to the elect. The participation in the servant mission of Jesus is about our eucharistic gathering. Thus, it is recommended that the elect attend Holy Thursday Mass. Certainly, the elect will be dismissed prior to the liturgy of the eucharist. [1069] Basically, Holy Thursday is Jesus, the Christ present washing our feet. Moreover, on Good Friday, it is Christ present crucified as well as Jesus offering us the cross. Furthermore, on Easter Sunday, it is the risen Lord present inviting us all into the gift of eternal life. [1070] Therefore, the elect fully participates in the mandatum which literally means "something given into another's hand" (commission).[1071] The penitential fast ends just prior to the Mass of the Lord's Supper on Holy Thursday. Thus, our paschal fast is not truly penitential but rather, it is an anticipatory fast that prepares us. It is proper to refrain from food and normal activities. The paschal mystery becomes the faithful's main concern.[1072] Certainly, the elect needs to spend time in prayer and reflection on Holy Saturday.

In fact, the texts from the Easter Vigil readings may serve this purpose of reflection. The elect and sponsors may share a basis or light lunch with their godparents and some parishioners. The elect may gather for prayer and faith sharing before returning home for final preparations.[1073] Preparation rites are done in anticipation of the celebration of the Mass and sacraments of initiation. The recitation of the Creed often called the redditio symboli (the return of the symbol), The Lord's Prayer (Our father) and the Ephphatha Rite compose the parts of this preparation.[1074]

Essentially, the liturgy of Baptism takes place after the homily. Basically, the elect are called forward while godparents are to present them. Sometimes a procession to the font is formed with an altar boy or Eucharistic minister carrying the Easter candle, the elect with godparents, and then the presider with assisting deacons or ministers.[1075] An invitation to prayer and singing of the Litany of the Saints as well as a pause for silent prayer for the elect in preparation to enter into the waters of baptism. At times, the Easter Vigil celebration commences with the Easter fire typically at the steps leading into the church. This may be utilized in order to restore the full Vigil experience. [1076] In the early church, a Christian community would actually keep vigil all night long. However, this is not plausible and the Easter fire is a reflection of this early church practice.[1077]

The rite calls for the presider to sing the blessing of the water which re-counts the various uses of water in the history of salvation. The presider will ask God to unseal the fountain of baptism then he lowers the Easter candle into the water to symbolize the candle breaking the seal of the water with the grace of God's Spirit. Thus, anyone who enters these waters will be filled with God's Spirit.[1078] This means that those receiving baptism becomes the bearers of this new life. Then the presider will invite the elect to reject sin. The renunciation of sin are responses to questions posed to the elect. Moreover, the profession of faith in the form of responses to questions is directed individually by the elect.[1079] The baptism of the elect follows the profession of faith which the elect responds altogether. Just as in the early church and especially eastern rite Catholics of today, the presider will request the elect to face the west, the direction of darkness and to renounce sin and evil. Then as the elect approaches the font, they must look to the east the rising sun and morning start as well as profess faith in Christ Jesus.[1080]

The anointing after baptism is as follows: "The God of power and Father of our Lord Jesus Christ has freed you from sin and brought you to new life through water and the Holy Spirit. He now anoints you with the chrism of salvation, so that, united with his people, you may remain forever a member of Christ who is Priest, Prophet, and King."[1081]

The presider utilizes the following formulary and states, "receive this baptismal garment": "N. and N., you have become a new creation and have clothed yourselves in Christ. Receive this baptismal garment and bring it un-stained to the judgment seat of our Lord Jesus Christ, so that you may have everlasting life."[1082]

The rite provides two options for baptism which includes immersion (full body or the head only) or the pouring of water over the head of the elect. This involves triple immersion (or pouring) using the Trinitarian formula. Moreover, godparents need to place the right hand on the shoulder of the elect.[1083]

The presentation of a lighted candle whereby the presider takes the Easter candle and states: "Godparents, please come forward to give to the newly baptized the light of Christ."[1084] Then the presider will have godparents' light candles from the Easter Candle and present it to the newly baptized: "You have been enlightened by Christ. Walk always as children of the light and keep the flame of faith alive in your hearts. When the Lord comes, may you go out to meet him with all the saints in the heavenly kingdom."[1085]

The presider's invitation is as follows: "My dear newly baptized, born again in Christ by baptism, you have become members of Christ and of his priestly people. Now you are to share in the outpouring of the Holy Spirit among us, the Spirit sent by the Lord upon his apostles at Pentecost ad given by them and their successors to the baptized. The promised strength of the Holy Spirit, which you are to receive, will make you more like Christ and help you to be witnesses to his suffering, death, and resurrection. It will strengthen you to be active members of the Church and to build up the Body of Christ in faith and love.[1086]

Confirmation follows and takes place where baptism was celebrated. The presider lays his hands over the newly baptized prays the prayer of invocation: "All-powerful God, Father of our Lord Jesus Christ, by water and the Holy Spirit you freed your sons and daughters from sin and gave them new life. Send your Holy Spirit upon them to be their helper and guide. Give them the spirit of wisdom and understanding, the spirit of right judgment and courage, the spirit of knowledge and reverence. Fill them with the Spirit of wonder and awe in your presence. We ask this through Christ our Lord."[1087]

The anointing with chrism, the sealing of the sacrament is next. This sealing sets the newly baptized apart for service of the Lord as the "indelible mark of the Spirit."[1088] Again, the godparents place their right hand on the shoulder of the newly baptized. The candles are relit for the renewal of baptismal promises. Thus, the presider sprinkles the faithful with the blessed water.[1089]

In the eastern rite, the main lines of the ritual are identical. However, in "The Barberini Euchologion" the renunciation of Satan and an affirmation of Jesus is as follows: "And after the Amen, the candidate is stripped and his shoes removed, and the priest turns him to the west. The candidate's hands being raised, the priest says thrice; 'I renounce Satan, and all his works and all his service and all his angels and all his pomp.' And the candidate or his sponsor answers each time. And again, the priest asks, saying: 'Have ye renounced Satan?" And he replies: 'We have renounced.' And the priest says: "Then blow upon him.' And the priest turns him to the east, his hands being lowered, and says: 'And I adhere to Christ, and I believe in one God, the Father Almighty, and the rest.' When the priest has spoken thrice, again he asks them: 'And have ye adhered to Christ?" And they answer: 'We have adhered.' And the priest says: 'Worship him.1090

Cyril of Jerusalem's Mystagogical Catecheses I is as follows: "2. First you entered the antechamber of the baptistery and faced towards the west. On the command to stretch out your hand, you renounced Satan as though he were there in person. 4. You were told, however, to address him as personally present, and with arms out. stretched to say: 'I renounce you, Satan.' Allow me to explain the reason for your facing west, for you should know it. Because the west is the region of visible darkness, Satan, who is himself darkness, has his empire in darkness; that is the significance of your looking steadily towards the west while you renounce that gloomy Prince of night... 5. Then in a second phrase you are taught to say, 'and all your'. All sin is 'the work of Satan' and sin too, you must renounce, since he who has escaped from a tyrant has also cast off the tyrant's livery... 6. Next you say, 'and all his pomp.' The Pomp of the Devil is the craze for the theatre, the horse races in the circus, the wild - beast hunts and all such vanity... 8. After this you say, 'and all your service'. The service of the Devil is prayer in the temple of idols, the honoring of lifeless images, the lighting of lamps or the burning of incense by springs or streams... 9. When you renounce Satan, trampling under foot every covenant with him then you annual that ancient 'league with Hell' and God's paradise opens be-fore you...II. That was what was done in the outer Chamber."[1091]

The liturgy of the Eucharist is next. Prior to the breaking of the bread, the presider may briefly speak about the Eucharist, the presider may briefly speak about the Eucharistic meal. The newly received are welcome to share in the community's Holy Communion with the Lord and the faithful.[1092] The blessing prayers in the Didache are as follows:

"Regarding the eucharist, give thanks [eucharistize] thus: First, concerning the cup: We give thanks to you, our Father, for the holy vine of David your servant, which you have made known to us through Jesus your servant. To you be glory unto the ages! Concerning the broken bread: We give thanks to you, our Father, for the life and knowledge which you have made known to us through Jesus your Servant. To you be glory unto the ages! As this broken bread was scattered over the hills, and then, when gathered, became one, so may your church be gathered from the ends of the earth into your kingdom.

For yours is the glory and the power through Jesus Christ, unto the ages! Let no one eat and drink of your enchaarist but those baptized in the name of the Lord; to this, too, the saying of the Lord is applicable: 'Do not give what is Holy to dogs (Mt 2.6).' 10. After you have been satisfied, give thanks [eucharistize] thus: We give you thanks, O holy

Father, for your holy name which you have enshrined in our hearts and for the knowledge and faith and immortality which you have made known to us through Jesus your Servant. To you be glory unto the ages! You, Master Almighty, have created all things for the sake of your Name, and have given for the sake of your Name, and have given food and drink to the sons of men for enjoyment, that they may give thanks to you. But to us you have granted spiritual food and drink for eternal life through Jesus your Servant. For all this we give thanks to you, for are mighty. To you be glory unto the ages! Armen. Be mindful, O Lord, of your Church, to deliver it from all evil, and to perfect it in your love; and gather it, the sanctified, from the four winds into your Kingdom which you have prepared for it. For yours is the power and the glory unto the ages! May grace come and this world pass away! Hosanna to the God of David!"[1093]

The final period is that of post baptismal catechesis or mystagogy. This involves reflection and prayer on the mysteries.[1094] Mystagogy (in Greek, mystagoghein) is a method by which the early church utilized to help the faithful live what they truly celebrate. In a sense, analogously what mystagogy is for liturgy is what the lectio divina is for Scripture.[1095] Certainly, mystagogy "is in the first place the accomplishment of a sacred action and in particular the celebration of the sacraments of initiation, baptism, and Eucharist."[1096] It is an epiphany of the mystery of God. Thus, one is initiated into the mystery via its celebration. Moreover, it is through the liturgy that mystery is revealed, communicated, and made known.[1097] Opus Dei, the work of God, was a way that Saint Benedict in his rule refers to the liturgy. Then, Opus Dei attributes God's action in the liturgy just as scripture, the word of God, is a word that attains what it signifies.[1098]

"...it shall not return to me empty, but it shall accomplish that which I purpose and succeed in the thing for which I sent it." (Isa 55:11)[1099]

Another meaning of mystagogy is "the oral or written explanation of the mystery that is hidden in the Scripture and celebrated in the liturgy. "[1100] Thus, the way of expression of mystery are both Scripture and liturgy. However, the methodology of explanation is mystagogy.[1101]

Essentially, the early Church fathers and fathers later on such as Cyril, Ambrose, John Chrysostom, and Theodore of Mopsuestia introduced their catechumens to the meaning of baptism, Eucharist, and the main parts of Christian liturgy in their mystagogical catecheses,[1102] Moreover, the identical hermeneutic was applied to the father's interpretation of the Scriptures. This correlation between Scripture and liturgy is solidified via mystagogy.[1103] Only the Lord can reveal the mystery of God; thus, mystery reveals itself.[1104] Mystery (mysterion) is the divine plan which the Lord Himself will make known.

"Surely the Lord God does nothing, without revealing his secret to his servants the prophets." (Amos 3:7).1105

"No wise men, enchanters, magicians, or diviners can show to the King the mystery that the King is asking, but there is a God in heaven who reveals mysteries." (Dan 2: 27-28)[1106]

Saint Paul indicated that "the mystery was made known to me by rev-elation" (Eph 3:3).[1107] Moreover, according to Paul, God's plan is "to gather up all things in [Christ]" (Eph 1:10).[1108] Thus, the mystery or Mystagogue is Jesus, the Christ who is not only the revealer but revealed fully in His death on the cross.[1109]

"Knowledge of the mysteries of the Kingdom of heaven has been granted to you, but to them it has not been granted." (Matt 13:11 NABRE; cf. Mark 4:10; Luke 8:10).

"Therefore, the one who entrust to his disciples the mystery of the Kingdom is Jesus, the prophet mighty in deed and word." (Luke 24:19).[1110]

According to Gregory of Nyssa, he wrote: "...initiates the people of Ephesus in the mysteries (mystagogheî) and imbues them though his instructions with the power of knowing what is that depth and height and breadth and length [of the knowledge of God]."[1111]

According to John Chrysostom, he wrote: "Paul is to be seen in prison, even in chains, instructing and initiating [mystagogounta: offering mystagogy], even in a court of justice, in shipwreck, in a storm, and in a thousand dangers."[1112]

According to Gregory of Nazianzus, he wrote in Christus patiens in the way similar to Greek tragedies, an anonymous person talking to

Judas: "You are the initiated into the mystery (mýstes) and you dishonor your fellow disciples by handing over for money your mystagogue (mystagogón)."[1113]

Thus, Gregory refers to Jesus as the mystagogue of his disciples and the twelve have become the initiated. However, the initiated will actually initiate others in the mystagogy.

According to Cyril of Alexandria, he wrote in his commentary on the Gospel of Luke in reference to Jesus teaching at Caperhaum: "It was useful and necessary that Christ often followed his mystagogy with miracles."[1114]

Thus, Cyril indicated that Jesus is the mystagogue who brought mystagogy to the crowds. In summary, the Nicene as well as post Nicene Fathers describe Jesus as the mystagogue. [1115] John, the apostle, wrote:

"No one has ever seen God. It is God the only Son, who is close to the Father's heart, who has made him known." (John 1:18)[1116]

Luke, the evangelist, wrote that the risen Christ "opened their minds to understand the scriptures" (Luke 24:45).[1117] Thus, it is the Risen Christ as the exegete of His mystery who acts as the revealer. Then, mystagogy is Christo-logical action and the revelation of the mystery of God is Jesus. At the celebration of the Eucharist, it is the Risen Christ who opens hearts and minds to comprehend the liturgy.[1118] The "word became flesh" (John 1:14) in Jesus Christ. The Roman Rite requires the ritual of placing the Book of the Gospels, the Evangelarium, on the altar. In Jesus, the Christ, the word of God becomes not only a body but rather a body offered.[1119]

"Sacrifices and offerings you have not desired, but a body you have pre-pared for me." (Heb 10:5; cf. Ps 40:6).[1120]

Certainly, the word of God found its fulfillment via Jesus, the Christ on the cross. Moreover, it is the total gift of self-unto death that the altar is in memorial as well as the place of thanksgiving. The book of gospels is placed on the altar a t the start of the eucharistic celebration. Thus, it becomes the hermeneutic of all that is celebrated in the liturgy by which the liturgy truly manifests the unity between Scripture and the

Eucharist.[1121] Origen, an early Church father, indicated this connection; he wrote: "It was not the visible bread that he held in his hands which God the Word called his body, but it was the word in whose sacrament the bread was to be broken. Nor was it the visible drink that he identified as his blood, but it was the Word in whose sacrament the libation was to be poured out."[1122]

Jerome wrote: "[A]s the Lord's flesh is true food and his blood is true drink, on an anagogical level, all the good we have in the present age is to feed on his flesh and drink his blood, not just at the sacrament but also in our reading of the scriptures."[1123]

Christians held a basic and simple liturgy in the early days of a persecuted church. However, in the fourth century when Christians could practice openly the church needed to impart the mystery of the liturgy to Catechumens.[1124] Essentially, the early church fathers saw baptism and Eucharist and then the liturgy altogether as a Whole. Similarly, their interpretation of the Scriptures and the liturgy had the common denominator of Jesus, the Risen Christ.[1125] The early church fathers applied the typological method of exegetical approach to both Scripture and Liturgy. Typology was comprehending the events and people (typoi) of the Old Testament as "anticipating and prefiguring the mystery of Christ."[1126] According to Jean Danielou, he wrote: "The application of this [typological] method to Scripture is called spiritual exegesis. When it is applied to liturgy it is called mystagogy."[1127]

The liturgy actually reflects gestures carried out by Jesus as well as a moral teaching which prefigures an eschatological reality. According to Cyril of Jerusalem, he wrote: "[T]his Chrism is prefigured in the Old Testament. When Moses conferring on his brother the divine appointment. Was ordering him high priest, he anointed him after he had bathed in water, and from that point he was called 'Christ' ('anointed'), clearly after the figurative Chrism... But what was done to [him) in figure was done to you, not in figure but in truth, because salvation began from Him who was anointed by the Holy Spirit in truth."[1128]

John Chrysostom in his baptismal catechesis wrote: "It is not only the priest who touches the head, but also the right hand of Christ, and this is shown by the very word of the one baptizing. He does not say: 'I baptize so-and-so' but: 'so-and-so is baptized' showing that he is only the minister of grace of and merely offers his hand because he has been ordained to this end by the Spirit. The one fulfilling all things is the Father and the Son and the Holy Spirit, the undivided trinity."[1129]

In the Scripture, there is a spiritual meaning underneath and within the graphé, human writing and analogously in the liturgy there is a hidden spiritual meaning within the érgon, the human action, or rite.[1130] This calls for a deeper exploration and understanding. Not only is mystagogy a basic initiation into liturgy but rather an understanding of the single mystery in both Scriptureand liturgy, namely the mystery of Christ.[1131] Cum Scriptura and sub-Scriptura the liturgy had its own unique way and thus it is quintessential of communicating the mystery of Christ.[1132] The leitourghia, communal prayer, is ergon, an action. Thus, the knowledge offered via the liturgy is not wholly intellectual. Rather, it requires a full investment of a person's faculties.[1133] One takes in information via the senses which is a conduit to meaning.[1134] Certainly, there is no true liturgical life without a knowledge of the mystery which is celebrated in the liturgy. Moreover, there is no real liturgy without mystagogy.[1135]

"Thus, when you have entered the land whichthe Lord will give you as he promised, you must observe this rite. When your children ask you, "What does this rite of yours mean?" You will reply, "It is the Passover sacrifice for the Lord, who passed over the houses of the Israelites in Egypt; when he struck down the Egyptians, he delivered our houses."[1136] (Exod 12:25-27, NABRE) Essentially, the question of what does this rite means is important, since recalling its meaning protects the rite from the risk of falling outside of human history. Thus, the loss of the historicity of the action of God is precarious. Just as it is dangerous if the liturgical rite is performed with a lack of knowledge of what it means.[1137] In fact, the liturgical rite could not be more historic since it contains the entire mystery of Jesus, the Risen Christ.

Basically, the catechumens and neophytes posed a similar question to the early church fathers. Their response included the events of salvation traced from the Old and New Testaments correlated in every single liturgical action. During the Last Supper, Jesus carried out the gesture that a slave would for his master, that is washing the feet of His disciples. Afterwards, Jesus states, "Do you realize what I have done for you?" (John 13:12, NABRE).[1138] However, Jesus becomes the exegete and the mystagogue and states: «If I, there-fore, the master and teacher, have washed your feet, you ought to wash one another›s feet.» (John :13 14, NABRE).[1139]

The whole mystery of Jesus, the Christ can be found in the Eucharistic gesture of the "breaking of the bread" and "handing over of the cup". However, this is true of the washing of the feet. Thus, it is vital to comprehend this gesture, and it is meaning in order to understand Jesus Christ, Lord and Savior.[1140] Mystagogy is much more than a method or various methods. It is the way one knows what Jesus does now for His church in the liturgy.[1141] Thus, it is a knowing of Christ via the liturgy since Christ Himself is the principle of knowledge and interpretation of the liturgy because Christ is the one and only true mystagogue of His mystery. The priest and Church perform mystagogy thus becoming a servant of Christ the mystagogue and this makes the Christian an epóptes, an eyewitness of this mystery.[1142]" Then mystagogy means com-prehending this mystery narrated via Scriptures and certainly celebrated in the liturgy. Mystagogy, the spiritual exegesis of the liturgy provides spiritual understanding of Christ in the same way as the spiritual exegesis of the Scriptures.[1143] The principle of Jerome: Ignoratio Scripturarum, Ignoratio Christi est ("Ignorance of the Scriptures is ignorance of Christ") is analogous to Ignoratio liturgiae, ignoration Christi est ("Ignorance of the meaning of the liturgy is ignorance of Christ").[1144]

Clement of Alexandria wrote: "For he who is still blind ad dumb, not having understanding, or the undazzled and keen vision of the contemplative soul, which the Savior confers, like the uninitiated (amýeteon) at the mysteries, or the unmusical at danus, not being yet pure and worthy of the pure truth, but still discordant and disordered and material, must stand outside of the divine choir.[1145]

CHAPTER III

DESIGN OF THE STUDY

This study was exploratory in nature. Perhaps, it is the only known empirical study of its type germane to RCIA. The fundamental goal was to examine demographic and motivational factors which predict success in RCIA in an urban setting. A survey approach was selected for a more broadly representative answer to questions in order to tell the full story of candidates/catechumen's experience in RCIA. Thus, there exists descriptive data as well as vitally important inferential statistical analysis in this study. Although the researcher utilized three different church groups in the state of Connecticut to randomly distribute surveys to completers or neophytes of RCIA, only twenty participants responded to the survey request.

This study may be defined as double-blind since the researcher was not present during the distribution and administration of the survey instrument. RCIA coordinators at three different sites collected data at their respective meeting places. Essentially, participants had completed a paper and pencil or pen survey during its administration. RCIA coordinators promptly and personally collected surveys immediately after participants had finished their respective survey. The construction of the survey items was designed and tested for reliability using co-efficient alpha (cronback) by the researcher who has a graduate degree in measurement under the tutelage of his thesis supervisor, an expert survey administrator. The present study focused on completers or neophytes of RCIA. Success was defined by a candidate receiving sacraments and remaining a practicing Catholic. An urban area in Connecticut was utilized by researchers for observation of the entire RCIA process for a four-year period. This included weekly meetings held on Sundays, listening to the teachings of catechists to catechumens/candidates, serving as a temporary sponsor, and attending the Easter Vigil Mass directing observing the rite being administered.

The population of this group was mainly Hispanic. A small pilot study was conducted at a different church in this urban environment for the purpose of constructing a reliable and valid survey instrument written in English and Spanish for the purpose of this study. A student -test was utilized to analyze demographic data while a Pearson Chi Square test was performed for motivating reasons. This non-parametrical test (Chisquare) is appropriate for nominal scale measurement with the power of the test measured by a phi coefficient (Ø).

RESEARCH HYPOTHESES:

The following hypotheses are stated in the null form:

Ho[1]   There are no statistically significant differences between the various ethnic groups represented in this study with respect to those participants who have completed RCIA.

Ho[2]   There are no statistically significant differences between the socio-economic level of participants represented in this study with respect to those individuals who have completed RCIA.

Ho[3]   There are no statistically significant differences between the participants levels of formal education in this study with respect to those individuals who have completed RCIA.

Hot[4]   There are no statistically significant differences between the age group of participants represented in this study with respect to those individuals who have completed RCIA.

Ho[5]   There are no statistically significant differences between those participants who felt fulfilled Spiritually as a result of experiencing RCIA with respect to those individuals who have completed RCIA

Ho[6]   There are no statistically significant differences between those participants who had a person in one's life who influenced one to enter RCIA and those who did not have such a person with respect to those individuals who have completed RCIA.

Ho[7]   There are no statistically significant differences between those participants who had a person in one's life that helped one remain and complete RCIA and those who did not have such a person.

CHAPTER IV

PRESENTATION AND ANALYSIS OF FINDINGS

Statistical Analysis germane to descriptive data include the following: (1) eight males, twelve females responded to the RCIA survey, (2) there were seventeen Hispanics and three whites in the sample, (3) the mean level of education was 10.9 grade (10.9) with a standard deviation of 2.67 (SD = 2.67) (4) the mean annual income was 21,677.95 dollars (21677.95) with a standard deviation of 22,915.11 (S.D. 22915.11(, (5) the mean age was forty-eight years (47.65) with a standard deviation of seventeen years (S.D. = 16.61), (5) at least one parent of neophyte attended church was fourteen out of twenty for seventy per-cent, (6) the religious affiliation of neophytes prior to RCIA was thirteen out of twenty were Catholics for sixty-five percent while the remaining seven neophytes did not affiliate with any religion, and finally (7) fourteen of the neophytes or seventy percent were single, three married or fifteen percent, two living together or ten percent, and one divorced or 0.5 percent of the sample.

Inferential Statistical analysis via non parametrical methods, namely a Pearson Chi Square indicated (x^2 (7) = 42.8, p < 0.01) statistical significance at the alpha .01 level with an effect size or power of 0.517 (Phi coefficient Q = 0.517) which falls within a medium to high or large effect for motivating reasons. Finally, a student -test was performed for demographic variables. The highest grade completed in school or education revealed a statistically significant of 18.233 ((19) = 18.233 p < 0.01) at the alpha level of .01.

The annual income revealed a statistically significant of 4.231((19) = 4.231, p <.01) at the alpha level of .01. The age of the neophyte at the time of the administration of the RCIA survey revealed a statistically significant of 12.831 ((19) = 12.831, p<.01) at the alpha level of .01. Thus, the demographic factors of education, age, and annual income demonstrated statistically significant differences. This statistical analysis of findings for motivating reasons indicates the hypothesis decision making of failing to retain (or accepting) the fifth, sixth, and seventh hypothesis. Thus, failing to retain these hypotheses in the null form has a type I error of .01.

All statistical analyses were processed by SPSS 21.0 for windows and the researcher's calculations by pen and paper. Since the comparison between variables was planned, the student- test was utilized in the analysis of demographic factors. It is important to note that the student - test is typically regarded as the most robust inferential test in this branch of mathematics. Since surveys were randomly assigned to participants, the normal distribution may be assumed. Moreover, the survey instrument was analyzed by use of coefficient or Cronbach's alpha as a measure of internal consistency of survey items Germane to motivating reasons. Thus, the coefficient alpha was 0.984.

Then, these items in an index are measuring similar domains. One may conclude that survey instruments were mathematically tested as reliable. This instrument was reliable and valid for the purpose of the study. In conclusion, the second, third, and fourth hypotheses written in the null form would render the decision to fail to retain these null hypotheses at the 0.01 alpha level which indicates a type I (one) error of 0.01 (seeing too much in the data). Furthermore, the researcher acknowledges that Hispanics are mostly or perhaps overly represented in this study. Thus, the researcher is reluctant to accept the first hypothesis. Therefore, quantitative analysis of the data suggests that a relationship exists in the second, third, fourth, fifth, sixth, and seventh hypotheses.

The researcher is of the belief that an effect was produced in this study. Nonetheless, the fact that a relatively small sample size of twenty lends caution in the interpretation of these findings. Certainly, a student t-test's robustness exists even with an n (sample size) of six. This attests to the appropriateness of its usage in examining this data.

Finally, the use of the Pearson Chi Square, a nonparametric test, was appropriate since the data examined for motivating reasons was nominal (categorical). The Phi coefficient (0) which is a correlation between dichotomous variables was used as a measure of effect size indicated a medium to large effect. Therefore, it seems that the most appropriate form of confirmatory analysis is the replication of this study.

DESCRIPTIVE STATISTICS

	N	Range	Minimum	Maximum	Mean	Mean
	Statistic	Statistic	Statistic	Statistic	Statistic	Std. Error
Male	1	0	8	8	8.00	
Female	1	.00	12.00	12.00	12.0000	
Black	1	.00	.00	.00	.0000	
Hispanic	1	.00	17.00	17.00	17.0000	
White	1	.00	3.00	3.00	3.0000	
Education	20	10.00	6.00	16.00	10.9000	.59780
Annual Income	20	80000	.00	80000.00	21677.9500	5123.97421
Parent Affiliation	1	.00	14.00	14.00	14.0000	
Religious Affiliation	0	.00				
Age	20	53.00	24.00	77.00	47.6500	3.71361
Married	1	.00	3.00	3.00	3.0000	
Single	1	.00	14.00	14.00	14.0000	
Divorced	1	.00	1.00	1.00	1.0000	
Living Together	1	.00	2.00	2.00	2.0000	
Parent not attending church	1	.00	6.00	6.00	6.0000	

ONE - SAMPLE STATISTICS

	N	Mean	Std. Deviation	Std. Error Mean
Male	1[a]	8.00		
Female	1[a]	12.0000		
Black	1[a]	.0000		
Hispanic	1[a]	17.0000		
White	1[a]	3.0000		
Education	20	10.9000	2.67346	.59780
Annual income	20	21677.9500	22915.10928	5123.97421
Parent affiliation	1[a]	14.0000		
Religious affiliation	0[a, b]			
Age	20	47.6500	16.60778	3.71361
Married	1[a]	3.0000		
Single	1[a]	14.0000		
Divorced	1[a]	1.0000		
Living together	1[a]	2.0000		
Parents not attending church	1[a]	6.0000		
Catholic	0[a]			
No religious	[b]0[a, b]			

STUDENT - TEST

	#	df	Slg.(2 tailed)	Mean Difference	95% confidence Interval of the difference	
					Lower	Upper
Education	18.233	19	.000	10.90000	9.6488	12.1512
Annual Income	4.231	19	.000	21677.95000	10953.3487	32402.5513
Age	12.831	19	.000	47.65000	39.8773	55.4227

DESCRIPTIVE STATISTICS

	N	Range	Minimum	Maximum	Mean	Mean
	Statistic	Statistic	Statistic	Statistic	Statistic	Std. Error
YDM	1	.00	15.00	15.00	15.0000	
NDM	1	.00	5.00	5.00	5.0000	
PIYES	1	.00	15.00	15.00	15.0000	
PINO	1	.00	5.00	5.00	5.0000	
PCYES	1	.00	16.00	16.00	16.0000	
PCNO	1	.00	4.00	4.00	4.0000	
PRYES	1	.00	19.00	19.00	19.0000	
PRNO	1	.00	1.00	1.00	1.0000	
FSYES	1	.00	20.00	20.00	20.0000	
FSNO	1	.00	.00	.00	.0000	
GMYES	1	.00	20.00	20.00	20.0000	
GMNO	1	.00	.00	.00	.0000	
TTYES	1	.00	20.00	20.00	20.0000	
TINO	1	.00	.00	.00	.0000	
CMYES	1	.00	14.00	14.00	14.0000	
CMNO	1	.00	6.00	6.00	6.0000	
RACE	0					
SEX	0					
MALE	1	.00	8.00	8.00	8.0000	
FEMALE	1	.00	12.00	12.00	12.0000	
WHITE	1	.00	3.00	3.00	3.0000	
HISPANIC	1	.00	17.00	17.00	17.0000	
BLACK	1	.00	.00	.00	.0000	
NO RELIGION	1	.00	7.00	7.00	7.0000	
MARRIED	1	.00	3.00	3.00	3.0000	
SINGLE	1	.00	14.00	14.00	14.0000	
DIVORCED	1	.00	1.00	1.00	1.0000	
SEPARATED	1	.00	.00	.00	.0000	
LIVING TOGETHER	1	.00	2.00	2.00	2.0000	
CATHOLIC	1	.00	13.00	13.00	13.0000	
PARENTS ATTEND CHURCH	1	.00	14.00	14.00	14.0000	
NOT ATTEND CHURCH	1	.00	6.00	6.00	6.0000	
Valid N (listwise)	0	.00				

STATISTICS

	YDM	NDM	PIYES	PINO	PCYES	PCNO	PRYES
N Valid	1	1	1	1	1	1	1
Missing	0	0	0	0	0	0	0
Mean	15.0000	5.0000	15.0000	5.0000	16.0000	4.0000	19.0000
Median	15.0000	5.0000	15.0000	5.0000	16.0000	4.0000	19.0000
Mode	15.00	5.00	15.00	5.00	16.00	4.00	19.00
Range	.00	.00	.00	.00	.00	.00	.00
Minimum	15.00	5.00	15.00	5.00	16.00	4.00	19.00
Maximum	15.00	5.00	15.00	5.00	16.00	4.00	19.00
Sum	15.00	5.00	15.00	5.00	16.00	4.00	19.00

STATISTICS

	PRNO	FSYES	FSNO	GMYES	GMNO	TTYES	TTNO
N Valid	1	1	1	1	1	1	1
Missing	0	0	0	0	0	0	0
Mean	1.0000	20.0000	.0000	20.0000	.0000	20.0000	.0000
Median	1.0000	20.0000	.0000	20.0000	.0000	20.0000	.0000
Mode	1.00	20.00	.00	20.00	.00	20.00	.00
Range	.00	.00	.00	.00	.00	.00	.00
Minimum	1.00	20.00	.00	20.00	.00	20.00	.00
Maximum	1.00	20.00	.00	20.00	.00	20.00	.00
Sum	1.00	20.00	.00	20.00	.00	20.00	.00

STATISTICS

	CMYES	CMNO	MALES	FEMALE	WHITE	HISPANIC	BLACK
N Valid	1	1	1	1	1	1	1
Missing	0	0	0	0	0	0	0
Mean	14.0000	6.0000	8.0000	12.0000	3.0000	17.0000	.0000
Median	14.0000	6.0000	8.0000	12.0000	3.0000	17.0000	.0000
Mode	14.00	6.00	8.00	12.00	3.00	17.00	.00
Range	.00	.00	.00	.00	.00	.00	.00
Minimum	14.00	6.00	8.00	12.00	3.00	17.00	.00
Maximum	14.00	6.00	8.00	12.00	3.00	17.00	.00
Sum	14.00	6.00	8.00	12.00	3.00	17.00	.00

STATISTICS

	AGE	NO RELIGION	MARRIED	SINGLE	DIVORCED	SPEARATED
N Valid	1	1	1	1	1	1
Missing	0	0	0	0	0	0
Mean	14.0000	6.0000	8.0000	12.0000	3.0000	17.0000
Median	14.0000	6.0000	8.0000	12.0000	3.0000	17.0000
Mode	14.00	6.00	8.00	12.00	3.00	17.00
Range	.00	.00	.00	.00	.00	.00
Minimum	14.00	6.00	8.00	12.00	3.00	17.00
Maximum	14.00	6.00	8.00	12.00	3.00	17.00
Sum	14.00	6.00	8.00	12.00	3.00	17.00

STATISTICS

	LIVING TOGETHER	CATHOLIC	PARENT ATTEND CHURCH	NOT ATTEND CHURCH
N Valid	1	1	1	1
Missing	0	0	0	0
Mean	2.0000	13.0000	14.0000	6.0000
Median	2.0000	13.0000	14.0000	6.0000
Mode	2.00	13.00	14.00	6.00
Range	.00	.00	.00	.00
Minimum	2.00	13.00	14.00	6.00
Maximum	2.00	13.00	14.00	6.00
Sum	2.00	13.00	14.00	6.00

DESCRIPTIVE STATISTICS

	N	MINIMUM	MAXIMUM	MEAN	STD. DEVIATION
DM	2	5.00	15.00	10.0000	7.07107
PI	2	5.00	15.00	10.0000	7.07107
PC	2	4.00	16.00	10.0000	8.48528
PR	2	1.00	19.00	10.0000	12.72792
FS	2	.00	20.00	10.0000	14.14214
GM	2	.00	20.00	10.0000	14.14214
TT	2	.00	20.00	10.0000	14.14214
CM	2	6.00	14.00	10.0000	5.65685
Valid N (listwise)	2				

RELIABILITY STATISTICS: COEFFICIENT ALPHA

Cronbach's Alpha	N of Items
984	8

MOTIVATING REASONS: FREQUENCIES

1. Discover RCIA from a member of the Church...

   Yes ||||| ||||| ||||| No |||||

      15 (75%)   5 (25%)

2. Particular Person who influenced you...

   Yes ||||| ||||| ||||| No |||||

      15 (75%)   5 (25%)

3. Particular Person who helped you remain/complete...

   Yes ||||| ||||| ||||| No ||||

      16 (80%)   4 (20%)

4. Primary Reason for entering RCIA...

   Yes ||||| ||||| ||||||||| No |

      19 (95%)   1 (5%)

5. Fulfilled Spiritually as a result of RCIA...

   Yes ||||| ||||| ||||||||| No

      20 (100%)   0

6. Group meetings in RCIA were beneficial...

   Yes ||||| ||||| ||||||||| No

      20 (100%)   0

7. Teaching and topics of discussion were relevant...

   Yes ||||| ||||| ||||||||| No

      20 (100%)   0

8. Continue Meeting with your RCIA group...

   Yes ||||| ||||| ||||||||| No

      14 (70%)   6 (30%)

	DM	PI	PC	PR	FS	GM	TT	CM	Total:
Yes	17.375	17.375	17.375	17.37	17.375	17.375	17.375	17.375	139
No	2.625	2.625	2.625	2.625	2.625	2.625	2.625	2.625	21
									160

$$x^2 = \frac{(15-17.375)^2}{17.375} + \frac{(5-2.625)^2}{2.625} + \frac{(15-17.375)^2}{17.375} + \frac{(5-2.625)^2}{2.625} + \frac{(16-17.371)^2}{17.371} +$$

[22.4496] [2.1488] [22.4496] [2.1488] [0

$$\frac{(4-2.625)^2}{2.625} + \frac{(19-17.375)^2}{17.375} + \frac{(1-2.625)^2}{2.625} + \frac{(20-17.371)^2}{17.371} + \frac{(0-2.625)^2}{2.625} +$$

[0.7202] [0.1520] [1.0060] [0.3966] [2.

$$\frac{(20-17.375)^2}{17.375} + \frac{(0-2.625)^2}{2.625} + \frac{(20-17.375)^2}{17.375} + \frac{(0-2.625)^2}{2.625} +$$

[0.3966] [2.625] [0.3966] [2.625]

$$\frac{(14-17.375)^2}{17.375} + \frac{(6-2.625)^2}{2.625} = 42.7939$$

[0.6556] [4.3393

	DM	PI	PC	PR	FS	GM	TT	CM	Total:
Yes	15	15	16	19	20	20	20	14	139
No	5	5	4	1	0	0	0	6	21
Total	20	20	20	20	20	20	20	20	160

$$f(E) = \frac{(139)(20)}{160} = \frac{2780}{160} = 17.375$$

$$f(E) = \frac{(21)(20)}{160} = \frac{420}{160} = 2.625$$

$$x^2 = \sum \frac{(fo - fE)^2}{fE}$$

*H*0: Response distributions for all treatment
(Null) Populations are equal.
*H*1: Not all of these response distributions
are equal.
df= (columns - 1) (rows -1)
df= (8-1)(2-1)=(7)(1)=7
df= 7, α=.05, x2=42.7939 = 42.8

Since the obtained x2 of 42.8 is greater than the critical value of x2 of 14.07, there is a significant statistical difference...

$$x^2{}_{obt} = 42.8, \propto = .05, x^2{}_{crit} = 14.07$$

$$x^2{}_{obt} = 42.8, \propto = .01, x^2{}_{crit} = 18.48$$

$$x^2(7) = 42.8, * p < .01$$

$$\text{Phi coefficient} = \sqrt{\frac{x^2}{N}}$$

$$\phi = \sqrt{\frac{42.79}{160}} = \sqrt{0.2674375} = 0.51714359707$$

A "medium to large" effect is produced by a ϕ > (phi coefficient) of 0.5171.

CHAPTER V

SUMMARY, CONCLUSIONS, AND RECOMMENDATIONS

My experience with the Rite of Christian Initiation of Adults with the Sacred Heart Church in Waterbury, Connecticut for over four years was very special. It was the largest number of catechumens and candidates in one place in the state of Connecticut. Following this group on a weekly basis including an RCIA retreat provided unique insight into how RCIA functions. The Sacred Heart RCIA made an important decision during this weekend retreat. They decided to become a full year catechumenate. The researcher who attended this retreat concurs with this decision. The researcher firmly believes that a candidate or catechumen must progress at one's own pace. RCIA is not really a program but rather a complex process. Certainly, a curriculum exists with catechists who differentiate instruction. However, each individual makes a unique journey in spiritual growth. In fact, one finds the true identity in one's walk with Our Lord Jesus, the Christ. This I-Thou relationship occurs in one's heart which encompasses thoughts and feelings in recognition of Jesus speaking to one's spirit. Certainly, an inner peace is present.

A certain state of conversion, a metanoia requires a surrender rather than a "fight or flight" response. When one enters more deeply into a per-sonal relationship with Jesus, one finds one's true self. Some people will initially resist by fighting it or running away which are defense mechanisms. Thus, it is a special and unique walk with different people taking varying paths at their own rate and fashion. RCIA allots for this timetable in the longer catechumenate format. Some people may progress faster and attain their sacraments sooner than others. Most importantly, one must find Jesus in one's life the Church has evolved over two thousand years and much change has happened in various ways.

However, the fundamental modification is allowing the Holy Spirit to permeate oneself. This is the constant of the ages. Jesus, the mystagogue, reaching one at the proper time. Thus, the achievement of the sacraments, the mysteries, is not an end in itself. The follow up which is the weakness of RCIA needs to be mended. Some RCIA groups are better than others in this follow up process. The researcher has observed the pastor or priest personally in-volved in this process in one group. Lay people who direct the process must be attentive to this follow up component.

The researcher found a group who is particularly good at recruiting former catechumens into sponsors and godparents. Moreover, a former catechumen has become a catechist. The researcher has found that the key to success is to create the appropriate atmosphere for growth to occur. RCIA coordinators must maintain a loving and welcoming environment. However, it is the parish family as a whole which must make an effort to promote such an environment. In the climate of the closing of some churches this will present more challenges. However, it is crucial that parishioners fully embrace the RCIA process. It is a team approach involving priests and lay people for the RCIA to function properly.

"God is in us, because we are in Christ. As members of the mystical body, Christians actually partake in the divine nature of The Trinity. We do not merely watch the dance; we dance the dance. We join hands with Christ and the Spirit flows through us and between us and our feet move always in the loving embrace of the Father. In that we are members of the mystical body of Christ, we see the joyful love of the Father through the eyes of the son. And with every breath, we breath the Holy Spirit."[1146]

"It takes one person to be an individual. It takes two people to make a couple. And it takes at least three people to make a community I like to use the English word "trey", derived from the French word "trei" meaning "three," as a simple, short memorable word for the "threesome" that creates an exponential explosion in potential - not only in the quantity, but also the quality of relationships creates the possibility for people to go beyond personal interest. It is, they say, the beginning of a sense of common cause a collective purpose - beyond what suits individual interests. A trey creates the stability and security that is essential for community because the ultimate reality if the universe depicted in the Trinity is a community of persons in relation to one another, we know the trey is the only way it is possible for people to relate to one another with the individuality of one, the reciprocity of two, and the stability, subjectivity, and objectivity of three."[1147]

The Rite of Christian Initiation of Adults (RCIA) has recently been referred to as The Order of Christian Initiation of Adults. It means that there is a bond which exists between those who have experienced a conversion via Jesus, the Christ. Therefore, the convert has an association with those who had a shared experience in seeking and finding Jesus. A personal relationship with Jesus emerges as a fresh new beginning via the Holy Cross. The vertical aspect of the cross is germane to the convert and his personal Lord and Savior. However, the horizontal shared experience of our Lord and Savior extends via the horizontal arm of the cross to an order or community of believers in a unique and special fashion. Essentially, this semantic usage of The Order of The Christian Initiation of Adults (OCIA) conveys this horizontal arm of the cross to those converts with a shared experience of being saved by the ultimate and boundless mercy and love of our Lord and Savior Jesus, the Christ.

RECOMMENDATIONS

The following recommendations are offered for future research and practice in RCIA.

1. Replication of this study with a large sample size is essential in substantiating the findings in regard to an analysis of demographic and motivational factors which predict success in completing the Rite of Christian Initiation of adults (RCIA) in an urban area.

2. An empirical investigation should be conducted comparing a half year catechumenate with a full year catechumenate.

3. In terms of practice, a training program for sponsors would be prudent in order to prevent catechumens from dropping out in the initial or early phase of RCIA.

4. In terms of practice, the entire faith community must be supportive to the RCIA process.

5. Finally, a better record keeping system for monitoring and tracking completers of RCIA must be implemented.

CONFIDENTIAL RCIA SURVEY

This survey is composed of two parts.
Part I is designed to collect demographic data. Answers provided by you will be strictly confidential.
Part II contains questions germane to your decision to enroll in RCIA.

Part I. Demographic Data
Please answer each statement by placing a circle around your choice and/or filling your response in the appropriate space.

Gender: Male/Female

Date of Birth: _____

Highest grade completed in school: _____

Ethnic Background: _____

Religious affiliation prior to RCIA: _____

If none, please state so on the line provided.

Marital Status: ☐ Single ☐ Married ☐ Divorced ☐ Separated
                    ☐ Living with partner (not married)

Number of Dependents: _____

Annual Income (approximate): _____

Please describe your family when you were growing up:
☐ Both parents were in the house
☐ Mother only was in the house
☐ Father only was in the house
☐ Other _____

Did at least one parent attend Church? ☐ Yes ☐ No

Part II: Motivating Reasons
Directions: Please circle either "yes" or "no" for each question listed below. Please briefly explain your response to each question on the space provided.

1.   How did you learn about the RCIA? Did you discover RCIA from a member of the Church?

               YES   NO

Please explain:

_____

_____

2.   Was there a particular person in your life who influenced you to enter RCIA?

               YES   NO

Please explain:

_____

_____

3.   Was there a particular person in your life who helped you remain and complete RCIA?

               YES   NO

Please explain:

_____

_____

4.   Please circle the response which most closely indicates your primary reason for entering RCIA?
      a) Found God in my life.
      b) Needed to participated in order to marry in the church.
      c) Wanted to learn more about the Catholic Faith.
      d) Other.

Please explain:

_____

_____

5.   Do you feel fulfilled spiritually as a result of participating in RCIA?

               YES   NO

Please explain:

_____

_____

_____

6.   Do you feel that the group meetings in RCIA were beneficial to you?
          YES   NO

Please explain:

_____

_____

_____

7.   Do you believe that the teachings and topics of discussion were relevant to your life?
          YES   NO

Please explain:

_____

_____

_____

8.   Would you have liked to continue meeting with your group or participate in another group connected with RCIA after completion of the Postbaptismal Catechesis or Mystagogy?
          YES   NO

If you indicated YES, then indicate which type of group or if Mystagogy is continuing, please describe your experience.

_____

_____

_____

ENCUESTA CONFIDENCIAL DE RCIA

Éste questionario está compuesto de dos partes.

La Primera parte está designada a colectar información demográfica. Las respuestas proporcionadas por usted seran estrictamente confidenciales,

La Segunda parte contiene preguntas relacionadas en su decisión de inscribirse en RCIA.

Parte I. Datos Demográficos.
Favor de contestar cada pregunta circulando su elección y/o brevemente explicando su respuesta en el espacio proporcionado.

Género: Masculino / Femenino

Fecha de Nacimiento: _____

Nivel más alto completado en la escuela: _____

Origen étnico: _____

Afiliación Religiosa anterior a RCIA: _____
En caso de no tener, favor de decirlo en la linea proveida.

Estado civil: ❏Soltero(a) ❏Casado(a) ❏ Divorciado(a) ❏ Separado(a)
❏Viviéndo en unión libre [no casado(a)}

Número de dependientes: _____

Ingreso anual (aproximadamente): _____

Favor de describir su familia durante su crianza:
❏ Vivia con ambos padres.
❏ Vivia con la Madre solamente.
❏ Vivia con el Padre solamente.
❏ Otro: _____
Almenós undo de sus padres asistia a la iglesia? ❏ Si ❏ No

Parte II. Razónes de motivación.
Instrucciones: Favor de circular cualquiera de las dos respuestas (Si/No) por cada pregunta en la lista. Favor de explicar brevemente su contestación en el espacio proporcionado.

1) Como usted se entero acerca del programa de RCIA? Descubrio usted RCIA por medio de un miembro de la iglesia?
                 SI   NO

Favor de explicar:

_____

_____

_____

2) Hubo en su vida una persona en particular que influyo en su entrada al RCIA?
                 SI   NO
Favor de explicar:

_____

_____

_____

3) Hubo una persona en su vida que la ayudo a permanecer y completar RCIA?
                 SI   NO

Favor de explicar:

_____

_____

_____

4) Favor de circular la respuesta que mas claramente indique la razón por la que ingreso a RCIA?
a) Encontre a Dios en mi vida.
b) Necesite participar para poder casarme por la iglesia.
c) Queria aprender mas hacerca de la fé Catholica.
d) Otra Razón: _____

Favor de explicar:

_____

_____

_____

5) Usted se siente lleno espiritualmente como resultado de la participacion en RCIA?
                 SI   NO

Favor de explicar:

_____

_____

_____

6) Usted siente que las juntas del grupo en el Rito de Initiation Cristiana de Adultos (RCIA) le beneficiaron a usted?

SI   NO

Favor de explicar:

_____

_____

_____

7) Usted cree que las ensenanzas y temas de discucion fueron relevantes en su vida?

SI   NO

Favor de explicar:

_____

_____

_____

8) Le hubiese gustado continuar con las juntas con su grupo o participar en otro grupo conectado con RCIA despues de completar la Cathequesis postbautismal o Mystagogy?

SI   NO

Si usted indico que si; que tipo de grupo o si la Mystagogy continua favor dedescribirsuexperiencia:

Favor de explicar:

_____

_____

_____

¿Qué es el Rito de Iniciación Cristiana de Adultos?

El Rito de la Iniciación Cristiana de Adultos (RCIA) es el proceso donde los adultos se preparan para recibir los sacramentos de bautismo, Eucaristía (comunión) y confirmación.

¿Y si no soy Católico? El RCIA te ayudará a ser un miembro de la iglesia Católica. Tú recibirás los sacramentos dentro de este programa.

¿Quién puede participar? (1) Los Católicos de 18 años de edad en adelante, quienes son bautizados, pero no recibieron los sacramentos de la Eucaristía ni la confirmación y (2) los personas que no son Católicos y no son bautizados.

¿Cuánto tiempo dura este proceso? Normalmente, este proceso dura dos años, pero este año, Sagrado Corazón tomará 6 meses para terminar las clases.

¿Cuándo empiezan las clases y a qué horas son las clases? Las clases, en este año, empiezan el día 4 de septiembre y empiezan a las 10:00 en la mañana, hasta a las 11:30 cada domingo, después de la misa de 9:00. Las clases se llevarán a cabo abajo en la escuela, en el sótano de la escuela.

¿Tienen cuidado para los niños (daycare)? Sí

¿Cuándo voy a recibir mis sacramentos? Normalmente, vas a recibir los sacramentos el día de Sábado de Gloria (el día antes de la Pascua).

¿Necesito llegar a la clase cada domingo y por qué necesito tomar estas clases? Sí. La iglesia quiere saber si realmente tú estás preparado para recibir los sacramentos.

¿Necesito hacer mis sacramentos en este programa para ser madrina o padrino? Sí.

¿Cómo puedo matricularme para el RCIA? Tú puedes llamar los coordinadores de RCIA, Dina o Xiomara Pantoni al 759-0586 o 982-8176.

Year-Round Catechumenal Process—model used at St. Joseph's Catholic Church Modesto, CA

How Long?

General guidelines of time required for adequate formation and delivery of the Deposit of Faith.

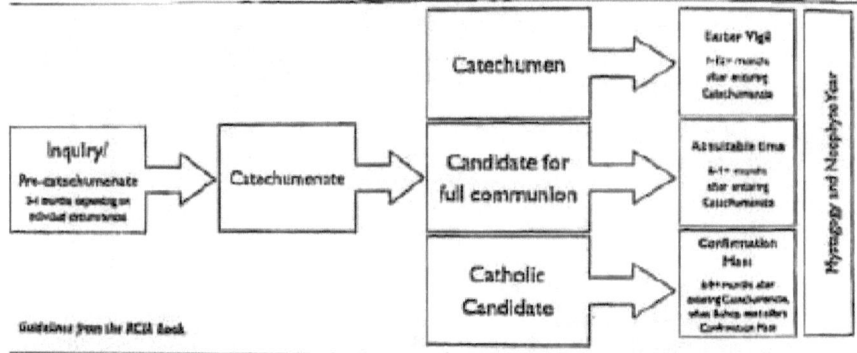

Guidelines from the RCIA Book.

Signs of conversion—readiness for the Rite of Acceptance (or Rite of Welcoming)
Unbaptized—(n.41) "The prerequisite for making this first step is that the beginnings of the spiritual life and the fundamentals of Christian teaching have taken root in the candidates."
Baptized, uncatechized—(n.103) "A program of training, catechesis suited to their needs, contact with the community of the faithful, and participation in certain liturgical rites are needed in order to strengthen them in the Christian life."
Baptized, Catechized, see Catholic—(n.477) "The baptized Christian is to receive both doctrinal and spiritual preparation, adapted to the individual pastoral requirements, for reception into the full communion of the Catholic Church. The candidate should learn to deepen an inner adherence to the Church, where he or she will find the fullness of his or her baptism."

Length of Catechumenate Period
Unbaptized—(Ap. 3l, n.6) "The period of the catechumenate... should extend for at least one year of formation... from at least the Easter season of one year until the next, preferably it should begin before Lent in one year and extend until Easter of the following year..." (n.76) "It may even last several years if necessary."

Minor Rites	When in the Process	When In the Liturgical year	Initiates What?
Celebrations of the Word	Catechumenate/Purification/Mystagogy	Ordinary Time/Lent/Easter Season	Forming/ Purifying Strengthening/
Minor Exorcisms	Catechumenate	anytime	Need for God's help
Blessings of Catechumens	Catechumenate	anytime	Courage, Joy, Peace
Anointing (unbaptized only)	Catechumenate	anytime	Need for God's help
Presentations Creed Lord's Prayer	Catechumenate or Purification/Enl	Lent or Ordinary Time after Christmas	Understanding heart of Church's faith and prayer
Penitential Rite (baptized only)	Purification/Enlightenment	Second Sunday of Lent	Preparation for Reconciliation
Scrutinies (unbaptized only)	Purification/Enlightenment	3rd, 4th, 5th Sundays of Lent (use Cycle A readings)	Self-searching/ repentance
Recitation of Creed	Purification/Enlightenment	Holy Saturday morning/afternoon	Preparation for Vigil

INFORMED CONSENT

I would like you to participate in a research study titled, "An Analysis of Demographic and Motivational Factors which Predict Success in Completing the Rite of Christian Initiation of adults in Selected Areas of the Northeast".

My definition of success includes remaining a practicing Catholic. Cer-tainly, the importance of this study is multifaceted. Essentially, there is little or no tracking of those who have completed the RCIA. Informal inquires with Pastors, Priests and RCIA Coordinators have concurred with this notion.

Therefore, I am seeking to further explore both demographic and motivational factors germane to follow up of these completers of RCIA. If you decide to participate in this study, your involvement will take no more than twenty minutes of your time. Your participation is completely voluntary, and you are free to refuse or stop at any time in the process of taking this RCIA Confidential survey.

All information will be number-coded and strictly confidential. Statistical analysis is for group data. You are not required to provide your name on this survey. Should you have any further questions, please feel free to contact me.

Cell phone (203) 228-4912

E-mail:
Aucella Laurence@hotmail.com
lfaphd@aol.com

Thank you and God bless you.
Dr. Laurence Aucella
Sincerely, Doctoral Candidate in Theological studies
Graduate Theological Foundation
Mishawaka, Indiana.

INFORMACION HACERCA DELCONSENTIMIENTO

Me gustaría que participara en un studio de investigación titulado, "Un análisis de factores demográficos y motivaciónales los cuales predicén el éxito en ter-minar el Rito de Iniciación Católica para Adultos (RCIA) en selecionadas areas en el Noreste".

Mi definicion de éxito incluye seguir siendo practicante Católico. Ciertamente, la importancía de este studio son multiples aspectos. Básicamente, hay poco o nada de segimiento en aquellas personas que han completado el RCIA. Preguntas informales con Pastores, Sacerdotes y Cordinadores de RCIA han estado de acuerdo con esta idea.

Por consiguiente, Yo estoy tratando de explorar más hacerca de los dos factores demográficos y motivaciónales relacionados con el seguimiento de los adultos que terminan el RCIA. Sí ústed decide participar en este studio, su participación no tomara más de veinte minutos de su tiempo. Su partici-pación es completamente voluntaría y usted es libre de negarse o abstenerse en cualquier momento durante el proceso de tomar esta encuesta confidencial de RCIA.

Toda la información será en número codificado y es estrictamente con-fidencial. Análisis estadísticos son parte de los datos del grupo. No es requerido que usted proporcione su nombre en esta encuesta.

Si usted tiene cualquier pregunta, por favor no dude en contactar me.

Celular (203) 228-4912

E-mail:
Aucella_Laurence@hotmail.com
Ifaphd@aol.com

Gracias y que Dios los Bendiga.
Sinceramente,
Dr. Laurence Aucella
Doctoral Candidate in Theological studies
Graduate Theological Foundation
Mishawaka, Indiana.

RCIA RETREAT

MERCY CENTER MADISON, CT
APRIL 5, 6 AND 7
SCHEDULE OF EVENTS

FRIDAY, APRIL 5, 2012
4:30 PM DEPARTURE FROM SACRED HEART CHURCH
    Dino Pantoni, Lucy Bryns and David Rivera - Driving

6:00 PM ARRIVAL AT MERCY CENTER/DINNER

7:00 PM PRAYER, OPENING REMARKS AND OVERVIEW OF RETREAT
Dino Pantoni

7:15 PM TALK #1 - MARY GALLAGHER
    Reviewing the Stages of the Catechumenate

8:00 PM SMALL GROUPS AND DISCUSSION

8:45 PM RECAP, REVIEW

9:00 PM EVINING PRAYER - FR. CARLOS

9:15 PM SNACKS AND THEN RETIRE

SATURDAY, APRIL 6, 2012
6:30 AM WAKE UP CALL, SHOWER, ETC

7:00 AM BREAKFAST

7:30 AM MORNING PRAYER- FR. CARLOS

8:00 AM TALK #2 MARY GALLAGHER
    Pre-Catechumenate - Where are we and where should we go?

8:30 AM SMALL GROUP AND DISCUSSION

9:15 AM RECAP, REVIEW

9:30 AM BREAK AND COFFEE

10:15 AM TALK #3 - MARY GALLAGHER
11:00 AM SMALL GROUP AND DISCUSSION

11:45 AM RECAP, REVIEW

12:00 NOON ANGELUS, FR. CARLOS

12:05 PM LUNCH AND BREAK

1:30 PM TALK #4-MARY GALLAGHE
      Catechumenate- where are we and where should go?

2:15 PM SMALL GROUP AND DISCUSSION

3:00 PM RECAP, REVIEW

3:15 PM CONFESSIONS

4:00 PM LITURGY

TALK/HOMILY #5 AND /OR STURDAY VIGIL MASS
      FR. ZAPATA: How the RCIA connect to the parish?

5:00 PM DINNER

6:30 PM TALK#6 - MARY GALLAGHER
      Mystagogy - Where are we and where should we go?

7:15 PM SMALL GROUP AND DISCUSSION

8:00 PM RECAP, REVIEW

8:15 PM EVENING PRAYER -FR. CARLOS

8:30 PM SNACKS AND THEN RETIRE

SUNDAY, APRIL 7, 2012
6:30 AM WAKE UP CALL, SHOWER, ETC

7:00 AM BREAKFAST

7:45 AM MORNING PRAYER- DINO

8:00 AM TALK #7 - MARY GALLAGHER
    Summary: What is God asking of us? Developing a pastoral plan.

8:45 AM SMALL GROUP AND DISCUSSION

9:30 AM RECAP, REVIEW

9:45 AM CONCLUSION -DINO PANTONI

What does this mean for Sacred Heart RCIA Program.

10:15 AM COMMENTS/EVALUATION

11:00 AM LEAVE MERCY CENTER

WORKS CITED

Akin, Jimmy. The Fathers Know Best. San Diego, California: Catholic answers, 2010.

Barron, Robert. Catholicism: A journey to the Heart of the Faith. New York: Image Books, a Division of Random House, Inc., 2011.

Beggiani, Seely. Aspects of Maronite History. Glen Allen, Va: Saint Maron Publications, 2003.

Bennett, Rod. Four Witnesses: The Early Church in Her Own Words. San Fran-cisco: Ignatius Press, 2002.

Bennett, William J. America: The Last Best Hope. Volume 1. Nashville, Tennessee: Thomas Nelson, inc., 2006.

Bennett, William J. America: The Last Best Hope. Volume 2. Nashville, Tennessee: Thomas Nelson, inc., 2007.

Bennett, William J. Tried by Fire. Nashville, Tennessee: Nelson Books, 2016.

Bevans, Stephen B. and Roger P. Schroeder, Constants in Context: A Theology of Mission for Today. New York: Orbis Books, 2004.

Boken, Kotter, Thomas. A Concise History of the Catholic Church. New York: Imagine Books, Published by Doubleday, 2004.

Boselli, Goffredo. The Spiritual Meaning of the Liturgy: School of prayer, Source of Life. Collegeville, Minnesota: Liturgycal Press, 2014.

Brown, Peter. Through the Eye of a Needle: Wealth, the Fall of Rome, and the Making of Christianity in the West, 350-550 A.D. Princeton: Princeton University Press, 2012.

Chinnici, Joseph P., and Angelyn Drics, Prayer and Practice in the American Catholic Community. New York: Orbis Books, 2000.

Davis, Cyparian. *The History of Black Catholics in the United States.* New York The Crossroad Publishing Company,1990.

Dawson, Christopher. *St. Augustine: His Age, Life, and Thoughts.* New York; Meridian Books, 1957.

Duquin, Lorence Hanley. *A Century of Catholic Converts.* Huntington, Indiana. Our Sunday Visitor, inc., 2003.

Flannery, Austin. *Vatican Council II: The Conciliar and Post Conciliar Documents.* New York: Constello Publishing Company, 1987.

Fox, Robin Lane. *Augustine: Conversions to Confessions.* New York: Basic Books, 2015.

Gelber L, and Romaeus Leuven, eds., Josephine Koeppel, trans. *The Collected Works of Edith Stein: Sister Teresa Benedicta of the Cross Discalced Carmelite. Self-Portrait in Letters 1916- 1942, Volume Five.* Washington, D.C.: ICS Publications, 1993.

Gillis, Chester. Roman Catholicism in America. New York: Columbia University Press, 1999.

Gonzalez, Justo L. *The Story of Christianity: The Early Church to the Dawn of Reformation, Vol. I.* New York: Harper Collins Publishers, 2010.

Goldstein, David. *Campaigners for Christ Handbook.* Boston: Astor Post Office, 1934.

Goldstein David and Martha Moore Avery. *Papers, MS.1986.167,* John I. Burns Library, Boston College.

Goldsworthy, Adrian. *Pax Rontana: War, Peace, and Conquest in the Roman World.* New York Yale University Press, 2016.

Guglielmi, Donald A. Staritsa: *The Spiritual Motherhood of Catherine Doherty.* Eugene, Oregon: Pickwick Publications, 2018.

Haggerty, Donald. *Conversions: Spiritual Insights into an Essential Encounter with God.* San Francisco: Ignatius Press, 2017.

Hahn, Scott. *Catholic Bible Dictionary.* New York: Doubleday, 2009.

Hahn, Scott, ed. Clement and *The Early Church of Rome: On the Dating of Clement's First*

Epistle to the Corinthians (Revered Thomas J. Herron, Dissertatioad Doctoratum in Facilitate Theologiae Blibiclae Pontificine Universitatis Giegorianae. Rome:1988), Emmaus Road Publishing, Steubenville, 2008.

Hahn, Scott. *Signs of Life. 40 Catholic Customs and Their Biblical Roots.* New York: Doubleday, 2009.

Hardon, John A. *The Catholic Catechism: A Contemporary Catechism of the Teaching of the Catholic Church.* New York: An Imagine Book Published bv Doubleday, 1981.

Hardon, John A. *Pocket Catholic Dictionary.* New York Imagine Books, Published by Doubleday, 1985.

Haykin, Michael A. *Rediscovering the Church Fathers: Who They Were and How They Shaped the Church.* Wheaton, Illinois: Crossway, 2011.

Hennesey, James. *American Catholics: A History of the Roman Catholic Community in the United States.* Oxford: Oxford University Press, 1981.

Herbermann, Charles G., ed., *The Catholic Encyclopedia.* New York The Gilmary Society, Published by the Encyclopedia Press, Inc., 1913.

Herron, Thomas J. *Clement and the early Church of Rome: on the Dating of Clement's First Epistle to the Corinthians edited by Scott Hahn.* Steubenville, Ohio: Emmaus Road Publishing, 2008.

Hitchcock, James. *History of the catholic Church: From the Apostolic Age to the Third Millenium.* San Francisco: Ignatius Press, 2012.

International Commission on English in the Liturgy. Rite of Christian Initiation of Adults: Study *Edition.* Collegeville, iMinnesota: The Liturgycal Press, 1988.

Jurgens, William A. *The Faith of the Early Fathers. Volume 1.* Collegeville, Minnesota: The Liturgical Press, 1970.

Kauffinan, Christopher, J. *Faith and Fratemalism: The History of the Knight of Columbus 1882-1982.* New York: Harper and Row, Publishers, 1982.

Lang, Jovian P. *Dictionary of the Liturgy.* New York Catholic Book Publishing Corp, 1989.

Law, Timothy Michael. *When God Spoke Greek: The Septuagint and the Making of the Christian* Bible. Oxford: Oxford University Press, 2013.

Libreria Editrice Vaticana. Catechism of The Catholic Church. Boston. Pauline Books & Media, 1994.

Lockyer, Herbert. *All the Apostles of the Bible.* Gand Rapids, Michigan. Zon dervan, 1972.

Louth, Andrew. *Eusebius: The History of the Church.* London, England. Penguin Books Books, 1989.

Masse, Benjamin L. *The Catholic Mind Through Fifty Years 1903-1953.* New York; The America Press, 1952.

Milavac, Aaron. *The Didache: Text, Translation, analysis, and Commentary.* Collegeville, Minnesota: Liturgical press, 2003.

McPeherson, James. *Battle Cry of Freedom: The Civil War Era.* Oxford: Oxford University Press,1988.

Morris, Thomas H. *The RCIA: Transforming the Church.* New York: Pau|ist Press, 1997.

National Conference of Catholic Bishops United States ofAmenca. Rite of Christian Initiation of Adults. New Jersey: Catholic Book Publishing Corp, 1988.

Neyer, Maria Amata and Eberhard Ave - Callemant, eds, and Hugh Candler Hunt, trans. *The Collected Works of Edith Stein: Letter to Roman Ingarden. Self-Portrait in Letters, Volume Twelve.* Washington, D.C: ICS Publications, 2014.

Oates, Whitney J. *Basic Writings of Saint Augustine. Volume II.* New York; Basic Books, 1948.

O'Connel, Gerald S.J. and Edward G. Farrugia, S J. *A Concise Dictionary of Theology.* New York: Paulist Press. 2000.

O'Reilly, Bill and Martin Dugard. *KillingLincoln: The Shocking Assassination That Changed America* Forever. New York: Henry Holt and Company, 2011.

O'Reilly, Bill and Martin Dugard. *Killing England: The Brutal Struggle for American Independence.* New York: Henry Holt and Company, 2017.

Osborne, Kenan B. *The Christian Sacraments of Initiation: Baptism, Confirmation, Eucharist* New York: Paulist Press, 1987.

Pope Benedict XVI. *Church Fathers: From Clement of Rome to Augustine.* San Francisco, Ignatius Press and By Libreria Editrice Vaticana, 2008.

Pope Benedict XVI. *Dogma and Preaching, Applying Christian Doctrine to Daily Life.* San Francisco: Ignatius Press, 2011.

Pope Benedict XVI. *Great Christian Thinkers: From the Early Church Through The Middle Ages.* Minneapolis; Fortress Press, 2011.

Pope Benedict XVI. *The Fathers.* Huntington, Indiana: Our Sunday Visitor Publishing Division and By Libreria Editrice Vaticana, 2008.

Price, Simon and Peter Thonemann. *The Birth of Classical Europe: A History from Troy to Augustine.* New York: Penguin Books, 2010.

Randall, Willard Sterne. *Unshackling America: How the War of 1812 Truly Ended the American Revolution.* New York: St. Martin's Press, 2017.

Riebling, Mark. *Church of Spies: The Pope's Secret War against Hitler.* New York: Basic Books, 2015.

Roth, Catharine, P. *On Wealth and Poverty.* New York: St. Vladimir's Seminary Press, 1984.

Sawicki, Marianne, ed, trans. *The Collected works of Edith Stein: Sister Teresa Benedicta of the Cross Discalced Carmelite. An Investigation Concerning the State,* Volume ten. Washington, D.C.: ICS Publications, 2006.

Scaperlanda, Maria Ruiz. *Edith Stein: The Life and Legacy of St. Teresa Benedicta of the Cross.* Manchester, New Hampshire: Sophia Institute Press, 2017.

Senior, Donald, John J. Collins, and Mary Ann Getty, Eds. *The Catholic Study Bible Third Edition: The New American Bible Revised Edition*. New York: Oxford University Press, 2010.

Stagaman, David J. *Authority in The Church*. Collegeville, Minnesota: The Liturgical Press, 1999.

Stravinskas, Peter, ed. *Our Sunday Visitor's Catholic Encyclopedia*. Huntington, Indiana: Our Sunday Visitor, Inc., 1991.

Sullivan, John. *Edith Stein: Essential Writings*. New York: Orbis Books, 2002.

Tanner, Norman. *Vatican II: The Essential Texts*. New York: Image Books, an imprint of the Crown Publishing Group, a division of Random House, inc., 2012.

Taylor, Alan. *American Colonies: The Penguin History of The United States*. New York: Penguin Books, 2001.

Traflet, Dianne Marie. *Saint Edith Stein: A Spiritual Portrait*. Boston: Pauline Books & media, 2008.

Vidmar, John. *The Catholic Church Through the Ages: A History Second Edition*. New York: Paulist Press, 2014.

White, Richard. *The Republic for Which It Stands: The United States During Reconstruction and the Gilded Age, 1865-1896*. New York: Oxford University Press, 2017. . . .

Wilken, Robert Louis. *The First Thousand Years: A Global history of Christianity*. New Haven: Yale University Press, 2012.

FOOTNOTES

1)   Michael A.G. Haykin. Rediscovering the Church Fathers: Who They Were and How They Shaped the Church (Wheaton, Illinois: Crossway, 2011), 94.

2)   Justo L. Gonzalez. The Story of Christianity: The Early Church to The Dawn of the Reformation (New York, NY: Harper Collins, 2010), 105-106.

3)   James Hennessey S. J., American Catholics: A History of the Roman Catholic Community in the United States (Oxford: Oxford University Press, 1981), 10.

4)   Chester Gillis. Roman Catholicism in America (New York: Columbia University Press, 1999), 48.

5)   Thomas F. Meechan, "The First Catholic Fourth of July", in the Catholic Mind Through Fifty Years 1903-1953, ed. Benjamin L. Masse, S.T (New York: The America Press), 160-161.

6)   James Hennessey, S.J., American Catholics: A History of the Roman Catholic Community in the United States (Oxford: Oxford University Press, 1981), 102.

7)   Ibid., 102.

8)   Vincent J. O'Malley, C.M., Saints of North America (Huntington, Indiana: Our Sunday Visitor Publishing Division, 2004), 19.

9)   Ibid., 19.

10)   Ibid., 19.

11)   Ibid., 19.

12)   Ibid., 17.

13)   Chester Gillis, Roman Catholicism In America (New York: Columbia University Press, 1999), 141.

14)   James Hennesey. S.T., American Catbolics: A History of the Roman Catholic Community in the United States. (Oxford: Oxford University Press, 1981), 103.

15)   Ibid., 103.

16)   Ibid., 103.

17) Ibid., 103.

18) Ibid., 103.

19) Ibid., 103.

20) Ibid., 104.

21) David Goldstein and Martha Moore Avery Papers, MS. 1986.167, John I. Burns Library, Boston College

22) Thomas H. Morris, The RCIA: Transforming the Church. (New York: Paulist Press, 1997), 9-10.

23) Austin Flannery, O.P., Vatican Council II: The Conciliar and Post Conciliar Documents (New York: Costello Publishing Company, 1987), 21.

24) Thomas H. Morris, The RCIA: Transforming the Church. (New York: Paulist Press, 1997), 10.

25) Ibid., 10.

26) Ibid., 27-28.

27) Ibid., 27-28.

28) Scott Hahn, Catbolic Bible Dictionary (New York: Doubleday, 2009), 19-21.

29) John A. Hardon, S. J., Catholic Dictionary: An Abridged and Updated Edition of Modern Catholic Dictionary (New York: Imagine Books, 2013), 9.

30) Bible Dictionary and Concordance, 8.

31) Scott Hahn, Catholic Bible Dictionary (New York: Doubleday, 2009), 36.

32) John A. Hardon, S. J., Catholic Dictionary: An Abridged and Updated Edition of Modern Catholic Dictionary (New York: Imagine Books, 2013), 16.

33) Scott Hahn, Catholic Bible Dictionary (New York: Doubleday, 2009), 51

34) Peter M. J. Stravinskas, ed., Our Sunday Visitor's: Catholic Encyclopedia (Huntington, Indiana: Our Sunday Visitor, Inc., 1991), 79.

35) Scott Hahn, Catholic Bible Dictionary (New York: Doubleday, 2009), 51-52.

36) Ibid., 58-59.

37) Ibid., 61.

38) Peter M. J. Stravinskas, ed., Our Sunday Visitor's: Catholic Encyclopedia (Huntington, Indiana: Our Sunday Visitor, Inc., 1991), 87.

39) Ibid., 89.

40) John A. Hardon, S. J., Catholic Dictionary: An Abridged and Updated Edition of Modern Catholic Dictionary (New York: Imagine Books, 2013), 29-30.

41) Ibid., 40.

42) Jovian P. Lang, OFM, Dictionary of the Liturgy (New York: Catholic Book Publishing Corp., 1989), 48.

43) Scott Hahn, Catholic Bible Dictionary (New York: Doubleday, 2009), 91.

44) Jovian P. Lang, OFM, Dictionary of the Liturgy (New York: Catholic Book Publishing Corp., 1989), 53.

45) Ibid., 86-87.

46) John A. Hardon, S. J., Catholic Dictionary: An Abridged and Updated Edition of Modern Catholic Dictionary (New York: Imagine Books, 2013), 76.

47) Peter M. J. Stravinskas, ed., Our Sunday Visitor's: Catholic Encyclopedia (Huntington, Indiana: Our Sunday Visitor, Inc., 1991), 179-180.

48) Jovian P. Lang, OFM, Dictionary of the Liturgy (New York: Catholic Book Publishing Corp., 1989), 90-91.

49) Gerald O'Collins, S.J. and Edward G. Farrugia, S.J. A Concise Diction-ary of Theology (New York: Paulist Press).

50) Jovian P. Lang, OFM, Dictionary of the Liturgy (New York: Catholic Book Publishing Corp., 1989), 92.

51) Peter M. J. Stravinskas, ed., Our Sunday Visitor's: Catholic Encyclopedia (Huntington, Indiana: Our Sunday Visitor, Inc., 1991),184.

52) John A. Hardon, S. J., Catholic Dictionary: An Abridged and Updated Edition of Modern Catholic Dictionary (New York: Imagine Books, 2013),78.

53) Ibid., 88.

54) Scott Hahn, Catholic Bible Dictionary (New York: Doubleday, 2009). 146.

55) Peter M. J. Stravinskas, ed., Our Sunday Visitor's: Catholic Encyclopedia (Huntington, Indiana: Our Sunday Visitor, Inc., 1991), 244-245.

56) John A. Hardon, S. J., Catholic Dictionary: An Abridged and Updated Edition of Modern Catholic Dictionary (New York: Imagine Books, 2013), 103-104.

57) Ibid., 104.

58) Jovian P. Lang, OFM, Dictionary of the Liturgy (New York: Catholic Book Publishing Corp., 1989), 131-132.

59) Ibid., 134-135.

60) John A. Hardon, S. J., Catholic Dictionary: An Abridged and Updated Edition of Modern Catholic Dictionary (New York: Imagine Books, 2013), 107.

61) Ibid., 448.

62) Jovian P. Lang, OFM, Dictionary of the Liturgy (New York: Catholic Book Publishing Corp., 1989), 136-138.

63) Peter M. J. Stravinskas, ed., Our Sunday Visitor's: Catholic Encyclopedia (Huntington, Indiana: Our Sunday Visitor, Inc., 1991), 855-857.

64) Ibid., 255.

65) Ibid., 258-259.

66) Jovian P. Lang, OFM, Dictionary of the Liturgy (New York: Catholic Book Publishing Corp., 1989),139-140.

67) John A. Hardon, S. J., Catholic Dictionary: An Abridged and Updated Edition of Modern Catholic Dictionary (New York: Imagine Books, 2013), 111.

68) Peter M. J. Stravinskas, ed., Our Sunday Visitor's: Catholic Encyclopedia (Huntington, Indiana: Our Sunday Visitor, Inc., 1991), 259.

69) Charles G. Herbermann, PH.D., LL.D, ed., The Catholic Encyclopedia Volume IV (New York: The Encyclopedia Press, Inc., 1913), 340.

70) Charles G. Herbermann, PH.D., LL.D., ed., The Catholic Encyclopedia Volume IX (New York: The Encyclopedia Press, Inc., 1913), 790.

71) Jovian P. Lang, OFM, Dictionary of the Liturgy (New York: Catholic Book Publishing Corp., 1989), 140.

72) Peter M. J. Stravinskas, ed., Our Sunday Visitor's: Catholic Encyclopedia (Huntington, Indiana: Our Sunday Visitor, Inc., 1991), 260.

73) Ibid., 260.

74) Jovian P. Lang, OFM, Dictionary of the Liturgy (New York: Catholic Book Publishing Corp., 1989), 140-141.

75) John A. Hardon, S. J., Catholic Dictionary: An Abridged and Updated Edition of Modern Catholic Dictionary (New York: Imagine Books, 2013), 112.

76) Libreria Editrice Vaticana, Catechism of The Catholic Church, 358-359.

77) Peter M. J. Stravinskas, ed., Our Sunday Visitor's: Catholic Encyclopedia (Huntington, Indiana: Our Sunday Visitor, Inc., 1991), 261.

78) Thomas H. Morris, The RCIA: Transforming the Church. (New York: Paulist Press, 1997), 26-27.

79) Scott Hahn, Catholic Bible Dictionary (New York: Doubleday, 2009), 167.

80) Ronald F. Youngblood, F.F. Bruce and R.K. Harrison, Nelson's Compact Bible Dictionary (Nashville: Thomas Nelson Publishers, 2004), 150.

81) Justo L. González, The Story of Christianity: The Early Church to The Dawn of The Reformation Volume I (New York: Harper Collins publishers, 2010), 31.

82) Peter M. J. Stravinskas, ed., Our Sunday Visitor's: Catholic Encyclopedia (Huntington, Indiana: Our Sunday Visitor, Inc., 1991), 270-271.

83) John A. Hardon, S. J., Catholic Dictionary: An Abridged and Updated Edition of Modern Catholic Dictionary (New York: Imagine Books, 2013),115.

84) Scott Hahn, Catholic Bible Dictionary (New York: Doubleday, 2009),175-177.

85) Ibid., 203-205.

86) Peter M. J. Stravinskas, ed., Our Sunday Visitor's: Catholic Encyclopedia (Huntington, Indiana: Our Sunday Visitor, Inc., 1991), 287.

87) Ronald F. Youngblood, F.F. Bruce and R.K. Harrison, Nelson's Compact Bible Dictionary(Nashville: Thomas Nelson Publishers, 2004), 174.

88) Jovian P. Lang, OFM, Dictionary of the Liturgy (New York: Catholic Book Publishing Corp., 1989), 162.

89) John A. Hardon, S. J., Catholic Dictionary: An Abridged and Updated Edition of Modern Catholic Dictionary (New York: Imagine Books,

1. 2013),131.

90) Peter M. J. Stravinskas, ed., Our Sunday Visitor's: Catholic Encyclopedia (Huntington, Indiana: Our Sunday Visitor, Inc., 1991), 307.

91) Ibid., 311.

92) Jovian P. Lang, OFM, Dictionary of the Liturgy (New York: Catholic Book Publishing Corp., 1989), 163.

93) Ibid., 172-173.

94) Peter M. J. Stravinskas, ed., Our Sunday Visitor's: Catholic Encyclopedia (Huntington, Indiana: Our Sunday Visitor, Inc., 1991), 331-332.

95) Jovian P. Lang, OFM, Dictionary of the Liturgy (New York: Catholic Book Publishing Corp., 1989), 176.

96) Ibid., 177.

97) Ibid., 180.

98) Stephen B. Bevans and Roger P. Schroeder, Constant's in Context: A Theology of Mission for Today (New York, N.Y.: Orbis Books, Mary Knoll, 2004), 21-22.

99) Scott Hahn, Catholic Bible Dictionary (New York: Doubleday, 2009), 255.

100) Ibid., 255-260.

101) Kenan B. Osborne, OFM, The Christian Sacraments of Initiation: Baptism, Confirmation, Eucharist (New York: Paulist press, 1987), 190-193.

102) Peter M. J. Stravinskas, ed., Our Sunday Visitor's: Catholic Encyclopedia (Huntington, Indiana: Our Sunday Visitor, Inc., 1991), 368-369.

103) Jovian P. Lang, OFM, Dictionary of the Liturgy (New York: Catholic Book Publishing Corp., 1989), 183-185.

104) Ibid., 466.

105) John A. Hardon, S. J., Catholic Dictionary: An Abridged and Updated Edition of Modern Catholic Dictionary (New York: Imagine Books, 2013),343.

106) Ibid., 400-401.

107) Scott Hahn, Catholic Bible Dictionary (New York: Doubleday, 2009), 670-671.

108) Peter M. J. Stravinskas, ed., Our Sunday Visitor's: Catholic Encyclopedia (Huntington, Indiana: Our Sunday Visitor, Inc., 1991), 836.

109) Jovian P. Lang, OFM, Dictionary of the Liturgy (New York: Catholic Book Publishing Corp., 1989), 551-554.

110) Ibid., 553-554.

111) Stephen B. Bevans and Roger P. Schroeder, Constants in Context: Biblical and Theological Foundations (New York, N.Y.: Orbis Books, 2004), 28.

112) James Hennesey, S. J., American Catholics: A History of the Roman Catholic Community in the United States (Oxford: Oxford University Press, 1981), 173.

113) Thomas H. Morris, The RCIA: Transforming the Church (New York; Paulist Press, 1997), 9-10.

114) Justo L. González, The Story of Christianity: The Early Church to The Dawn of the Reformation (New York; Harper Collins, 2010), 105-106.

115) Ibid., 107.

116) Ibid., 101.

117) Thomas Boken Kotter, A Concise History of the Catholic Church (New York: Image Books, 2004),37.

118) Michael A.G. Haykin, Rediscovering the Church Fathers: Who They Were and How They Shaped the Church (Wheaton, Illinois: Crossway, 2011), 46.

119) Justo L. González, The Story of Christianity: The Early Church to The Dawn of the Reformation (New York: Harper Collins; 2010), 35.

120) Ibid., 35.

121) Ibid., 35.

122) Ibid., 35.

123) Ibid., 35.

124) Ibid., 35.

125) Stephen B. Bevans and Roger P. Schroeder, Constants in Context: Bi-lical and Theological Foundations (New York; Orbis Books, 2004), 24.

126) Ibid., 22.

127) Ibid., 25.

128) Ibid., 26.

129) Ibid., 27.

130) Ibid., 27.

131) Ibid., 28.

132) Robert Barron, Catholicism: A Journey to the Heart of The Faith (New York; Imagine Books, 2011), 129.

133) Ibid, 131.

134) Stephen B. Bevans and Roger P. Schroeder, Constants in Context: Biblical and Theological Foundations (New York; Orbis Books, 2004), 29,

135) Scott Hahn, Catholic Bible Dictionary (New York: Doubleday, 2009), 51-52.

136) Ibid., 51-52. .

137) Stephen B. Bevans and Roger P. Schroeder, Constants in Context: A Theology of Mission for Today (New York; Orbis Books, 2004), 28.

138) Ibid., 28.

139) Justo L. González, The Story of Christianity: The Early Church to The Dawn of the Reformation (New York: Harper Collins; 2010), 33.

140) Ibid., 33.

141) Ibid., 35.

142) Ibid., 36.

143) William j. Bennett, Tried By Fire (Nashville, Tennessee, Nelson Books, 2016), 13.

144) Herbert Lockyer, All the Apostles of the Bible (Grand Rapids, Michigan; Zondervan,1972), 255-257.

145) Thomas J. Harron, Clement and the Early Church of Rome; On the Dating of Clement's First Epistle to the Corinthians (Steubenville, Ohio: Emmaus Road Publishing, 2008), 82-83.

146) Ibid., 11.

147) William A. Jurgens, The Faith of the Early Fathers, Volume I (Collegeville, Minnesota: The Liturgical Press, 1970), 7.

148) Ibid., 7.

149) Ibid., 7.

150) Ibid., 7.

151) Thomas J. Herron, Clement and the Early Church of Rome, On the Dating of Clement's First Epistle to the Corinthians (Steubenville, Ohio: Emmaus Road Publishing, 2008), 11.

152) Ibid., 9.

153) Jimmy Akin, The Fathers Know Best (San Diego, California: Catholic Answers, 2010) 57.

154) Ibid., 57.

155) Thomas J. Herron, Clement and the Early Church of Rome: On the Dating of Clement's First Epistle to the Corinthians (Steubenville, Ohio: Emmaus Road Publishing, 2008), 87.

156) Ibid., 87.

157) Ibid., 88.

158) Ibid., 91-92.

159) Ibid., 91-92.

160) Charles G. Herbermann, The Catholic Encyclopedia, Volume I (New York: The Encyclopedia Press, 1913), 638-639.

161) Aaron Milavec, The Didache; Text, Translation, Analysis, and Commentary (Collegeville, Minnesota: Liturgical Press, 2003), 41.

162) Ibid., 42

163) Ibid., 42-43.

164) Ibid., xii.

165) Ibid., xiii - xiv.

166) Thomas J. Herron, Clement and The Early Church of Rome; On the Dating of Clement's First Epistle to the Corinthians (Steubenville, Ohio: Emmaus Road Publishing, 2009) 71.

167) Ibid., 72-73.

168) Ibid., 73.

169) Ibid., 86.

170) Ibid., 87.

171) Ibid., 82.

172) Ibid., 83.
173) Ibid., 83.
174) Ibid., 87.
175) Ibid., 89.
176) Ibid., 90.
177) Ibid., 90.
178) Ibid., 92.
179) Ibid., 87.
180) Ibid., 17.
181) William A. Jurgens, The Faith of the Early Fathers, Volume I (Collegeville, Minnesota: The Liturgical Press, 1970), 17.
182) Ibid., 17.
183) Justo L. González, The Story of Christianity: The Early Church to The Dawn of the Reformation (New York; Harper Collins, 2010), 52.
184) Pope Benedict XVI, Church Fathers; From Clement of Rome to Augustine (Vatican City: Libreria Editrice Vaticana, 2008), 13.
185) Ibid., 13.
186) Justo L. González, The Story of Christianity: The Early Church to The Dawn of the Reformation (New York; Harper Collins, 2010),51.
187) Ibid., 52.
188) Thomas J. Herron, Clement and the Early Church of Rome: On the Dating of Clement's First Epistle to the Corinthians (Steubenville, Ohio: Emmaus Road Publishing, 2008), 75.
189) Justo L. Gonzalez, The Story of Christianity: The Early Church to The Dawn of The Reformation (New York: Harper Collins, 2010), 53.
190) Ibid., 54.
191) William a, Jurgens, The Faith of the Early Fathers, Volume I (Collegeville, Minnesota: The Liturgical Press, 1970), 31.
192) Justo L. Gonzalez, The Story of Christianity: The Early Church to The Dawn of The Reformation (New York: Harper Collins, 2010), 54.
193) Ibid., 55-56.
194) Ibid., 56.

195) William J. Bennett, Tried by Fire: The Story of Christianity's First Thon-sand Years (Nashville, Tennessee: Nelson Books, 2016), 45.

196) Rod Bennett, Four Witnesses: The Early Church in Her Own Words (San Francisco: Ignatius Press, 2002), 155.

197) Ibid., 155.

198) Pope Benedict XVI, Church Fathers: From Clement of Rome to Augustine (Vatican City: Libreria Editrice Vaticana, 2008), 18.

199) Rod Bennett, Four Witnesses: The Early Church in Her Own Words (San Francisco Ignatius Press, 2002), 155.

200) Justo L. Gonzalez, The Story of Christianity: The Early Church to The Dawn of The Reformation (New York: Harper-Collins, 2010), 56.

201) Ibid., 56-57.

202) Ibid., 57.

203) Ibid., 57.

204) Ibid., 59.

205) Ibid., 57.

206) Ibid., 61.

207) Ibid., 62.

208) Michael A.G. Haykin, Rediscovering the Church Fathers: Who They Were And How They Shaped The Church (Wheaton, Illinois: Crossway, 2011), 50.

209) Ibid., 50.

210) Ibid., 50-51.

211) Ibid., 51.

212) Ibid., 51.

213) Ibid., 52.

214) Ibid., 53.

215) Ibid., 53-54.

216) Ibid., 55.

217) Ibid., 55-56.

218) Justo L. Gonzalez, The Story of Christianity: The Early Church to The Dawn of The Reformation (New York: Harper-Collins, 2010), 63.

219) Ibid., 64-66.

220) Pope Benedict XVI, Church Fathers: From Clement of Rome to Augustine (Vatican City: Libreria Editrice Vaticana, 2008), 43

221) Ibid., 44.
222) William J. Bennett, Tried by Fire: The Story of Christianity's First Thon-sand Years(Nashville, Tennessec, Nelson Books, 2016), 55.
223) Justo L. Gonzalez, The Story of Christianity: The Early Church to The Dawn of The Reformation (New York: Harper Collins, 2010),53.
224) Ibid., 70.
225) Ibid., 71-73.
226) Ibid., 76-77.
227) Ibid., 76.
228) Ibid., 77.
229) Gerald O' Collins and Edward G, Farrugia, A Concise Dictionary of Theology: Revised and Expanded Edition (New York: Paulist Press, 2000), 57.
230) Justo L. Gonzalez, The Story of Christianity: The Early Church to The Dawn of The Reformation (New York: Harper-Collins, 2010), 77.
231) Ibid., 78.
232) David J. Stagaman, Authority in The Church (Collegeville, Minnesota: The Liturgical Press, 1999), 76.
233) Ibid., 76-77.
234) Ibid., 77.
235) Ibid., 77-78.
236) Ibid., 78.
237) Ibid., 78.
238) Ibid., 83.
239) Justo L. Gonzalez, The Story of Christianity: The Early Church to The Dawn of The Reformation (New York: Harper-Collins, 2010), 81.
240) David J. Stagaman, Autbority in The Church (The Liturgical Press, 1999), 83. Collegeville, Minnesota:
241) Ibid., 86.
242) Ibid., 84.
243) Ibid., 85.
244) Ibid., 87.
245) Ibid., 87.

246) Justo L. Gonzalez, The Story of Christianity: The Early Church to The Dawn of The Reformation (New York: Harper-Collins, 2010), 181.

247) John Vidmar, The Catholic Church Through the Ages: A History Second Edition (New York: Paulist Press, 2014), 30-31.

248) Ibid., 31.

249) Gerald O' Collins and Edward G. Farrugia, A Concise Dictionary of Theology (New York: Paulist Press, 2000), 177.

250) Stephen B. Bevans and Roger P. Schroeder, Constant's in Context: A Theology of Mission for Today (New York: Orbis Books, Mary knoll, 2004), 87.

251) Ibid., 88.

252) Ibid., 89.

253) Ibid., 90.

254) Ibid., 90.

255) Ibid., 91.

256) Ibid... 91.

257) Justo L. Gonzalez. The Story of Christianity: The Early Church to The Dawn of The Reformation (New York: Harper-Collins, 2010), 98-99.

258) Stephen B. Bevans and Roger P. Schroeder, Constant's in Context: A Theology of Mission for Today (New York: Orbis Book, Maryknoll, 2004), 82.

259) Ibid., 75.

260) Ibid... 78.

261) Ibid... 78.

262) Ibid., 78.

263) Ibid., 78.

264) Ibid., 78.

265) Ibid., 79.

266) Ibid., 79.

267) Ibid., 78.

268) Justo L. Gonzalez, The Story of Christianity: The Early Church to The Dawn of The Reformation (New York: Harper-Collins, 2010), 139.

269) Stephen B. Bevans and Roger P. Schroeder, Constant's in Context: A Theology Mission for Today (New York: Orbis Books, Mary knoll, 2004), 80.

270) Justo L. Gonzalez, The Story of Christianity: The Early Church to The Dawn of The Reformation (New York: Harper Collins, 2010), 181-182.

271) Stephen B. Bevans and Roger P. Schroeder, Constant's in Context: A Theology of Mission for Today (New York: Orbis Books, Mary knoll, 2004), 82.

272) David J. Stagaman, Authority in The Church (Collageville, Minnesota: The Liturgical Press, 1999), 83-84.

273) Justo L. Gonzalez, The Story of Christianity: The Early Church to The Dawn of The Reformation (New York: Harper-Collins, 2010), 184.

274) Ibid., 185-186.

275) Ibid., 186.

276) Ibid., 186.

277) Ibid., 187.

278) William J. Bennett Tried by Fire: The Story of Christianity's First Thon-sand Years (Nashville, Tennessee: Nelson Books, 2016), 122-123.

279) Ibid., 123-124.

280) Justo L. Gonzalez, The Story of Christianity: The Early Church to The Dawn of The Reformation (New York: Harper Collins, 2010), 184.

281) Ibid., 188-189.

282) Ibid., 190.

283) William J. Bennett Tried by Fire: The Story of Christianity's First Thon-sand Years(Nashville, Tennessee: Nelson Books, 2016), 125.

284) Ibid., 126.

285) Justo L. Gonzalez, The Story of Christianity: The Early Church to The Dawn of The Reformation (New York: Harper-Collins, 2010), 191.

286) William J. Bennett Tried by Fire: The Story of Christianity's First Thou-sand Years (Nashville, Tennessee: Nelson Books, 2016), 129.

287) Stephen B. Bevans and Roger P. Schroeder, Constant's in Context: A Theology of Mission for Today (New York: Orbis Books, Mary knoll, 2004), 102.

288) Ibid., 102.

289) Ibid., 100.

290) Ibid., 103-104.

291) Ibid., 104.

292) Ibid., 104.

293) Ibid., 104.

294) Justo L. Gonzalez, The Story of Christianity: The Early Church to the Dawn of The Reformation (New York: Harper-Collins, 210),191.

295) Ibid., 194.

296) Ibid., 194.

297) Ibid., 195.

298) Ibid., 196.

299) Ibid., 197.

300) Ibid., 197.

301) Ibid., 197.

302) Ibid., 201.

303) James Hitchcock, History of the Catholic Church: from The Apostolic Age to The Third Millenium (San Francisco: Ignatius Press, 2012), 83.

304) Justo L. Gonzalez, The Story of Christianity: The Early Church To The Dawn of The Reformation (New York: Harper-Collins, 210), 202-203.

305) Ibid., 204.

306) Ibid., 205.

307) Ibid., 207.

308) James Hitchcock, History of the Catholic Church: From the Apostolic Age to the Third Millenium (San Francisco: Ignatius Press, 2012), 84.

309) Ibid., 84.

310) Justo L. Gonzalez, The Story of Christianity: The Early Church to the Dawn of The Reformation (New York: Harper-Collins, 2010), 206.

311) Ibid., 206.

312) Ibid., 213.

313) Ibid., 209.

314) Ibid., 216-217.

315) Pope Benedict XVI, The Father (Huntington, Indiana: Our Sunday Visitor Publishing Division, Our Sunday Visitor, Inc., 2008), 84-85.

316) Ibid., 85.

317) Ibid., 85.

318) Justo L. Gonzalez, The Story of Christianity: The Early Church to The Dawn of The Reformation (New York: Harper-Collins, 2010), 217.

319) Ibid., 209-210.

320) Ibid., 210-211.

321) Stephen B. Bevans and Roger P. Schroeder, Constant's in Context: A Theology of Mission for Today (New York: Orbis Books, Mary knoll, 2004), 126-127.

322) Justo L. Gonzalez, The Story of Christianity: The Early Church To The Dawn of The Reformation (New York: Harper-Collins, 2010), 213-214.

323) Ibid., 214.

324) Ibid., 219-220.

325) Ibid., 221.

326) Ibid., 223.

327) Ibid., 224.

328) Ibid., 224.

329) Ibid., 234.

330) William J. Bennett Tried by Fire: The Story of Christianity's First Thou-sand Years

331) (Nashville, Tennessee: Nelson Books, 2016), 194-195.

332) Justo L. Gonzalez, The Story of Christianity: The Early Church to The Dawn of The Reformation (New York: Harper-Collins, 2010), 234-236.

333) Ibid., 237.

334) Robin Lane Fox, Augustine: Conversions to Confessions (New York: Basic Books, 2015), 177.

335) Ibid., 162.

336) Ibid., 163-164.

337) Justo L. Gonzalez, The Story of Christianity: The Early Church to the Dawn of The Reformation (New York: Harper-Collins, 2010), 241-242.

338) Gerald O' Collins and Edward G. Farrugia, A Concise Dictionary of Theology: Revised and Expanded Edition (New York: Paulist Press, 2000),149.

339) Justo L. Gonzalez, The Story of Christianity: The Early Church to The Dawn of The Reformation (New York: Harper-Collins, 2010), 242.

340) Gerald O' Collins and Edward G. Farrugia, A Concise Dictionary of Theology: Revised and Expanded Edition (New York: Paulist Press, 2000), 149.

341) Ibid., 149.

342) Justo L. Gonzalez, The Story of Christianity: The Early Church to The Dawn of The Reformation (New York: Harper-Collins, 2010), 243.

343) Ibid., 245.

344) Ibid., 245-246.

345) Adrian Goldsworthy, Pax Romana: War, Peace and Conquest in the Roman World (New York: Yale University Press, 2016), 299.

346) John Vidmar, The Catholic Church Through the Ages: A History (New York: Paulist Press, 2014), 33.

347) Robin Lane Fox, Augustine: Conversions to Confessions (New York: Basic Books 2015), 167.

348) Ibid., 168-169.

349) Ibid., 172.

350) Ibid., 178.

351) Robert Louis Wilken, The First Thousand Years: A Global History of Christianity (New Heaven, Yale University Press, 2012), 185.

352) Ibid., 185.

353) Justo L. Gonzalez, The Story of Christianity: The Early Church to The Dawn of The Reformation (New York: Harper-Collins, 2010), 246.

354) Robert Louis Wilken, The First Thousand Years: A Global History of Christianity (New Heaven, Yale University Press, 2012), 185.

355) Robin Lane Fox, Augustine: Conversions to Confessions (New York: Basic Books, 2015), 348.

356) Ibid., 348.

357) Ibid., 348-349.

358) Ibid., 349.

359) Ibid., 349.

360) Ibid., 349-350.

361) Ibid., 350.

362) Ibid., 350.

363) Ibid., 351.

364) Ibid., 391.

365) Justo L. Gonzalez, The Story of Christianity: The Early Church to The Dawn of The Reformation (New York: Harper-Collins, 2010), 246-247.

366) Robin Lane Fox, Augustine: Conversions to Confessions (New York: Basic Books, 2015), 502.

367) Ibid., 502.

368) Ibid., 502-503.

369) Robert Louis Wilken, The First Thousand Years: A Global History of Christianity (New Heaven, Yale University Press, 2012), 186-187.

370) Ibid., 187.

371) Ibid., 188.

372) Ibid., 188.

373) Robin Lane Fox, Augustine: Conversions to Confessions (New York: Basic Books, 2015), 557.

374) Adrian Goldsworthy, Pax Romana: War, Peace and Conquest in the Roman World (New York: Yale University Press, 2016), 405.

375) Whitney J. Oates, Basic Writings of Saint Augustine Volume II. (New York: Basic Book, 2015), 554.

376) Robin Lane Fox, Augustine: Conversions to Confessions (New York: Basic books, 2015), 554.

377) Ibid., 555.

378) Ibid., 555.

379) Ibid., 563.

380) Justo L. Gonzalez, The Story of Christianity: The Early Church to The Dawn of The Reformation (New York: Harper-Collins, 2010), 252.

381) Christopher Dawson, "St. Augustine And His Age" in St. Augustine: His Age, Life, and Thought, (New York: Meridian Books, 1957), 44-45.

382) Ibid., 45.

383) Catharine P. Roth, On Wealth and Poverty (New York: St. Vladimir's Seminary Press, 1984), 8.

384) Ibid., 7.

385) Ibid., 8.

386) Justo L. Gonzalez, The Story of Christianity: The Early Church to The Dawn of The Reformation (New York: Harper-Collins, 2010), 225.

387) Ibid., 226.

388) Ibid., 227.

389) Catharine P. Roth, On Wealth and Poverty (New York: St. Vladimir's Seminary Press, 1984), 10.

390) Justo L. Gonzalez, The Story of Christianity: The Early Church to The Dawn of The Reformation (New York: Harper-Collins, 2010), 227,

391) Ibid., 227.

392) Ibid., 227-228.

393) Catharine P. Roth, On Wealth and Poverty (New York: St. Vladimir's Seminary Press, 1984), 10.

394) Justo L. Gonzalez, The Story of Christianity: The Early Church to The Dawn of The Reformation (New York: Harper-Collins, 2010), 229,

395) Ibid., 229-321.

396) Catharine P. Roth, On Wealth and Poverty (New York: St. Vladimir's Seminary Press, 1984), 10-11.

397) Simon Price and Peter Thonemann, The Birth of Classical Europe: A History from Troy to Augustine (New York: Penguin Books, 2010), 307.

398) Robert Louis Wilken, The First Thousand Years: A Global History of Christianity (New Haven: Yale University Press, 2012), 233.

399) Justo L. Gonzalez, The Story of Christianity: The Early Church to The Dawn of The Reformation (New York: Harper-Collins, 2010), 254.

400) Ibid., 255.

401) Ibid., 255.

402) Andrew Louth, Eusebius: The History of the Church (London, England: Penguin Books, 1989), 349.

403) Stephen B. Bevans and Roger P. Schroeder, Constant's in Context: A Theology of Mission for Today (New York: Orbis Books, Mary knoll, 2004), 78.

404) Seely Beggiani, Aspects of Maronite History (Glen Allen, VA: Saint Maron Publications, 2003), 4.

405) Robert Louis Wilken, The First Thousand Years: A Global History of Christianity (New Haven: Yale University Press, 2012), 224.

406) Seely Beggiani, Aspects of Maronite History (Glen Allen, VA: Saint Maron Publications, 2003), 4.

407) Ibid., 3.

408) Ibid., 3.

409) Ibid., 4-6.

410) Ibid., 7.

411) Robert Louis Wilken, The First Thousand Years: A Global History of Christianity (New Haven: Yale University Press, 2012), 224-225.

412) Ibid., 225.

413) John Vidmar, The Catholic Church Through the Ages: A History Second Edition (New York: Paulist Press, 2014), 62-63.

414) Justo L. Gonzalez, The Story of Christianity: The Early Church to The Dawn of The Reformation (New York: Harper-Collins, 2010), 256.

415) Ibid., 296.

416) Ibid., 295-297.

417) Ibid., 297.

418) Ibid., 298-299.

419) Ibid., 300.

420) Ibid., 300.

421) Ibid., 300-301.

422) Ibid., 301.

423) Ibid., 301-302.

424) Stephen B. Bevans and Roger P. Schroeder, Constant's in Context: A Theology of Mission for Today (New York: Orbis Books, Mary knoll, 2004), 102-103.

425) Ibid., 103.
426) Robert Louis Wilken, The First Thousand Years: A Global History of Christianity (New Haven: Yale University Press, 2012), 225.
427) Stephen B. Bevans and Roger P. Schroeder, Constant's in Context: A Theology of Mission for Today (New York: Orbis Books, Mary knoll, 2004), 103.
428) Ibid., 103.
429) Ibid., 103.
430) Robert Louis Wilken, The First Thousand Years: A Global History of Christianity (New Haven: Yale University Press, 2012), 225.
431) Ibid., 226.
432) Ibid., 226-227.
433) Ibid., 227.
434) Ibid., 227.
435) Justo L. Gonzalez, The Story of Christianity: The Early Church to The Dawn of The Reformation (New York: Harper-Collins, 2010), 302 -303.
436) Ibid., 303.
437) Ibid., 303.
438) Robert Louis Wilken, The First Thousand Years: A Global History of Christianity (New Haven: Yale University Press, 2012), 228.
439) Ibid., 228.
440) Ibid., 228.
441) Ibid., 239.
442) Stephen B. Bevans and Roger P. Schroeder, Constants in Context: A Theology of Mission for Today (New York: Orbis Books, 2004), 99-101.
443) Ibid., 101.
444) Ibid., 101.
445) Ibid., 105
446) Ibid., 105.
447) Robert Louis Wilken, The First Thousand Years: A Global History of Christianity (New Haven: Yale University Press, 2012), 241-241.
448) Stephen B. Bevans and Roger P. Schroeder, Constant's in Context: A Theology of Mission for Today (New York: Orbis Books, Mary knoll, 2004), 105.

449) Ibid., 105.
450) Ibid., 105.
451) Ibid., 105, 108.
452) Ibid., 108.
453) Robert Louis Wilken, The First Thousand Years: A Global History of Christianity (New Haven: Yale University Press, 2012), 242.
454) Ibid., 242-243.
455) Ibid., 243.
456) Ibid., 243.
457) Stephen B. Bevans and Roger P. Schroeder, Constant's in Context: A Theology of Mission for Today (New York: Orbis Books, Mary knoll, 2004
458) Ibid., 113.
459) Ibid., 113.
460) Ibid., 113.
461) Ibid., 114
462) Ibid., 114.
463) Ibid., 114.
464) Ibid., 114.
465) Robert Louis Wilken, The First Thousand Years: A Global History of Christianity (New Haven: Yale University Press, 2012), 213.
466) Ibid., 211.
467) Ibid., 211.
468) Ibid., 211.
469) Ibid., 211.
470) Ibid., 215.
471) Ibid., 216.
472) Ibid., 217.
473) Ibid., 217.
474) Ibid., 217.
475) Ibid., 217.
476) Ibid., 218.
477) Ibid., 218.
478) Ibid., 219.
479) Ibid., 219.

480) Timothy Michael Law, When God Spoke Greek: The Septuagint and the Making of the Christian Bible (Oxford: Oxford University Press, 2013), 88-89.480)

481) Ibid., 59.

482) Robert Louis Wilken, The First Thousand Years: A Global History of Christianity (New Haven: Yale University Press, 2012), 219.

483) Ibid., 220.

484) Justo L. Gonzalez, The Story of Christianity: The Early Church to The Dawn of The Reformation (New York: Harper-Collins, 2010), 305.

485) Ibid., 305-306.

486) Ibid., 306.

487) Ibid., 312.

488) Ibid., 312.

489) Ibid., 312-313.

490) Ibid., 313

491) Peter Brown, Through the Eye of a Needle: Wealth, the Fall of Rome, and the Making of Christianity in the West, 350-550 A.D. (Prinuto: Prinuton University Press, 2012), 527.

492) Ibid., 528.

493) Ibid., 528.

494) Ibid., 529-530.

495) Justo L. Gonzalez, The Story of Christianity: The Early Church to The Dawn of The Reformation (New York: Harper-Collins, 2010), 257.

496) Ibid., 345.

497) Ibid., 345.

498) Ibid., 345.

499) Ibid., 357.

500) Ibid., 359.

501) Ibid., 360.

502) Ibid., 360.

503) Ibid., 360.

504) James Hennesey S.J., American Catholics: A History of the Roman Catholic Community in the United States (Oxford: Oxford University Press, 1981), 10.

505) Cyprian Davis, O.S.B., The History of Black Catholics in the United States (New York: The Crossroad Publishing Company, 1990),21.
506) Ibid., 21.
507) Ibid., 22.
508) Ibid., 22.
509) Ibid., 21.
510) Ibid., 22-23.
511) James Hennesey S.J., American Catholics: A History of the Roman Catholic Community in the United States (Oxford: Oxford University Press, 1981), 10.
512) Ibid., 11.
513) Ibid., 11-12.
514) Ibid., 12.
515) Alan Taylor, American Colonies: The Penguin History of the United States (New York: Penguin Books, 2001), 77.
516) Ibid., 77-78.
517) Ibid., 78.
518) James Hennesey S.J., American Catholics: A History of the Roman Catholic Community in the United States (Oxford: Oxford University Press, 1981),10.
519) Alan Taylor, American Colonies: The Penguin History of the United States (New York: Penguin Books, 2001), 78-79
520) Ibid., 79.
521) James Hennesey S.J., American Catholics: A History of the Roman Cath-olic Community in the United States (Oxford: Oxford University Press, 1981), 13.
522) Ibid., 13.
523) Ibid., 13.
524) Alan Taylor, American Colonies: The Penguin History of the United States (New York: Penguin Books, 2001), 83.
525) Ibid., 83.
526) Ibid., 84.
527) Ibid., 84.
528) Ibid., 85.
529) Ibid., 86-88.
530) Ibid., 86-88.

531) Ibid., 84-85.

532) Ibid., 87.

533) Ibid., 87.

534) Ibid., 89.

535) Ibid., 90.

536) James Hennesey S.J., American Catholics: A History of the Roman Cath-olic Community in the United States (Oxford: Oxford University Press, 1981),17-18.

537) Alan Taylor, American Colonies: The Penguin History of the United States (New York: Penguin Books, 2001), 90.

538) James Hennesey S.J., American Catholics: A History of the Roman Cath-olic Community in the United States (Oxford: Oxford University Press, 1981), 18.

539) Ibid., 18.

540) Ibid., 18-19.

541) Ibid., 19.

542) Ibid., 19.

543) Ibid., 20.

544) Chester Gills, Roman Catholicism in America (New York: Columbia University Press, 1999), 49.

545) James Hennesey S.J., American Catholics: A History of the Roman Catholic Community in the United States (Oxford: Oxford University Press, 1981), 20.

546) Ibid., 20-21.

547) Ibid., 21.

548) Ibid., 21-22.

549) Ibid., 31.

550) Ibid., 31

551) Ibid., 34-35.

552) Ibid., 32-33.

553) Ibid., 33.

554) Ibid., 34-35.

555) Ibid., 35.

556) Alan Taylor, American Colonies: The Penguin History of the United States (New York: Penguin Books, 2001), 394-395.

557) William J. Bennett, America: The Last Best Hope (Nashville: Thomas Nelson, Inc., 2006), 55.

558) Ibid., 60.
559) Ibid., 60.
560) Ibid., 55.
561) Ibid., 61.
562) James Hennesey S.J., American Catholics: A History of the Roman Catholic Community in the United States (Oxford: Oxford University Press, 1981), 55-56.
563) Ibid., 44-45.
564) Ibid., 56.
565) Ibid., 56.
566) Chester Gillis, Roman Catholicism in America (New York: Columbia University Press, 1999), 56.
567) James Hennesey S.J., American Catholics: A History of the Roman Catholic Community in the United States (Oxford: Oxford University Press, 1981), 48.
568) Ibid., 49.
569) Ibid., 50.
570) Ibid., 49-50.
571) Ibid., 50.
572) Ibid., 50.
573) Ibid., 51.
574) Ibid., 51.
575) Ibid., 51.
576) Ibid., 51.
577) Ibid., 51.
578) Ibid., 51.
579) Angelyn Dries, OSF, The Missionary Movement in American Catholic History (MaryKnoll, New York: Orbis Books, 1998), 17.
580) Ibid., 17-18.
581) Ibid., 18.
582) James Hennesey S.J., American Catholics: A History of the Roman Catholic Community in the United States (Oxford: Oxford University Press, 1981), 53.
583) 582)
584) 583)
585) 584)

586) Ibid., 18.

587) James Hennesey S.J., American Catholics: A History of the Roman Catholic Community in the United States (Oxford: Oxford University Press, 1981), 65.

588) Ibid., 67-68.

589) Ibid., 68.

590) William J. Bennett, America: The Last Best Hope Vol. I (Nashville: Thomas Nelson, Inc.,2006), 102.

591) Ibid., 103.

592) James Hennesey S.J., American Catholics: A History of the Roman Catholic Community in the United States (Oxford: Oxford University Press, 1981), 69.

593) Ibid., 69-71.

594) Ibid., 71.

595) Ibid., 72.

596) Ibid., 72.

597) Ibid., 72-73.

598) Benjamin L. Masse S.J., The Catholic Mind Through Fifty Years 1903-1953 (New York: The America Press, 1952), 147.

599) James Hennesey S.J., American Catholics: A History of the Roman Catholic Community in the United States (Oxford: Oxford University Press, 1981), 74-75.

600) Ibid., 73-74.

601) Ibid., 74.

602) Ibid., 74.

603) Ibid., 74-75.

604) Bill O' Reilly and Martin Dugard, Killing England: The Brutal Struggle for American Independence (New York: Henry Holt and Company, 2017), 310.

605) Ibid., 310-34.

606) Ibid., 311.

607) Ibid., 312.

608) James Hennesey S.J., American Catholics: A History of the Roman Catholic Community in the United States (Oxford: Oxford University Press, 1981), 75.

609) Ibid., 75.

610) Ibid., 75.

611) Ibid., 75.

612) Ibid., 76.

613) Ibid., 77.

614) Ibid., 77.

615) Ibid., 81.

616) Ibid., 82.

617) Ibid., 82-83.

618) Ibid., 83.

619) Ibid., 85.

620) Ibid., 85-86.

621) Ibid., 86.

622) Ibid., 89.

623) Willard Sterne Randall, Unshackling America: How the War of 1812 Truly Ended The American Revolution (New York: ST. Martin's Press, 2017), 191.

624) James Hennesey S.J., American Catholics: A History of the Roman Catholic Community in the United States (Oxford: Oxford University Press, 1981), 89.

625) Ibid., 90.

626) Ibid., 101.

627) James Mc Pherson, Battle Cry of Freedom: The Civil War Era (Oxford: Oxford University Press, 1988), 170-174.

628) James Hennesey S.J., American Catholics: A History of the Roman Catholic Community in the United States (Oxford: Oxford University Press, 1981),147.

629) Ibid., 143.

630) Ibid., 144.

631) Ibid., 144.

632) Ibid., 144.

633) Ibid., 144-145.

634) Ibid., 145.

635) Cyprian Davis, O.S. B., The History of Black Catholics in The United States (New York: The Crossroad Publishing Company, 1990), 39-40.

636) Ibid., 40.

637) James Hennesey S.J., American Catholics: A History of the Roman Catholic Community in the United States (Oxford: Oxford University Press, 1981), 145-146.

638) Ibid., 146.

639) Ibid., 146.

640) Cyprian Davis, O.S. B., The History of Black Catholics in The United States (New York: The Crossroad Publishing Company, 1990), 49.

641) Ibid., 49.

642) James Hennesey S.J., American Catholics: A History of the Roman Catholic Community in the United States (Oxford: Oxford University Press, 1981), 154.

643) Ibid., 147.

644) Ibid., 147.

645) Ibid., 147.

646) Ibid., 147.

647) Ibid., 147-148.

648) Ibid., 148.

649) Ibid., 148-149.

650) Ibid., 149.

651) Ibid., 149.

652) Ibid., 149.

653) Ibid., 149.

654) Ibid., 150.

655) Ibid., 150.

656) Ibid., 150-151.

657) Ibid., 156-157.

658) Ibid., 157.

659) Ibid., 159.

660) Bill O'Reilly and Martin Dugard, Killing Lincoln: The Shocking Assassination That Changed America Forever (New York: Henry Holt and Company, 2011), 208-211.

661) James Hennesey S.J., American Catholics: A History of the Roman Catholic Community in the United States (Oxford: Oxford University Press, 1981), 159.

662) Bill O'Reilly and Martin Dugard, Killing Lincoln: The Shocking Assassination That Changed America Forever (New York: Henry Holt and Company, 2011), 102 - 103.

663) Ibid., 197-203.

664) Ibid., 117.

665) Ibid., 250-251.

666) Ibid., 247-248.

667) Ibid., 265-266, 278.

668) Ibid., 278.

669) James Hennesey S.J., American Catholics: A History of the Roman Catholic Community in the United States (Oxford: Oxford University Press, 1981), 159.

670) Bill O'Reilly and Martin Dugard, Killing Lincoln: The Shocking Assassination That Changed America Forever (New York: Henry Holt and Company, 2011), 294.

671) James Hennesey S.J., American Catholics: A History of the Roman Catholic Community in the United States (Oxford: Oxford University Press, 1981), 159-160.

672) Ibid., 160.

673) Ibid., 160.

674) Ibid., 160.

675) Ibid., 161.

676) Ibid., 162.

677) Ibid., 119.

678) Ibid., 120.

679) James Hennesey S.J., American Catholics: A History of the Roman Cat-olic Community in the United States (Oxford: Oxford University Press, 1981), 162.

680) Ibid., 162-163.

681) Cyprian Davis, O.S.B. The History of Black Catholics in the United States (New York; The Crossroad Publishing Company, 1, 1990),155.

682) Ibid., 152-153.

683) Ibid., 153-154

684) Ibid., 155-156.

685) Ibid., 155.

686) Ibid., 156.

687) Ibid., 160

688) Ibid., 160.

689) Ibid., 161.

690) Ibid., 162.

691) James Hennesey S.J., American Catholics: A History of the Roman Cath-olic Community in the United States (Oxford: Oxford University Press, 1981), 163.

692) Angelyn Dries, O.S.F., The Missionary Movement in American Catholic History (New York: Orbis Books, 1998), 29-30.

693) Ibid., 30.

694) Ibid., 30.

695) Ibid., 30.

696) Ibid., 30-31.

697) Ibid., 31.

698) Vincent J. O'Malley, C.M., Saint of North America (Huntington, Indiana: Our Sunday Visitor, Inc., 2004), 114.

699) Ibid., 114.

700) Ibid., 114.

701) Ibid., 114-115.

702) Ibid., 115.

703) Ibid., 115.

704) James Hennesey S.J., *American Catholics: A History of the Roman Catholic Community in the United States* (Oxford: Oxford University Press, 1981), 165

705) Ibid., 164.

706) Ibid., 165.

707) Ibid., 165.

708) Ibid., 165.

709) Ibid., 167.

710) Ibid., 168.

711) Ibid., 168.

712) Ibid., 168.

713) Ibid., 169.

714) Ibid., 170.

715) Ibid., 171.

716) Angelyn Dries, O.S.F., The Missionary Movement in American Catholic History (New York: Orbis Books, 1998), 268.

717) James Hennesey S.J., American Catholics: A History of the Roman Catholic Community in the United States (Oxford: Oxford University Press, 1981), 172.

718) Ibid., 172.

719) Bill O'Reilly and David Fisher, Legends and Lies: The Real West (New York: Henry Holt and Company, 2015), 135-139.

720) Ibid., 139.

721) Ibid., 139.

722) James Hennesey S.J., American Catholics: A History of the Roman Catholic Community in the United States (Oxford: Oxford University Press, 1981), 173.

723) Ibid., 173.

724) Ibid., 173.

725) Ibid., 173.

726) Ibid., 174.

727) Ibid., 174.

728) Vincent J. O'Malley, C.M., Saint of North America (Huntington, Indiana: Our Sunday Visitor, Inc., 2004), 440 - 441.

729) Ibid., 441.

730) Ibid., 440.

731) Ibid., 441.

732) Ibid., 441.

733) Ibid., 441.

734) Ibid., 442.

735) Ibid., 442.

736) Ibid., 443

737) James Hennesey S.J., American Catholics: A History of the Roman Cath-olic Community in the United States (Oxford: Oxford University Press, 1981), 174.

738) Ibid., 174-175.

739) Ibid., 175.

740) Ibid., 175.

741) Ibid., 175.

742) Ibid., 175.

743) Ibid., 175.

744) Ibid,. 175.

745) Ibid., 175.

746) Ibid., 175.
747) Ibid., 176.
748) Ibid., 176.
749) Ibid., 176.
750) Ibid., 176.
751) Charles G. Herbermann, PH.D., LLD, ed et al., The Catholic Encyclopedia Volume III (New York: The Encyclopedia Press, Inc., 1913), 1.
752) Ibid., 1.
753) Ibid., 1.
754) Ibid., 1.
755) ibid., 1.
756) Ibid., 1.
757) Ibid., 2.
758) Ibid., 2.
759) Ibid., 2.
760) Ibid., 2.
761) Ibid., 2.
762) Ibid., 2.
763) Ibid., 2.
764) Ibid., 2.
765) Ibid., 2.
766) Ibid., 2.
767) Ibid., 3.
768) Ibid., 3.
769) Ibid., 3.
770) Ibid., 2-3.
771) James Hennesey S.J., American Catholics: A History of the Roman Catholic Community in the United States (Oxford: Oxford University Press, 1981), 177
772) Ibid., 177.
773) Ibid., 177.
774) Ibid., 179.
775) Ibid., 179.
776) Ibid., 177.

777) Christopher J. Kauffman., Faith and Fraternalism: The History of the Knights of Columbus 1882-1982 (New York: Harper and Row, Publishers, 1982), 17.

778) Ibid., xiii.

779) Ibid., 11-12.

780) Ibid., 16.

781) Charles W. Burpee., Burpee's the Story of Connecticut, vol. II (New York: The American Historical Company, Inc., 1939), 827.

782) Janet Maher and John Wiehn., Waterbury Irish; From the Emerald Isle to the Brass City (Charleston, SC: The History Press, 2015), 52.

783) Ibid., 52.

784) Ibid., 58-59.

785) Charles W. Burpee., Burpee's the Story of Connecticut, vol. II (New York: The American Historical Company, Inc., 1939) 827.

786) Janet Maher and John Wiehn., Waterbury Irish: From the Emerald Isle to the Brass City (Charleston, SC: The History Press, 2015),58.

787) Ibid., 61.

788) James Hennesey S.J., American Catholics: A History of the Roman Catholic Community in the United States (Oxford: Oxford University Press, 1981), 181-183.

789) Ibid., 186.

790) Ibid., 177.

791) Ibid., 186.

792) Ibid., 187.

793) Ibid., 187.

794) Ibid., 189.

795) Ibid., 186.

796) Ibid., 187.

797) Ibid., 188, 191.

798) Ibid., 193.

799) Ibid., 193

800) Ibid., 193.

801) Ibid., 193.

802) Ibid., 194.

803) Ibid., 196.

804) Ibid., 196.
805) Ibid., 195.
806) Ibid., 195.
807) Ibid., 195.
808) Ibid., 195.
809) Ibid., 196.
810) Ibid., 197.
811) Ibid., 200.
812) Benjamin L. Masse S. J., The Catholic Mind Through Fifty Years 1903-1953 (New York; The America Press, 1952), 147.
813) James Hennesey S.J., American Catholics: A History of the Roman Catholic Community in the United States (Oxford: Oxford University Press, 1981), 206-207.
814) Ibid., 207.
815) Ibid., 207.
816) Ibid., 208.
817) Ibid., 209.
818) Ibid., 210.
819) Ibid., 217.
820) Ibid., 218.
821) Ibid., 219.
822) Ibid., 219.
823) Ibid., 219.
824) Ibid., 219.
825) Ibid., 220.
826) Ibid., 222-223.
827) Ibid., 223.
828) Ibid., 223.
829) Ibid., 223.
830) Ibid., 223.
831) Ibid., 223.
832) ibid., 223.
833) Ibid., 224.
834) Ibid., 224.
835) Ibid., 225.
836) Ibid., 225.
837) Ibid., 225.

838) Hew Strachar, The First World War (New York: Penguin Books, 2013), 227.

839) Ibid., 227.

840) Ibid., 206.

841) Ibid., 227.

842) James Hennesey S.J., American Catholics: A History of the Roman Catholic Community in the United States (Oxford: Oxford University Press, 1981), 225.

843) Ibid., 225.

844) William J. Bennett, America The Last Best Hope vol. II: From a World at war To the Triumph of Freedom 1914-1989 (Nashville: Thomas Nelson, Inc., 2007), 19.

845) Ibid., 19.

846) James Hennesey S.J., American Catholics: A History of the Roman Catholic Community in the United States (Oxford: Oxford University Press, 1981), 226.

847) Ibid., 226.

848) Ibid., 226.

849) Ibid., 227.

850) Ibid., 227.

851) Ibid., 228.

852) Ibid., 228.

853) Ibid., 228.

854) Ibid., 229.

855) Ibid., 229.

856) Ibid., 229.

857) Ibid., 230.

858) Ibid., 230.

859) Ibid., 231.

860) Ibid., 232.

861) John Sullivan, Edith Stein: Essential Writings (New York: Orbis Books, 2002),

862) Dianne Marie Traflet, Saint Edith Stein: A Spiritual Portrait (Boston: Pauline Books & Media, 2008), 5.

863) Maria Ruiz Scaperlanda, Edith Stein: The Life and Legacy of St. Teresa Benedicta of the Cross (Manchester, New Hampshire: Sophia Institute Press, 2017), xiii.

864) L. Gelber and Romaens Leuren, eds, The Collected Works of Edith Stein: Sister Teresa Benedicta of the Cross Discalced Carmelite 1891-1942 Volume Five (Washington, D.C., ICS Publications, 1993), 1-2.

865) Maria Amata Neyer and Eberhard Avé-Lallemant, The Collected Works of Edith Stein Volume 12: Letters to Roman Ingarden (Washington, D.C., ICS Publications, 2014), xvi.

866) Marianne Sawicki, The Collected Works of Edith Stein; Sister Teresa Bene-dicta of the Cross Discalced Carmelite 1891-1942. Volume Ten (Washing-ton, D.C., ICS Publications, 2006), XIV-XVI.

867) Dianne Marie Traflet, Saint Edith Stein: A Spiritual Portrait (Boston: Pauline Books & Media, 2008), 31.

868) Ibid., 32.

869) Ibid., 32.

870) Ibid., 33.

871) Ibid., 37.

872) Ibid., 38.

873) Ibid., 40.

874) Ibid., 40.

875) Maria Ruiz Scaperlanda, Edith Stein: The Life and Legacy of St. Teresa Benedicta of the Cross (Manchester, New Hampshire: Sophia Institute Press, 2017),68.

876) Ibid., 69.

877) Ibid., 70.

878) L. Gelber and Romaens Leuven, eds, The Collected Works of Edith Stein: Sister Teresa Benedicta of the Cross Discalced Carmelite 1891-1942 Volume Five (Washington, D.C., ICS Publications, 1993), 6-7.

879) Maria Amata Neyer and Eberhard Avé-Lallemant, The Collected Works of Edith Stein Volume 12: Letters to Roman Ingarden (Washington, D.C., ICS Publications, 2014), 33.

880) Ibid., 88-89.

881) Ibid., 90-91.

882) Dianne Marie Traflet, Saint Edith Stein: A Spiritual Portrait (Boston: Pauline Books & Media, 2008), 41.

883) Ibid., 42-43.

884) Ibid., 43-44.

885) Ibid., 44.

886) Maria Ruiz Scaperlanda, Edith Stein: The Life and Legacy of St. Teresa Benedicta of the Cross (Manchester, New Hampshire: Sophia Institute Press, 2017), 76.

887) Ibid., 76.

888) L. Gelber and Romaens Leuven, eds, The Collected Works of Edith Stein: Sister Teresa Benedicta of the Cross Discalced Carmelite 1891-1942 Volume Five (Washington, D.C., ICS Publications, 1993), 47.

889) Maria Ruiz Scaperlanda, Edith Stein: The Life and Legacy of St. Teresa Benedicta of the Cross (Manchester, New Hampshire: Sophia Institute Press, 2017), 78.

890) L. Gelber and Romaens Leuven, eds, The Collected Works of Edith Stein: Sister Teresa Benedicta of the Cross Discalced Carmelite 1891-1942 Volume Five (Washington, D.C., ICS Publications, 1993), 105.

891) Maria Ruiz Scaperlanda, Edith Stein: The Life and Legacy of St. Teresa Benedicta of the Cross (Manchester, New Hampshire: Sophia Institute Press, 2017), 79.

892) Dianne Marie Traflet, Saint Edith Stein: A Spiritual Portrait (Boston: Pauline Books & Media, 2008), 46.

893) Ibid., 46.

894) L. Gelber and Romaens Leuven, eds, The Collected Works of Edith Stein: Sister Teresa Benedicta of the Cross Discalced Carmelite 1891-1942 Volume Five (Washington, D.C., ICS Publications, 1993), 104.

895) Dianne Marie Traflet, Saint Edith Stein: A Spiritual Portrait (Boston: Pauline Books & Media, 2008), 46-47.

896) Ibid., 47.

897) L. Gelber and Romaens Leuven, eds, The Collected Works of Edith Stein: Sister Teresa Benedicta of the Cross Discalced Carmelite 1891-1942 Volume Five (Washington, D.C., ICS Publications, 1993), 185.

898) Dianne Marie Traflet, Saint Edith Stein: A Spiritual Portrait (Boston: Pauline Books & Media, 2008), 47.

899) L. Gelber and Romaens Leuven, eds, The Collected Works of Edith Stein: Sister Teresa Benedicta of the Cross Discalced Carmelite 1891-1942 Volume Five (Washington, D.C., ICS Publications, 1993), 100-101.

900) Ibid., 51.

901) Dianne Marie Traflet, Saint Edith Stein: A Spiritual Portrait (Boston: Pauline Books & Media, 2008), 48-49.

902) Maria Ruiz Scaperlanda, Edith Stein: The Life and Legacy of St. Teresa Benedicta of the Cross (Manchester, New Hampshire: Sophia Institute Press, 2017), 85.

903) Dianne Marie Traflet, Saint Edith Stein: A Spiritual Portrait (Boston: Pauline Books & Media, 2008), 49.

904) L. Gelber and Romaens Leuven, eds, The Collected Works of Edith Stein: Sister Teresa Benedicta of the Cross Discalced Carmelite 1891-1942 Volume Five (Washington, D.C., ICS Publications, 1993), 185.

905) Dianne Marie Traflet, Saint Edith Stein: A Spiritual Portrait (Boston: Pauline Books & Media, 2008), 49.

906) Ibid., 50.

907) Ibid., 50.

908) Maria Ruiz Scaperlanda, Edith Stein: The Life and Legacy of St. Teresa Benedicta of the Cross (Manchester, New Hampshire: Sophia Institute Press, 2017), 85-86.

909) Ibid., 91.

910) Ibid., 93.

911) Ibid., 94.

912) Ibid., 95.

913) Ibid., 96.

914) Dianne Marie Traflet, Saint Edith Stein: A Spiritual Portrait (Boston: Pauline Books & Media, 2008), 53.

915) Ibid., 54.

916) Ibid., 54.

917) Ibid., 54.

918) Maria Ruiz Scaperlanda, Edith Stein: The Life and Legacy of St. Teresa Benedicta of the Cross (Manchester, New Hampshire: Sophia Institute Press, 2017), 96.

919) Ibid., 97.

920) Ibid., 97.
921) Ibid., 98.
922) Ibid., 98,101.
923) Ibid., 101.
924) Ibid., 102.
925) Ibid., 102.
926) Ibid., 102.
927) Ibid., 102.
928) Ibid., 103.
929) Dianne Marie Traflet, Saint Edith Stein: A Spiritual Portrait (Boston: Pauline Books & Media, 2008), 72.
930) Ibid., 72-73.
931) Ibid., 73-74.
932) Ibid., 74.
933) Ibid., 74.
934) Ibid., 75.
935) Ibid., 76.
936) Ibid., 77-78.
937) Ibid., 78.
938) Maria Ruiz Scaperlanda, Edith Stein: The Life and Legacy of St. Teresa Benedicta of the Cross (Manchester, New Hampshire Sophia Institute Press, 2017), 114-116.
939) Ibid., 116.
940) Ibid., 117.
941) Ibid., 117.
942) L. Gelber and Romaens Leuven, eds, The Collected Works of Edith Stein: Sister Teresa Benedicta of the Cross Discalced Carmelite 1891-1942 Volume Five (Washington, D.C., ICS Publications, 1993), 234-235.
943) Maria Ruiz Scaperlanda, Edith Stein: The Life and Legacy of St. Teresa Benedicta of the Cross (Manchester, New Hampshire: Sophia Institute Press, 2017), 118.
944) Ibid., 118.
945) Mark Riebling, Church of Spies: The Pope's Secret War Against Hitler (New York: Basis Books, 2015), 8.
946) Ibid., 8.
947) Ibid., 9.

948) Ibid., 9.

949) Ibid., 11.

950) Ibid., 12.

951) Ibid., 13.

952) Ibid., 15.

953) Ibid., 15.

954) Maria Ruiz Scaperlanda, Edith Stein: The Life and Legacy of St. Teresa Benedicta of the Cross (Manchester, New Hampshire Sophia Institute Press, 2017), 125.

955) Ibid., 125.

956) Ibid., 127.

957) Ibid., 127.

958) Dianne Marie Traflet, Saint Edith Stein: A Spiritual Portrait (Boston: Pauline Books & Media, 2008), 86.

959) Ibid., 86.

960) Ibid., 86.

961) L. Gelber and Romaens Leuven, eds, The Collected Works of Edith Stein: Sister Teresa Benedicta of the Cross Discalced Carmelite 1891-1942 Volume Five (Washington, D.C., ICS Publications, 1993), 308-309.

962) Mark Riebling, Church of Spies: The Pope's Secret War Against Hitler (New York: Basis Books, 2015), 33.

963) Ibid., 33.

964) Ibid., 34.

965) Ibid., 34.

966) Ibid., 61.

967) Ibid., 62.

968) Ibid., 62.

969) Ibid., 63.

970) Maria Ruiz Scaperlanda, Edith Stein: The Life and Legacy of St. Teresa Benedicta of the Cross (Manchester, New Hampshire: Sophia Institute Press, 2017), 135.

971) Ibid., 135.

972) L. Gelber and Romaens Leuven, eds, The Collected Works of Edith Stein: Sister Teresa Benedicta of the Cross Discalced Carmelite 1891-1942 Volume Five (Washington, D.C., ICS Publications, 1993), 324-325.

973) Maria Ruiz Scaperlanda, Edith Stein: The Life and Legacy of St. Teresa Benedicta of the Cross (Manchester, New Hampshire: Sophia Institute Press, 2017), 138.

974) Ibid., 138.

975) Ibid., 138.

976) Ibid., 142.

977) L. Gelber and Romaens Leuven, eds, The Collected Works of Edith Stein: Sister Teresa Benedicta of the Cross Discalced Carmelite 1891-1942 Volume Five (Washington, D.C., ICS Publications, 1993), 341-342.

978) Maria Ruiz Scaperlanda, Edith Stein: The Life and Legacy of St. Teresa Benedicta of the Cross (Manchester, New Hampshire: Sophia Institute Press, 2017), 143.

979) L. Gelber and Romaens Leuven, eds, The Collected Works of Edith Stein: Sister Teresa Benedicta of the Cross Discalced Carmelite 1891-1942 Volume Five (Washington, D.C., ICS Publications, 1993), 347-348.

980) Maria Ruiz Scaperlanda, Edith Stein: The Life and Legacy of St. Teresa Benedicta of the Cross (Manchester, New Hampshire: Sophia Institute Press, 2017), 146.

981) Ibid., 146.

982) Ibid., 146-147.

983) Ibid., 147.

984) Ibid., 147.

985) Ibid., 149.

986) Ibid., 149-150.

987) L. Gelber and Romaens Leuven, eds, The Collected Works of Edith Stein: Sister Teresa Benedicta of the Cross Discalced Carmelite 1891-1942 Volume Five (Washington, D.C., ICS Publications, 1993), 350-351.

988) Ibid., 352.

989) Ibid., 353.

990) Maria Ruiz Scaperlanda, Edith Stein: The Life and Legacy of St. Teresa Benedicta of the Cross (Manchester, New Hampshire: Sophia Institute Press, 2017), 152-153.

991) James Hennesey S.J., American Catholics: A History of the Roman Catholic Community in the United States (Oxford: Oxford University Press, 1981), 276.

992) Ibid., 278

993) Ibid., 275.

994) Ibid., 276.

995) Ibid., 276.

996) Ibid., 283.

997) Ibid., 284.

998) Ibid., 284.

999) Ibid., 286-287.

1000) Vincent J. O'Malley, C.M., Saint of North America (Huntington, Indiana: Our Sunday Visitor Publishing Division, Inc., 2004),486 - 487.

1001) Ibid., 487.

1002) Donald A. Guglielmi, Staritsa: The Spiritual Motherhood of Catherine Doherty (Eugne, Oregon: Pickwick Publications, 2018), 140.

1003) Vincent J. O'Malley, C.M., Saint of North America (Huntington, Indiana: Our Sunday Visitor Publishing Division, Inc., 2004), 487.

1004) Donald A. Guglielmi, Staritsa: The Spiritual Motherhood of Catherine Doherty (Eugne, Oregon: Pickwick Publications, 2018), 22.

1005) Vincent J. O'Malley, C.M., Saint of North America (Huntington, Indiana: Our Sunday Visitor Publishing Division, Inc., 2004), 488.

1006) Ibid., 488.

1007) Ibid., 488.

1008) Donald A. Guglielmi, Staritsa: The Spiritual Motherhood of Catherine Doherty (Eugne, Oregon: Pickwick Publications, 2018), 28-29.

1009) Ibid., 29.

1010) Ibid., 29.

1011) Ibid., 29.

1012) Ibid., 29.

1013) Ibid., 29.

1014) Ibid., 31.
1015) Ibid., xvi.
1016) Ibid., 33.
1017) Ibid., 34.
1018) Ibid., 36.
1019) Ibid., 36.
1020) Ibid., 37.
1021) Ibid., 39.
1022) Ibid., 39.
1023) Ibid., 67-68.
1024) Ibid., 67.
1025) Ibid., 69.
1026) Ibid., 69-70.
1027) Ibid., 72.
1028) Ibid., 72-73.
1029) Ibid., 73.
1030) Ibid., 89-90.
1031) Ibid., 90.
1032) Lorene Hanley Duquin, A Century of Catholic Converts (Huntington, Indiana: Our Sunday Visitor, inc., 2003), 49-50.
1033) Thomas H. Morris, the RCIA: Transforming the Church (New York: Paulist Press, 1997),9.
1034) James Hennesey S.J., American Catholics: A History of the Roman Catholic Community in the United States (Oxford: Oxford University Press, 1981), 310.
1035) Ibid., 310.
1036) Ibid., 310.
1037) Ibid., 311.
1038) Ibid., 311.
1039) Ibid., 311.
1040) Ibid., 311.
1041) Ibid., 312.
1042) Norman Tanner, S.J., Vatican II: The essential Texts (New Yorke Image Books, and imprint of the Crown Publishing Group, a division of Random House, inc., 2012), 41.

1043) James Hennesey S.J., American Catholics: A History of the Roman Catholic Community in the United States (Oxford: Oxford University Press, 1981), 312.

1044) Thomas H. Morris, the RCIA: Transforming the Church (New York: Paulist Press, 1997), 10.

1045) Donald Haggerty, Conversion: Spiritual Insights into an Essential Encounter with God (San Francisco: Ignatius Press, 2017), 24.

1046) Ibid., 21.

1047) Ibid., 21.

1048) Ibid., 21-22.

1049) Thomas H. Morris, the RCIA: Transforming the Church (New York: Paulist Press, 1997), 10-11.

1050) International Commission on English in the Liturgy, Rite of Christian Initiation of Adults: Study Edition (Collegeville, Minnesota: The Liturgical Press, 1988), 5-6.

1051) Ibid., 6-7.

1052) Ibid., 8.

1053) Ibid., 8-9.

1054) Jovian P. Lang, OFM, Dictionary of the Liturgy (New York: Catholic Book Publishing Corp., 1989), 577.

1055) International Commission on English in the Liturgy, Rite of Christian Initiation of Adults: Study Edition (Collegeville, Minnesota: The Liturgical Press, 1988), 9.

1056) Thomas H. Morris. The RCIA: Transforming the Church (New York: Paulist Press, 1997), 183.

1057) Donald Senior, John J. Collins, and Mary Ann Getty, Eds, The Catholic Study Bible Third Edition: The New American Bible Revised Edition (New York: Oxford University Press, 2010), 1206.

1058) Thomas H. Morris, The RCIA: Transforming the Church (New York: Paulist Press, 1997), 182-183.

1059) Donald Senior, John J. Collins, and Mary Ann Getty, Eds, The Catholic Study Bible Third Edition: The New American Bible Revised Edition (New York: Oxford University Press, 2010), 1660.

1060) International Commission on English in the Liturgy, Rite of Christian Initiation of Adults: Study Edition (Collegeville, Minnesota: The Liturgical Press, 1988), 78.

1061) Ibid., 79.

1062) Thomas H. Morris, The RCIA: Transforming the Church (New York: Paulist Press, 1997), 168-169.

1063) Ibid., 169.

1064) Ibid., 170.

1065) Ibid., 194. 1066)

1066) Jovian P. Lang, OFM. Dictionary of the Liturgy (New York: Catholic Book Publishing Corp., 1989), 180.

1067) Thomas H. Morris. The RCIA: Transforming the Church (New York Paulist Press,1997), 194.

1068) Ibid., 188-189.

1069) Ibid., 188.

1070) Ibid., 189-190.

1071) Ibid., 191.

1072) Ibid., 192.

1073) Ibid., 192-194.

1074) Ibid., 199.

1075) Ibid., 198-199.

1076) Ibid., 199.

1077) Ibid., 200-201.

1078) Ibid., 201.

1079) Ibid., 201.

1080) International Commission on English in the Liturgy, Rite of Christian In-itintion of Adults: Study Edition (Collegeville, Minnesota: The Liturgical Press, 1988), 143.

1081) Ibid., 144.

1082) Thomas H. Morris. The RCIA: Transforming the Church (New York Paulist Press, 1997), 201-202.

1083) International Commission on English in the Liturgy, Rite of Christian Initiation of Adults: Study Edition (Collegeville, Minnesota: The Liturgical Press, 1988), 144.

1084) Ibid., 144.

1085) Ibid., 145.

1086) Ibid., 146.

1087) Thomas H. Morris, The RCIA: Transforming the Church (New York: Paulist Press,1997), 203.

1088) Ibid., 203.

1089) Kenan B. Osborne, OFM., The Christian Sacrament of Initiation: Baptism, Confirmation, Eucharist (New York: Paulist Press, 1987), 71.

1090) Ibid., 73.

1091) Thomas H. Morris, The RCIA: Transforming the Church New Yorkc Paulist Press, 1997), 204.

1092) Kenan B. Osborne, OFM., The Christian Sacrament of Initiation: Ba tism, Confirmation, Eucharist (New York: Paulist Press, 1987), 176-177.

1093) Thomas H. Morris, The RCIA: Transforming the Church New York Paulist Press, 1997), 210.

1094) Goffredo Boselli, The Spiritual Meaning of the Liturgy: School of Prayer, Source of Life (Collegeville, Minnesota: Liturgical Press, 2014), v

1095) Ibid., 4.

1096) Ibid., 4.

1097) Ibid., 4.

1098) Ibid., 4.

1099) Ibid., 5.

1100) Ibid., 5.

1101) Ibid., 3-5.

1102) Ibid., 5.

1103) Ibid., 5.

1104) Ibid., 6.

1105) Ibid., 6.

1106) Ibid., 6.

1107) Ibid., 6.

1108) Ibid., 6.

1109) Ibid., 6.

1110) Ibid., 7.

1111) Ibid., 8.

1112) Ibid., 8.

1113) Ibid., 8.

1114) Ibid., 9.

1115) Ibid., 9.
1116) Ibid., 9.
1117) Ibid., 10.
1118) Ibid., 11.
1119) Ibid., 11.
1120) Ibid., 11.
1121) Ibid., 12.
1122) Ibid., 12.
1123) Ibid., 13.
1124) Ibid., 13.
1125) Ibid., 14.
1126) Ibid., 14.
1127) Ibid., 14-15.
1128) Ibid., 15.
1129) Ibid., 15-16.
1130) Ibid., 16.
1131) Ibid., 16.
1132) Ibid., 16.
1133) Ibid., 16.
1134) Ibid., 17.
1135) Ibid., 17.
1136) Ibid., 17-18.
1137) Ibid., 19-20.
1138) Ibid., 20.
1139) Ibid., 20.
1140) Ibid., 20.
1141) Ibid., 21.
1142) Ibid., 21.
1143) Ibid., 21.
1144) Ibid., 21.
1145) Richard Rohr and Mike Morrell, The Divine Dance: The Trinity and Your Transformation. (New Kensington, Pa: Whitaker House, 2016), 64.
1146) Ibid., 101.
1147) Ibid., 101.

www.ingramcontent.com/pod-product-compliance
Lightning Source LLC
Chambersburg PA
CBHW021712120626
46545CB00004B/1516